Efficient Macro Concept

Efficient Macro Concept

U.S. Monetary, Industrial, and Foreign Exchange Policies

William Mannen

LEXINGTON BOOKS
Lanham • Boulder • New York • London

Published by Lexington Books
An imprint of The Rowman & Littlefield Publishing Group, Inc.
4501 Forbes Boulevard, Suite 200, Lanham, Maryland 20706
www.rowman.com

Unit A, Whitacre Mews, 26-34 Stannary Street, London SE11 4AB

British Library Cataloguing in Publication Information Available

Library of Congress Cataloging-in-Publication Data

Names: Mannen, William, 1986- author.
Title: Efficient macro concept : U.S. monetary, industrial, and foreign exchange policies / William Mannen.
Description: Lanham : Lexington Books, [2018] | Includes bibliographical references and index.
Identifiers: LCCN 2018005404 (print) | LCCN 2017057037 (ebook) | ISBN 9781498560030 (Electronic) | ISBN 9781498560023 (cloth : alk. paper)
Subjects: LCSH: Monetary policy—United States. | Banks and banking—United States. | Industrial policy—United States. | Foreign exchange—Law and legislation—United States.
Classification: LCC HG540 (print) | LCC HG540 .M36 2018 (ebook) | DDC 339.5/30973—dc23
LC record available at https://lccn.loc.gov/2018005404

∞™ The paper used in this publication meets the minimum requirements of American National Standard for Information Sciences Permanence of Paper for Printed Library Materials, ANSI/NISO Z39.48-1992.

Printed in the United States of America

Contents

Part I

The Money Supply in Historical Perspective

ONE

Beyond Monetary Policy

The United States must implement a new monetary-industrial policy that is more aggressive than conventional forms of monetary policy in transmitting money into the real economy. Such an industrial policy operates outside of the banking sector and other credit channels in an effort to drive gains in production. It serves as a step beyond monetary policy, but in certain institutional respects it resembles central banking. The early Federal Reserve managed a discount window through which it made out loans to member banks or purchased their acceptances. A new Economic Development Account System (EDAS) and a Credit Note Facility (CNF) similarly set up the institutional means by which to transfer money to manufacturing firms for driving investment and employment. EDAS and CNF therefore work to strengthen the real economy over the long-term. An industrial account system partly modeled on the Federal Reserve serves as a practical and flexible way to promote Gross Domestic Product (GDP) growth in an age of globalization and international competition.

A new industrial policy comports with the pattern of a money supply increasingly managed by central banking institutions over the course of American history. The federal government failed to permanently establish a central bank during the 1800s. The early Federal Reserve was a decentralized organization and not consolidated until the mid-1930s. By the early 1950s, the Fed began to pursue a more autonomous monetary policy for handling the business cycle. In the 1960s, the Fed initiated a bond purchasing program intended to shore up investment and employment over the longer-term.

A new industrial policy helps manage the money supply to the extent it offers accounts or other miscellaneous purchasing power to private sector firms that seek to voluntarily join any such system. As the individual policy options will demonstrate, the federal government in no way usurps the freedom of choice of these firms. Industrial policy only manages the money supply by redirecting monetary resources into major scale economies instead of entirely leaving national production vulnerable to market forces.

A historical case can be made for a new industrial policy. An effort to boost the nation's production of goods should implicate efficient accounting systems that bear similarity to central banking. The Federal Reserve's record of stabilizing the money supply is far from perfect. Among their mistakes, Reserve officials failed to coordinate effectively in the early 1930s and allowed inflation to build up in the late 1960s and 1970s. But markets operate more safely when a central bank stands ready to tighten in a period of growth and inflation and to ease in a period of contraction and deflation. Perhaps this paradigm does not always work out so smoothly, but it at least offers a guide for how to ideally stabilize the turbulent financial markets of the twenty-first century. An optimal market is therefore one partly managed by a central bank.

However, almost by definition the Federal Reserve must operate in countercyclical terms. It can push back against speculative excess and surging prices, or it can try to jumpstart a new process of investment and hiring. In spite of the Fed's goal of full employment, it cannot in practice maintain an artificially defined rate of full employment at the risk of fueling ever more inflation or speculation. The Fed is also not institutionally equipped to drive secular economic expansion. The Fed's most reliable tool, developed since the 1920s, remains open market policy. Paying out Interest on Excess Reserves (IOER) on the deposits of member banks increases the funds that the Fed can use to purchase securities in the open market. But the Fed cannot maintain quantitative easing forever. Interest rates eventually need to drift upwards to take pressure off a bull market in stocks and to alleviate the "hunt for yield" in riskier investments. Not surprisingly, the Fed finally began raising its policy rate while also announcing a plan to reduce its portfolio in the recovery from the Great Recession.

A central bank should not be responsible for attempting to drive gains in GDP or employment over the long-term. In the same vein, while a central bank can manage the money supply to stabilize the monetary and banking system, it cannot fuel economic development. Industrial policy, on the other hand, does serve as a mechanism for real economic expansion and development over the long-term, to the point where it can do so more efficiently than a return to outmoded protectionism.

The establishment of the Federal Reserve vastly changed the landscape of American money and banking. Every national bank was required to join the System and to hold its reserves in deposits at local Reserve Banks. A new industrial policy does not impact the money supply in such dramatic terms. Firms are only eligible to join, and their numbers would be far outnumbered by the member banks of the Federal

Reserve System. An EDAS and CNF do not overall transform the money supply in the same way as the Federal Reserve in 1913. But such an industrial policy is more aggressive than monetary policy because the member firms are directly involved in manufacturing and capital investment. When the Fed purchases securities from its institutional dealers in order to target interest rates, the proceeds of the purchases eventually flow into the larger economy. Through EDAS and CNF, money flows directly into the real economy to fund investment and employment. But otherwise, monetary policy and industrial policy are similar in the way they funnel money into the private economy through a series of institutions and transactions.

A new industrial policy is historically shaped not only by central banking but also by the transition from a gold standard to a fiat monetary standard in the 1970s. Under commodity standards, a nation's money supply was based on a commodity such as gold or silver. Members of the public were able to convert fiduciary currency into gold until 1933. Afterwards, only official settlements were paid for in gold. Because a currency paid for only so much in gold, exchange rates were fixed. The gold standard broke down in the early 1970s amid problems involving the U.S.'s balance of payments and trade deficit.

Though the U.S. resorted to fiat money under near emergency conditions, the shift to fiat was ultimately a fortuitous turn of events. Under fiat, governments can allow their currencies to float in the open markets and are relieved of the political burden of defending exchange rates at inopportune times. Under fiat, government enjoys the prerogative of creating currency irrespective of its stock of bullion. During the gold standard, on the other hand, the free market determined the rate at which gold or silver was converted into money. Fiat standards therefore imply an increasingly managed money supply in that money is now purely national.

The most visible result of fiat money is floating exchange rates. But other implications of fiat evaded mainstream political discussion. A fiat standard allows a new industrial policy to operate more efficiently and with less friction than it would have under gold. The reasons for this are obscure and minute, but they are still critical when envisioning the workings of a new industrial policy. Under fiat, government is able to create fiduciary currency in a flexible and timely manner while also ensuring through institutional means that currency creation does not produce debilitating inflation.

Utilizing technical aspects of fiat money also shapes a new foreign exchange policy. The U.S. has only a limited experience with manipulating dollar rates around the world. Foreign exchange policy is in many ways an outgrowth of central banking. During the gold standard, central banks sometimes intervened in the forex markets to maintain their currency's ratio to gold. The New York Federal Reserve Bank and the Treasury occasionally purchased foreign exchange or dollars in the late 1920s and 1930s in an effort to pump up the fragile interwar gold standard. The Fed later engaged in currency swaps in the 1960s.

The beginning of peacetime fiat in the 1970s conceivably facilitated forex operations now that governments were no longer constrained by gold reserves and adjustable currency pegs. But the idea of implementing a new foreign exchange policy never took hold in the U.S. The dollar started a long overdue slide that lasted through the 1970s. Funding such a policy appeared to be a waste of money, and the World Trade Organization (WTO) prohibits devaluing currency to assist exports in any event. A new foreign exchange policy appears futile and in contravention of international law. But technical aspects of fiat money can help to reduce costs and avoid WTO restrictions.

The argument being made here for new monetary-industrial and foreign exchange policies does not operate within the parameters of theoretical economics. Theories are not tested or proven in order to justify the argument. Such an argument presumes that government should attempt to spur a process of renewed GDP growth. The argument does not concede that governments are necessarily subject to assumptions like comparative advantage. The argument instead focuses on formulating new policy proposals that are potentially capable of generating national economic expansion.

The exercise undertaken in this work is not bound by any specific academic discipline. Such an exercise instead involves a series of policy options in historical context. A historical context forces a more practical discussion of what can and cannot work instead of focusing on abstract theories that are not germane. The policy options are outlined from the perspective of a narrative recounting the increasingly managed U.S. money supply. The majority of this work is historical, proceeding from the Revolutionary War through the dollar appreciation of the 1980s. The second part outlines the policy options. These options should not be considered in abstract terms but as the result of historical progress. They should be thought of as literally the next step after monetary policy in helping government transmit money into the real economy.

TWO

The Development of a Specie Standard

The U.S. did not begin its history on a specie basis. The Continental Congress and the state governments instead issued fiat money during the Revolutionary War. Particularly in the case of the Continental bill emissions, the experience was nothing short of disastrous. The assumptions of that era dictated that a monetary regime be fixed to specie in order to foster a uniform and sound currency. No institutional machinery or precedent existed to guide the competent management of a fiat standard. Governments only resorted to fiat during the exegesis of war. The reliance on fiat by Congress and among the states during the Revolution was in fact to be expected given the dearth of specie in the U.S., which was at least partly attributable to the country's colonial past. The colonies had not been allowed to mine and produce specie because of the mercantilist practices of the British authorities. Specie had flowed into the colonies either through earnings on trade or payments made in connection with the British military presence in North America. Estimates are that specie was only about a quarter of the total money supply of the U.S. in the late 1700s.[1]

From 1775 to 1779, the Continental Congress issued $241.5 million in paper money, which was injected into the economy through its expenditures. These bills were not classified as legal tender but were still intended to operate as hand-to-hand money that holders could redeem for specie. But in reality Congress was not prepared to unconditionally redeem the bills because it could not impose taxes without the cooperation of the states. Congress had little alternative except to attempt to allocate repayment obligations to the states in proportion to their populations. The state governments only aggravated the situation by issuing an additional $209.5 million worth of paper notes.[2]

The infusion of paper money inevitably led to depreciation of the Continental bills and even to instances of their rejection by members of the public. Congress eventually requested the states to enforce the transactional use of the bills in commerce. In 1780, Congress took further steps to stabilize the money supply by taxing out of existence $119.4 million in the depreciated bills. But it did not exactly rectify matters by then issuing $4.4 million new interest bearing tenders that were of a reduced value compared to the old issues.[3] The old bills no longer operated as money by May 1781 and were mainly purchased by speculators at a fraction of their original market value.[4]

The monetary situation did not significantly improve under the Articles of Confederation because the states were still authorized to issue their own depreciated paper money. At the heart of the monetary turmoil lay the limited supply of specie in the U.S. To more effectively fund the war effort, but also to address larger monetary problems, Congress unanimously elected Robert Morris as Superintendent of Finance in early 1781. Morris was by profession a part owner of a prominent, Philadelphia-based shipping company. During his tenure in Congress earlier in the war, he had served on the Secret Committee, charged with covertly purchasing military supplies in France and other allied nations and transporting them back across the Atlantic.

Morris brought much needed acumen to financial questions and saw the clear need to establish a specie standard to restore monetary order. He had all along disagreed with Congress's inclination to incrementally print paper money in the 1770s. He warned in his correspondence with other members of Congress that the Continental bills were becoming depreciated and rejected by the public.[5] When later serving as Superintendent, he derided the bills as a "useless load" in a letter to Benjamin Franklin and cast doubt that they could be used to pay for war-related provisions, at one point asserting, "If I could buy anything with it, I would not until the last necessity, but it will buy nothing, so that it must be burnt as soon as it honestly can."[6] Only in 1783 did he decide upon bill emissions as a means to paying soldiers in an emergency effort to expedite the disbanding of the Continental Army.[7]

Congress instructed Morris to make a report with recommendations regarding coinage in January 1782.[8] Foreign coins, especially the Spanish silver dollar, widely circulated in the states.[9] In his report, Morris focused on the need for the states to maintain uniform parities to specie. But the domestic exchanges that set up convertibility ratios between paper notes and specie differed widely in the states, which potentially inhibited and at least complicated interstate commerce. Morris saw a monometallic silver standard as the most effective way to adopt a uniform currency. A bimetallic standard composed of both gold and silver might theoretically appear more suited to a specie poor economy such as the U.S., in that the full supply of specie could be brought into use, but Morris considered a bimetallic standard difficult to administer. Deciding on silver instead of gold, Morris proposed an extremely small money unit equivalent to .1440 of a Spanish silver dollar. A dollar made up of 373 grains of fine silver would therefore equal 1,440 units. A cent of about 100 units would consist of 25 grains of fine silver, along with two grains of copper. Morris intended to allow even the smallest coins of the state governments to convert into these units without requiring any need for further adjustments in valuation. These units would then have harmonized the parity of state coinage systems to silver.[10]

By contrast, Thomas Jefferson recommended to Congress a bimetallic standard centered on the Spanish silver dollar. After Morris resigned as Superintendent, a committee submitted a proposal similar to Jefferson's for a bimetallic standard based on the dollar.[11]

Though Congress did not act on Morris's idea, his proposal in 1782 was still notable in its foreshadowing of future bullion standards. When addressing gold's advantage of easier portability than silver, Morris wrote, "It will always be in our Power to carry a Paper Circulation to every proper Extent. There can be no doubt therefore that our Money Standard ought to be affixed to Silver."[12] Morris said nothing more on this point in his report, but he implied that the public could have substituted paper for coin. This implication was all the more apparent because his proposed money unit was not supposed to take the form of a coin.[13] The plan was still in legal terms a silver coinage system, in that paper could be redeemed for coin. But in effect the public could have used paper money instead of coin in the normal course of business while holding silver in reserve with banks, similar to later bullion standards in which governments consolidated their specie reserves and used them to fund the balance of payments. Morris condemned the virtually unredeemable bills emitted by Congress during the war, though he recognized paper's function when buttressing a silver standard.

Morris's proposal would also have escaped Gresham's Law, which predicts that under a bimetallic standard the public will want to hoard the more valuable coins and pass on the lower valued or shabbier pieces. Morris's reluctance to commit to a bimetallic standard also reflected the perceived danger of gold being driven from circulation as its mint ratio with silver became undervalued in relation to its market ratio. A silver standard could not have avoided alternating periods of inflation and deflation due to fluctuations in the mining and production of silver. But a monometallic standard would have stabilized market expectations by monetizing a single commodity.

While Morris might have envisioned the adoption of a bullion standard over the long-term, he still emphasized in his report the creation of a mint to coin silver. The immediate coinage of silver would in his view strengthen the public credit and engender market confidence.[14] Even before Congress asked him to submit a report, Morris had already contacted an expert to prepare for the construction of a mint in Philadelphia. Congress voted its approval for a U.S. Mint in late February 1782, and Morris was able to hire the necessary personnel and oversee the lodging of equipment. The Mint produced sample silver coins that Morris delivered to members of Congress for their inspection in April 1783, but by then funds were lacking. The project came to a halt, and Morris paid off the personnel hired to manage the machinery.[15]

The Confederation Congress undertook no other major initiatives regarding coinage. The effective creation of a national monetary standard was only made possible after adoption of the Constitution. Given the experience with fiat paper money in the 1770s and 1780s, the new Constitution unsurprisingly limited the power to mint and coin money to the federal government while also explicitly prohibiting the states from engaging in these activities.[16] Contrary to conclusions reached in Morris's 1782 report, Congress ultimately refrained from implementing a monometallic silver standard under the new Constitution. President Washington had actually expected to appoint Morris as the first Treasury Secretary. By 1789, Morris was serving as U.S. Senator from Pennsylvania. When Washington offered him the position, Morris responded that he had already become too controversial a figure due to his role as Superintendent and instead vouched for Washington's former chief of staff, Alexander Hamilton, who had corresponded with Morris in depth on financial matters.[17]

As Treasury Secretary, Hamilton submitted his report on a mint to Congress in January 1791 recommending that both gold and silver be made full legal tender. Hamilton premised his recommendation on the theoretical logic that a bimetallic standard expanded the money supply by monetizing two commodities.[18] By contrast, Morris's reluctance towards a bimetallic standard was based on the realities of attempting to administer two metals at once. Hamilton still recognized that the mint ratio of gold to silver needed to mirror the ratio of their market values. He conceded that if a discrepancy opened up between the mint and market ratios, then the undervalued metal at the mint would be hoarded. Hamilton derived a market ratio of 15:1 gold to silver.[19] As a result, Hamilton recommended a mint ratio of 15:1, with the gold dollar worth 24 ¾ grains of fine gold and the silver dollar worth 371 ¼ grains of fine silver.[20]

Congress acted on most of Hamilton's recommendation when passing the Mint Act of 1792. The U.S. Mint coined gold and silver at a rate of 15:1. Gold was more valuable than silver because it translated into more money than silver at the mint ratio. But despite Hamilton's efforts to ensure consistency in the mint and market ratios, the two began to deviate from each other. Gold's market ratio rose to 15.6:1, causing it to become undervalued at the mint ratio and driven from circulation.[21] By 1821, a report issued by a committee of the House of Representatives conceded that gold was no longer used for transactional purposes by the public.[22] The driving of gold from circulation did not imply a total failure to produce gold. From the late 1790s into the early 1830s, the Mint coined $15.5 million in gold compared to $36.3 million in silver.[23]

Under the workings of the specie standard, the federal government purchased and coined gold and silver bullion that members of the public brought to the Mint at rates consistent with the mint ratio. By imposing a tax, government earned a profit called seigniorage. Market forces drove fluctuations in the gold stock. One theory held that as the gold stock expanded and prices rose, the real value of gold per ounce declined, and speculators were less inclined to mine gold and bring it to the Mint. Deflation, on the other hand, drove up the real value of gold and incentivized the prospecting and mining for specie, especially as low prices put downward pressure on real wages. These assumptions supposedly led to a self-correcting cycle. Whether or not this theory can be accepted in part or full, private actors controlled the bringing of gold and silver to the Mint. In the depths of monetary stagnation in the early nineteenth century, Congress might have ordered federal agents to prospect for new mines and even directly subsidized the exploitation of such mines, but these activities were clearly beyond the realm of government in what was taken to be an entirely market-driven phenomenon. Moreover, because Gresham's Law implied that a bimetallic standard was unworkable over the long run, Congress was even hampered in its ability to designate an optimal mint ratio.

The reality of the commodity standard did not stop numerous individuals from proposing inflationist schemes in the popular press, particularly after Congress briefly suspended convertibility during the War of 1812. Through pamphlets and editorials, Thomas Law, a former civil servant, promoted an inflationist paper currency that could be used to assist in the building of new infrastructure. Law plotted out a National Currency Board that issued perpetual loans to state governments at 2.5 percent to 4 percent interest that then re-issued the loans in the market at 5 percent interest. Borrowers repaid interest but not principal. The Board made out these loans in the form of notes that circulated as money. Law predicted that when market interest rates were under 5 percent, borrowers would draw out loans from private creditors. But unlike the Board, private creditors would obligate the borrowers to repay principal, disincentivizing the borrowers from switching to private loans even at lower interest rates.[24] In any case, Law's idea envisioned the use of paper money, here in the form of loans issued by the Board, as a direct lever in promoting real growth by funding public works projects. The scheme was also purely inflationist, in that the Board would be issuing inconvertible notes to the states. Only when the states had become saturated with infrastructure might the issuance of Board notes finally stop.

Hamilton described a more practical scenario in his report on a national bank in 1790 while serving as Treasury Secretary. Hamilton predicted that banknotes, or early forms of checks, of the U.S. Bank would function as paper money. Banknotes would expand the money supply by entering the stream of commerce and funding commercial transactions.[25] If the federal government were to deposit its revenue with the Bank as well as to partly capitalize the Bank, then the Bank would be furnished with added liquid resources to inject into the real economy. But the First U.S. Bank probably helped restrain the reckless expansion of banks and note circulation through its ability to accumulate the banknotes of state banks. During the existence of the First U.S. Bank, the number of state banks rose from 3 in 1790 to 88 in 1811.[26] When the charter of the U.S. Bank expired in 1811 and the institution was liquidated, state banks rapidly increased from 88 to 208 over a four year stretch from 1811 to 1815. At the same time, banknote circulation doubled from $2.3 million to $4.6 million.[27] Congress also authorized the U.S. Bank to only issue banknotes within stable limits. Though the new banknotes were receivable for federal taxes and qualified as money-like instruments, the U.S. Bank's charter capped banknote circulation at $10 million in excess of deposits.[28]

The views of Law and Hamilton implicated the issue of how to establish a money supply optimally correlated to real wealth, whether real wealth were to be interpreted in the form of produce, wares, or infrastructure. A reliance on banknotes followed from European practices, but the poverty of specie in the early American economy gave banknotes and other paper money substitutes an added importance.

Because of the hoarding and export of gold, agitation for a monometallic silver standard began in the early 1830s. Samuel Ingham, Treasury Secretary under President Jackson, proposed a silver standard on the view that silver coin already circulated in far greater magnitude than gold. Ingham noted that paper money tended to finance commercial intercourse anyway, so that a paper money standard backed by silver could more realistically provide a circulating medium than gold.[29] But Congress again rejected silver monometallism and instead revised the mint ratio upwards to 16:1 in gold to silver in 1834.[30]

The slump in monetary growth was not broken until the discovery of gold in California in 1848. By the early 1850s, gold production had expanded to $225 million due to the California discoveries.[31] The U.S. in fact became the world's leading gold producer for the rest of the nineteenth century.[32] By contrast, silver coinage excluding small pieces over this same period amounted to only $41.2 million.[33] The discoveries contributed to a moderate rise in domestic prices, but the price rises were not severe. Because of its more abundant supply, gold became overvalued at the Mint while circulation in silver contracted, which led to the depletion of fractional silver coins. Silver had already begun to sell at a premium in the currency markets.[34] In an attempt to pump smaller pieces back into circulation, Congress in 1853 required the Mint to issue silver coins of less weight and to stop producing silver coins of over $5.[35]

The deflation of the 1840s raised the real price of gold, so that the 1848 gold discovery came at an extremely opportune time. But the initial discovery along the American River in northern California was apparently inadvertent and occurred near the construction site for a dam. The real price of gold did not therefore somehow trigger an intensified process of prospecting in the region that then led to discovery, though the high real price of gold arguably drove the subsequent Gold Rush.[36] Moreover, the California discovery prompted gold prospecting in Australia, which resulted in discoveries soon afterwards.[37]

The antebellum era featured an initial and ongoing deflation that reflected the nation's dearth of specie. In the wake of the California gold discovery and the Gold Rush, this deflation turned to inflation. Proposals such as Morris's for a silver standard were well considered in light of the lack of a robust supply of gold, but this issue became moot after the California Gold Rush.

NOTES

1. Peter L. Rousseau, "Monetary Policy and the Dollar," in *American Economic Policy in the 1790s*, ed. Douglas Irwin and Richard Sylla (Chicago: University of Chicago Press, 2010), 139–40.
2. Davis Rich Dewey, *Financial History of the United States*, Sixth Edition (New York: Longmans, Green and Co., 1918), 36–38.
3. Ibid., 38–40.
4. Ibid., 41.
5. Ellis Paxson Oberholtzer, *Robert Morris: Patriot and Financier* (New York: The Macmillan Co., 1903), 26.
6. Oberholtzer, *Robert Morris*, 116.
7. Ibid., 201–03.
8. Ibid., 151.
9. Rousseau, "Monetary Policy and the Dollar," 139.
10. Robert Morris, "Robert Morris to President of Congress: 15 Jan. 1782," published 2000, University of Chicago, http://press-pubs.uchicago.edu/founders/documents/a1_8_5s2.html.
11. Edwin Walter Kemmerer, *Gold and the Gold Standard: The Story of Gold Money Past, Present, and Future* (New York: McGraw Hill Co., 1944), 58.
12. Morris, "Robert Morris to President of Congress."
13. Ibid.
14. Ibid.
15. Oberholtzer, *Robert Morris*, 154–55.
16. Kemmerer, *Gold and the Gold Standard*, 59–60.
17. Oberholtzer, *Robert Morris*, 237–38.
18. Alexander Hamilton, "On the Establishment of a Mint," in *The Works of Alexander Hamilton: Comprising His Correspondence, and His Political and Official Writings, Exclusive of the Federalist, Civil and Military*, vol. III, ed. John C. Hamilton (New York: John F. Trow, 1850), 157.
19. Hamilton, "On the Establishment of a Mint," 158–62.
20. Ibid., 180.

21. Kemmerer, *Gold and the Gold Standard,* 67–69.
22. Ibid., 74–75.
23. Ibid., 69–70.
24. Murray Rothbard, *The Panic of 1819: Reactions and Policies* (1962, reprint, Auburn, AL: Ludwig von Mises Institute, 2007), 152–53.
25. Alexander Hamilton, "National Bank," in *The Works of Alexander Hamilton: Comprising His Correspondence, and His Political and Official Writings, Exclusive of the Federalist, Civil and Military,* vol. III, ed. John C. Hamilton (New York: John F. Trow, 1850), 108–09.
26. Dewey, *Financial History,* 127.
27. Rothbard, *Panic of 1819,* 5.
28. Dewey, *Financial History,* 100.
29. Kemmerer, *Gold and the Gold Standard,* 72–3.
30. Ibid., 75.
31. Ibid., 79–80.
32. Hugh Rockoff, "Some Evidence on the Real Price of Gold, Its Costs of Production, and Commodity Prices," in *A Retrospective on the Classical Gold Standard: 1821–1931,* ed. Michael D. Bordo and Anna J. Schwartz (Chicago: University of Chicago Press, 1984), 625.
33. Kemmerer, *Gold and the Gold Standard,* 79.
34. Ibid., 80.
35. Ibid., 82.
36. Rockoff, "Real Price of Gold," 625.
37. Ibid., 626.

THREE

The U.S. Banks and Antebellum Panics

The money supply was impacted not only by fluctuations in the stock of specie but also by the structure of banking systems and the emergence of asset bubbles. The latter became especially problematic due to the boundless tracts of federal land for sale. Often directly the result of government policies, investors poured money into land and construction, which helped to fuel the Panics of 1819 and 1837 and the turmoil of 1839. The government also failed to develop a full-fledged central banking authority during this period. The Bank of North America and the First and Second U.S. Banks were all positioned to ultimately grow into the role of a central bank. But widespread distrust of banking forced the expiration of the public charters of all three institutions. The failure of the U.S. to develop a central bank in the 1800s would bear consequences stretching as far into the future as the Great Depression.

Upon his appointment as Superintendent of Finance in 1781, Robert Morris faced the task of establishing an institution that could assist the Continental Congress in waging the Revolutionary War. Morris recommended the establishment of a new bank called the Bank of North America. He had already set up the Pennsylvania Bank, but this was not an actual bank. Investors subscribed funds with Morris that he used to pay for military expenditures. The Bank of North America, however, served as a formal institution that functioned primarily to make out loans to Congress, which reached $923,308 in 1782 before falling to $349,534 in 1783. In turn, Congress subscribed $200,000 to the Bank's capital stock using newly imported specie from France. The relationship between the Bank and Congress was mutually beneficial. The Bank helped raise loans for Congress and earned interest. Congress owned shares in the Bank and earned dividends. The government and a private institution cooperated to direct money flows into the hands of Congress more efficiently than if Congress had relied ad hoc on a larger number of private creditors. But the Bank was only able to raise $70,000 in private capital. The official arrangements between the Bank and Congress were discontinued at war's end, and the Bank obtained a Pennsylvania charter in 1787.[1]

At the start of the Washington Administration, the need arose for an institution patterned upon the Bank of North America, particularly in its ability to financially assist the federal government. Hamilton had drafted a letter to Morris in 1781 outlining his plan for a bank of this sort. The plan was in many ways consistent with Morris's thinking but conceived on a larger scale. Now serving as Treasury Secretary, Hamilton worked to charter a U.S. Bank with a capital stock of $10 million, the amount originally envisioned for the Bank of North America. The Bank housed the federal revenue and served as a facilitator of credit for the government. Both specie and government securities counted as capital stock, with the federal government's share of the total capital coming to 20 percent. The Bank made out an immediate loan to the federal government of $2 million. After the government's debt to the Bank rose to $6.2 million in 1796, Congress was forced into selling the government's stock shares and using the proceeds to pay off its loans. By 1802, all of the government's bank shares had been sold off, bringing in $671,860 net of loan payments on top of $1.1 million in dividends.[2]

The U.S. Bank was not an official central bank, and it lacked the resources to serve in such a role. Hamilton in his capacity as Treasury Secretary purchased securities to stabilize the market after panics in 1791 and 1792, the first involving Bank scrip and the second Treasurys.[3] These actions served as a forerunner for open market operations later undertaken by the Treasury during the National Banking era. But had the U.S. Bank not been limited to a twenty-year charter, and had it been allowed to build up a specie reserve and a portfolio of Treasury securities, then it could have conceivably developed into a central bank capable of engaging in open market operations and serving as a lender of last resort. Nonetheless, political opposition to the Bank on several grounds forced its charter to expire in 1811, ranging from the proliferation of state banks to the extensive foreign ownership of Bank stock. Even the federal government's reacquisition of its starting capital might have cast doubt on the continued usefulness of the Bank.

To stabilize the monetary situation at the end of the War of 1812 and to provide for a uniform and sound currency, Congress passed legislation for a Second U.S. Bank that President Madison signed into law in April 1816.[4] The Bank began operations in January 1817.[5] Treasury Secretary Alexander Dallas considered the establishment of a Second U.S. Bank a necessary step for facilitating the resumption of specie payments, which had been suspended outside of New England during the war.[6]

In order to spur state banks into restoring specie payments by late February 1817, the Bank entered into an agreement with state banks obligating it to purchase up to $6 million in state banknotes before presenting notes for specie from the state banks. The Bank also committed itself to other provisions, such as assisting the state banks in a crisis and holding their public deposits. The Treasury backed this agreement because it helped prop up state banknotes as a form of revenue for the government.[7] The price of resumption was for the Bank to adopt expansionary policies against a specie reserve under $3 million.[8] The head of the Bank, William Jones, also ordered the Bank's branches to redeem the banknotes of all other branches. This policy in effect caused specie to drain from the Eastern branches while branches in the South and West recklessly emitted notes.[9]

The Bank exacerbated conditions of banknote depreciation and land speculation in the first few years of its charter as its specie reserve further dwindled. By 1819, the Bank's new president, Langdon Cheves, was forced into reversing course and pursuing a tighter policy, such as contracting the amount of credit supplied to state banks and regularly converting their banknotes into specie.[10] As the Panic of 1819 broke, banks contracted loans and suspended payments. The economy experienced deflation, bank failures, and other commercial bankruptcies. Cheves probably could have pursued countercyclical policies in response to these deteriorating conditions, but he was more concerned with maintaining the Bank's solvency.[11]

When establishing the Second U.S. Bank, Congress capped the Bank's total note circulation at $35 million.[12] Note circulation never reached this cap during Jones's tenure and in fact stayed a little under $10 million. Note circulation was even smaller under Cheves's stewardship.[13] After the Panic, note circulation reached $6 million in the second half of 1821 before mildly dropping off. By the time of Cheves's retirement from the presidency in early 1823, note circulation hovered at around $5 million.[14]

Cheves's successor, Nicholas Biddle, reverted to a more expansionary policy and worked to inject greater liquidity into Western states and territories. These regions depended on the U.S. Bank's paper money to finance local commerce more than other areas.[15] Under Biddle's stewardship, banknote circulation expanded from $5 million at the beginning of 1824 to $14 million in the first half of 1830.[16] While note circulation more than doubled in amount, this expansion remained well under the $35 million authorized by Congress in 1816. Biddle was constrained by the requirement that Bank officials at the main office sign all of the Bank's notes. But he was able to formulate a workaround called the branch draft, in which the branches issued checks that could only be presented at the main office. These checks were functionally equivalent to the notes issued at the main office, in that they operated as paper money. Biddle also involved the Bank in the speculative trading of bills of exchange used to finance agricultural trade.[17]

The Bank was relatively successful in expanding the money supply in the 1820s. But its status as a quasi-official creature of federal law ended as a result of the Bank War of 1832. Andrew Jackson opposed the U.S. Bank as a pawn of elites and foreign interests. Jackson asserted in a message submitted to Congress in December 1829 that "[b]oth the constitutionality and the expediency of the law creating this bank are well questioned by a large portion of our fellow citizens, and it must be admitted by all that it has failed in the great end of establishing a uniform and sound currency."[18]

Bank officials initiated the process of renewing the Bank's charter in 1831, which was scheduled to expire in 1837. Many political operatives worried that petitioning for re-charter before the 1832 presidential election was tactically risky. But Henry Clay, now serving in the Senate, along with other partisans of the Bank thought that the issue should be exploited in 1832. Clay and his allies assumed that robust support for the Bank in both houses of Congress assured passage of a bill for renewal, which would then force Jackson to decide whether to veto the bill. Clay believed that Jackson would avoid using his veto against the Bank during an election year. If Jackson did use his veto, such a supposed blunder would cost him reelection. Clay would in fact be running against Jackson in 1832, and the Bank War of that year defined the divide between Democrats and National Republicans, who eventually formed the Whig Party. In July 1832, both the Senate and House passed a bill for renewal of the charter. On July 10, Jackson submitted his veto, and Congress failed to override the veto with a two-thirds majority. Subsequent events proved Clay's gambit to be a severe miscalculation. Jackson was decisively reelected in November after waging a populist campaign against the Bank.[19] Jackson's reelection at least temporarily put an end to the question of renewal of the Bank's federal charter.

Jackson the next year appointed Roger Taney, who had been serving as Attorney General, to be Acting Treasury Secretary with the specific objective of transferring federal revenue from the U.S. Bank to several state "pet" banks. Martin van Buren succeeded his fellow Democrat Jackson to the presidency in 1837 and sought a more permanent solution to storing federal revenue, which had been turning in surpluses because of public land sales. In the aftermath of the Panic of 1837, van Buren requested Congress to pass legislation for an Independent Treasury allowing the Treasury Department to directly handle the flow of federal revenue as it was received. Van Buren disapproved of a subsequent bill establishing an Independent Treasury because it permitted banknotes issued by banks that paid out specie to be receivable for federal taxes instead of only specie. As an adherent to hard money, van Buren favored a specie-only restriction for the payment of federal taxes. Senator John Calhoun of

South Carolina supported the President's position and inserted such a provision into the bill, but easy money representatives prevented the bill from passing in the House. After the congressional elections of 1838, however, the hard money forces gained a numerical upper hand in Congress. A deal was reached delaying the specie-only restriction for the receipt of federal taxes until June 1843. Congress then passed a bill for an Independent Treasury made up of regional subtreasuries that van Buren signed into law on July 4, 1840.[20]

The expiration of the Second U.S. Bank's federal charter prevented it from developing into a veritable central bank. Yet the outcome of the Bank War during the Jackson Administration was not a fait accompli. A Third U.S. Bank could have still been chartered. A Whig takeover of Congress and the White House in 1840 indeed put the recently enacted Independent Treasury into immediate peril, since the Whigs continued to support the Bank in their party platform. The Whigs worked to repeal the legislation establishing the Independent Treasury in August 1841, but they were unable to complete their victory by instituting a new U.S. Bank. The newly sworn in president, war hero William Henry Harrison, died of either pneumonia or enteric fever soon after taking office. Harrison's Vice President, John Tyler, was nominally a Whig, but he hailed from Virginia and sided with the Democrats on the issue of the Bank. Tyler vetoed two bills establishing some form of federally chartered banking institution.[21]

Tyler thereafter submitted his own proposal for housing the federal revenue, which was contained within a message to Congress in December 1841. Tyler proposed a Board of Control that would hold and manage the federal revenue and maintain offices at different locations. The Board would only be authorized to issue Treasury notes in lieu of gold or silver at the discretion of creditors, and even these note issues would be capped at $15 million. The Board would be further authorized to hold a limited number of private deposits, in exchange for which the Board would issue Certificates of Deposit. Relatively speaking, the most radical departure in Tyler's proposal was to allow the Board to deal in short-dated bills. But even this provision appeared largely intended to enable the Board to earn a small premium to pay for its own operating expenses. Tyler obviously did not envision anything that could somehow develop into a central banking authority since he had already vetoed bills establishing such institutions. He declared that the Board of Control "is made to rest on an actual specie basis, in order to redeem the notes at the places of issue" and "produces no dangerous redundancy of circulation."[22]

While the Board was authorized to issue up to $15 million in notes, these issues were not intended to de facto add to the money supply as, for instance, Biddle's branch drafts were institutionally equipped to do. Tyler's proposal could be interpreted as falling just short enough of an Independent Treasury to cater to Whig prejudices. But Tyler was unsuccessful even according to this interpretation. The Whigs had already passed two compromise bills that Tyler had vetoed, and they were in no mood to negotiate any further.[23] The Independent Treasury was formally restored in 1846 after the Democrats had regained control of Congress and the White House.[24]

One wonders how the Board of Control might have evolved as an institution notwithstanding Tyler's own views. Tyler only sketched out a plan, and members of Congress would likely have modified it had it ever passed into law. But the Whigs were not necessarily inclined to limit the Board's prerogatives. The most noteworthy aspect of the plan was Tyler's concession that the Board be authorized to deal in bills and drafts. While Tyler stated that these market operations would be employed "in so far as may be necessary for government purposes exclusively," such as to pay for operating expenses, he mentioned only a few other objective constraints. Tyler insisted that the Board would buy and sell bills "resting on a real and substantial basis, payable at sight, or having but a short time to run, and drawn on places not less than one hundred miles apart." The Board could also only conduct these operations if the state governments did not prohibit such activities within their jurisdictions.[25]

What Tyler described came to be known as the real bills doctrine, which restricted a central bank's mandate to purchases of only self-liquidating, so-called real bills arising out of commercial or agricultural transactions. Tyler might not have intended to arm the Board with powers over rudimentary monetary policy, but that is beside the point. Federal Reserve Banks were incidentally granted the authority to deal in government securities under the original Federal Reserve Act in 1913, and this incidental authority inadvertently made possible the development of open market policy. Under the plan as laid out by Tyler, albeit in draft form, the Board of Control would have been authorized to issue cash in exchange for real bills at low interest rates. These operations would have preceded the rediscounting of real bills by Federal Reserve Banks by over half a century. At the same time, the Board would at least partially have met the definition of a bank because of its authorization to hold public and private deposits. The Board would have in this respect more closely resembled a bank than the Federal Reserve. Finally, Tyler probably contemplated a highly centralized organization, with the satellite agencies only intended to assist the Board in managing the flow of federal revenue. Because Tyler wanted the Board to be primarily responsible for managing the federal revenue, such a centralized institution would not have been at odds with his underlying views.

Yet Tyler left ambiguous whether the Board of Control itself or the peripheral agencies would oversee the dealing in bills, and this ambiguity is a critical one. The Board would also not have been authorized to issue notes on a fractional reserve basis. But the cautious assertion can be made that this plan, at least what we know of it and considering what might have become of it, could have potentially laid the groundwork for an institution capable of developing into a central banking authority by the second half of the 1800s. Such an institution would have more effectively developed into a central banking authority than the Independent Treasury, while the Board of Control could also have achieved a higher degree of centralization and efficiency than the early Federal Reserve System.

State law dominated banking with the demise of the Second U.S. Bank as a federally chartered institution. In a trend that would continue through most of the twentieth century, state governments imposed restrictions on bank branching, including unit banking laws that prohibited branches outright. These laws prevented interstate consolidation in the banking industry. But while most states continued to regulate against branching, a handful of states also relaxed entry requirements by passing free banking laws. Free banking laws emerged as an alternative to chartering individual banks. Under free banking laws, new enterprises were authorized to issue notes after posting designated state or federal bonds with state officials as collateral. Sixteen states eventually experimented with free banking laws. In New York alone, 133 banks were created soon after the state legislature passed a free banking law.[26] States were incentivized into passing free banking laws because they boosted demand for their own bond issues. This idea for collateralizing government bonds was later incorporated into the National Banking System. Such liberal requirements permitted the creation of "wildcat" banks in remote, frontier regions that did not even hold deposits. Owners of wildcat banks were still obligated to comply with collateral requirements, but otherwise these so-called banks often functioned more as a way for their owners to obtain hard money than to legitimately collect deposits and make out loans. At the opposite extreme, the Suffolk banking system in New England during this period implemented early forms of branch banking.[27]

The trend towards decentralization in banking overlapped with a period of financial distress in the late 1830s and early 1840s. The Jackson Administration helped to spark a crisis when it issued the Specie Circular in July 1836 requiring the federal government to only accept specie in payment for public land sales beginning in August of that year. The Circular served as part of an attempt to stop Western land speculation and to curtail note expansion but it in fact accelerated the flow of specie from East Coast banks to the West. Both Jackson and van Buren blocked efforts to repeal the Circular. A panic broke out the following spring in New York and other major financial centers, marked by bank runs, suspensions of specie payments, hoarding, and spiking interest rates. The Bank of England worsened the situation in the U.S. by raising its discount rate to 5 percent in September 1836 after having kept it at 4 percent for nearly ten years.[28] As a result, U.S. commodity exports plummeted at a time when banks desperately needed gold inflows.

The economy rebounded quickly and the Circular was repealed in 1838. Investors again poured money into land-related speculation, this time through the conduit of state public works projects. Looking ahead to when newly sold public land would become taxable after a brief moratorium, state governments began selling bonds to fund canals, roads, and other internal improvements. One such project was the Michigan and Illinois Canal, whose construction had been ongoing since the mid-1830s. By 1839, the Governor of Illinois coordinated with the local Board of Canal Commissioners to sell $500,000 in state bonds to fund renewed construction. The Board was only able to sell $100,000 in Chicago, forcing the state to then sell another $1 million in bonds denominated in sterling through an investment bank in London at 6 percent interest. Unfortunately, the investment bank imploded after making an advance to the state of Illinois but before selling any bonds.[29]

Funding the Michigan and Illinois Canal typified the process by which a bubble in state government debt grew, with state governments relying on construction boards and local banks to sell their bonds in capital markets. When demand eventually dried up in the early 1840s, major financial institutions, including the Bank of the U.S., now operating essentially as an investment bank under Pennsylvania charter, were caught stranded holding huge portfolios of state bonds that had not yet been sold in the capital market. The Bank of the U.S. defaulted after having become seriously overleveraged from state government debt and cotton speculation, which from a political standpoint only further hurt the prospects for chartering a Third U.S. Bank. As land prices imploded and construction stopped, states repudiated those bonds that had not yet been sold in the open markets.

Putting aside panics and looking instead to overall real output before the Civil War, the lack of data for computing gross product makes deriving a correlation between monetary trends and real growth difficult. Paul David estimated that the annual GDP growth rate per capita averaged 1 percent to 1.5 percent until 1840. It then continued to gradually increase in subsequent decades.[30] By contrast, Walt Rostow dated a "take-off" in growth in the 1840s due to formative instances of industrialization such as railroad construction.[31] The American economy from the end of the eighteenth century into the early nineteenth century was overwhelmingly agricultural, but agriculture's share of GDP contracted as the century progressed.

Regarding the terms of trade, or the ratio of the prices of exports to imports, external factors distorted the period of Neutral Trade from the outbreak of the French Revolutionary Wars in 1793 to the Embargo on European trade imposed by President Jefferson in 1807. The blockade of European ports due to war came as a boon to U.S. traders and shippers since the U.S. remained a neutral party. Total merchandise exports rose from $1.7 million in 1793 to over $60 million by 1806.[32] But the gains in exports were artificial and temporary. Many U.S. shippers earned outsized profits by re-exporting merchandise through the West Indies. Consistent with these trends, shipping remained a lucrative industry into the first half of the nineteenth century, including both the sale of ships and freight earnings. The sale of ships rose from around $200,000 in 1790 to $1 million by 1806 while at the same time freight earnings increased from $5.9 million to $34.6 million.[33]

International pressures also helped to accelerate domestic production. When Jefferson imposed the Embargo, U.S. consumers were largely shut off from European imports. Merchandise imports declined sharply from $138.5 million in 1807 to $59.4 million by 1809, after the Embargo had gone into effect.[34] Domestic industries needed to be created in order to offset the contraction in imports. Cotton mills operating in the U.S. rose from 15 to 62 within the narrow time span of 1808–09. Over the same period spindles utilized at such sites increased from 8,000 to 31,000.[35] The emergence of textiles and woolens industries sparked a protectionist movement after the War of 1812 that gained momentum in the 1820s.

Attempting to estimate the effects of the supply of specie on exports through the price specie flow mechanism would be difficult to fully determine. Price specie flow predicts that a domestic price rise will render exports uncompetitive relative to cheaper merchandise sold in a deflationary import market. The flow mechanism can be further plotted out as a self-adjusting process involving exports and domestic price levels. The idea can only be intuitively understood when trading partners share a common medium of exchange such as gold. Price specie flow would predict higher rates of exports in the early 1800s given a comparatively smaller stock of U.S. specie, but the era of Neutral Trade distorts any such hypothesis. However, inflation in the early 1850s may have temporarily exerted downward pressure on U.S. exports. The merchandise trade surplus reached $39,544 in 1843 amid deflationary conditions. Merchandise trade again notched a large surplus of $29,421 in 1847 but then turned to a deficit of $16,394 the following year. The deficit continued to widen in the early 1850s until coming to $72,672 in 1854, after which it stabilized.[36] These data cannot conclusively prove the effect of price specie flow, especially since merchandise trade was in deficit during most years immediately following 1820, but nor do they decisively refute it.

While price specie flow cannot be positively identified, monetary growth in the early 1850s did help to push the economy out of recession. The trough or end-point of the contraction is dated to December 1854. The subsequent expansion peaked in June 1857, with the economy reentering recession until December 1858. The economy again expanded into the early fall of 1860.[37] By the mid-1850s, a few years after the gold stock began expanding, the economy had recovered from its weakened state a decade earlier. The Panic of 1857 broke this growth period, but it was relatively brief, and specie payments resumed soon afterwards.[38]

NOTES

1. Dewey, *Financial History*, 54–56.
2. Ibid., 100–01.
3. Richard Sylla, "The Financial Foundations: Public Credit, the National Bank, and Securities Markets," in *Founding Choices: American Economic Policy in the 1790s*, ed. Douglas Irwin and Richard Sylla (Chicago: University of Chicago Press, 2010), 77–78.
4. Dewey, *Financial History*, 150.
5. Ibid., 151.
6. Ibid., 146.
7. Ralph C.H. Catteral, *The Second Bank of the United States* (Chicago: University of Chicago Press, 1903), 24–25.
8. Catteral, *Second Bank*, 29.
9. Ibid., 33–35.
10. Ibid., 77.
11. Edwin J. Perkins, "Langdon Cheves and the Panic of 1819: A Reassessment," *The Journal of Economic History* 44, no. 2 (1984): 459–60.
12. Ralph C.H. Catterall, "The Issues of the Second Bank of the United States," *Journal of Political Economy* 5, no. 4 (1897): 421.
13. Catterall, "Second Bank of the United States," 429.
14. Ibid., 424.
15. Ibid., 425.
16. Ibid., 424.
17. Ibid., 425–26.
18. John J. Knox, *A History of Banking in the United States* (New York: Bradford Rhodes & Co., 1900), 62–63.
19. Ibid., 68–70.
20. Dewey, *Financial History*, 235–36.
21. Ibid., 239–42.
22. Alexander Gurdon, *John Tyler: President of the United States, Up to the Close of the Second Session of the Thirty Seventh Congress* (New York: Harper & Brothers, 1843), 211.
23. Dewey, *Financial History*, 243.
24. Ibid., 252–53.
25. Gurdon, *John Tyler*, 211.
26. John Thom Holdsworth, "Lessons of State Banking before the Civil War," *Proceedings of the Academy of Political Science in the City of New York* 1, no. 2 (1911): 220–21.
27. Holdsworth, "Lessons of State Banking," 217.
28. Wallace E. Huffman and James R. Lothian, "The Gold Standard and the Transmission of Business Cycles, 1833–1932," in *A Retrospective on the Classical Gold Standard: 1821–1931*, ed. Michael D. Bordo and Anna J. Schwartz (Chicago: University of Chicago Press, 1984), 465–66.
29. J.W. Putnam, "An Economic History of the Michigan and Illinois Canal," *Journal of Political Economy* 17, no. 5 (1909): 284–85.
30. Paul A. David, "The Growth of Real Product in the United States Before 1840: New Evidence, Controlled Conjectures," *Journal of Economic History* 27, no. 2 (1967): 155–56.
31. W.W. Rostow, "The Take-Off Into Self-Sustained Growth," *The Economic Journal* 66, no. 261 (1956): 26.
32. Douglass North, "The United States Balance of Payments, 1790–1860," in *Trends in the American Economy in the Nineteenth Century*, ed. Conference on Research in Income and Wealth (Princeton: Princeton University Press, 1960), 591–92.
33. North, "Balance of Payments," 600.
34. Ibid., 592.
35. F.W. Taussig, *The Tariff History of the United States*, Fifth Edition (New York: G.P. Putnam's Sons and the Knickerbocker Press, 1910), 32.
36. North, "Balance of Payments," 605.

37. National Bureau of Economic Research, "U.S. Business Cycle Expansions and Contractions," NBER, http://www.nber.org/cycles/cyclesmain.html, accessed August 2017.

38. Clement Juglar, *A Brief History of Panics and Their Periodical Occurrence in the United States* (New York: G.P. Putnam's Sons, 1916), 89.

FOUR

Greenbacks, Gold, and Silver Purchases

The postbellum era witnessed the effort to restore convertibility, the use of limited silver purchases, and the continuation of a wartime financial system, but at an ulterior level the U.S. was subject to a secular deflation caused by slumping growth in the world's gold stock. No major gold discoveries were made until the late 1880s.

The Civil War led to a suspension of convertibility and adoption of a provisional fiat standard. The suspension of specie payments during wartime was hardly a surprising decision. But the federal government did not immediately resort to fiat at the outbreak of hostilities. There was even initially some belief that it could sustain specie payments through a protracted conflict. After Congress granted him broad powers to borrow money, Treasury Secretary Salmon P. Chase convened with Eastern bankers in August 1861 to coordinate the selling of government debt. Chase agreed for the Treasury to borrow three installments of $50 million in loans in exchange for selling 3-year Treasury notes yielding 7.3 percent interest to the banks. Under these arrangements, the banks would directly deposit gold into the Department's subtreasuries. But this would result in the banks' gold reserves becoming seriously depleted after they deposited the money. To offset the loss in gold for the banks, the Treasury was committed to making timely war-related expenditures in order to pump the gold back into the economy and eventually bank deposits. Chase also permitted the banks to sell the Treasury notes in the open market as a way to replenish their reserves. The Treasury and the banks intended gold to expeditiously flow into and out of government vaults and thereby keep the money supply stabilized while the Union was fighting the war. But any serious crisis, which could hardly be unexpected in wartime, might seriously upset these money flows by increasing hoarding and preventing the transfer of gold back into bank deposits.[1]

Because of changes in federal law, Chase and the bankers could have set up alternative channels whereby the Treasury held its borrowed gold in the form of deposits with the banks. The Treasury could have drawn on these accounts whenever it wanted to make payments. But Chase was unsure that this system would work, particularly in regards to Western banks. The banks therefore directly transferred gold into the subtreasuries. Chase also issued Treasury notes to the public pursuant to statutory authority.[2]

Perhaps inevitably, panicky conditions hit markets in December. Chase released his *Annual Report* towards the end of the year, which deemphasized the use of taxes to raise revenue for the duration of the war and instead proposed legislation to virtually coerce the banks into increasing their holdings of Treasurys. Bankers had looked forward to Chase presenting a more systematic means for increasing taxable revenue instead of relying predominantly on borrowing. In addition, a war scare erupted with the U.K. after a U.S. Navy officer seized two Confederate emissaries aboard the British vessel *Trent*.[3] The ensuing panic on the New York Stock Exchange and gold hoarding eventually forced the Eastern banks to suspend specie payments on December 30. The Treasury followed suit soon afterwards. If banks were now unable to lend gold to the federal government, there was no reason for the Treasury to redeem its own notes at the gold window.[4]

With the federal government having now affirmatively gone off gold, Congress issued a combined $300 million in greenbacks, or non-interest bearing legal tender notes, by the summer of 1862. Congress issued an additional $150 million in March 1863 mainly to replace existing notes. During this time, the value of the greenback against gold gyrated depending upon the performance of Union armies on the battlefield.[5] Congress capped the supply of greenbacks at $400 million in 1864 while also limiting a supplementary amount to $50 million, "as may be temporarily required for the redemption of temporary loan."[6]

When the banks and the Treasury suspended specie payments at the end of 1861, the public started hoarding gold. But the Treasury still paid interest in gold to its creditors, which helped the banks maintain their gold reserves. The only region where gold continued to circulate during the war, and indeed throughout the greenback era, was the West Coast. California's state constitution outlawed the establishment of banking institutions. With no banks to suspend payments, California was not as affected by the crisis of late 1861 as the financial centers on the other side of the country. When Congress started issuing greenbacks, businesses agreed to payment in greenbacks only if their value was at par with gold. The state legislature thereafter sanctioned contracts that contained gold payment clauses.[7]

But gold ceased to circulate in most parts of the country, and as the greenbacks depreciated following Union defeats in 1862, the market premium on gold simultaneously rose. Chase attempted to drive down the premium through a handful of measures, but they all failed. Among them included a proposal to issue notes convertible to gold used for paying customs duties, a tax on the contractual buying of gold, Treasury sales of $11 million in gold in the New York money market, and legislation that criminalized gold futures contracts. The New York gold sales temporarily worked in pushing down the premium, but the Treasury could not continue these market operations on a long-term basis. The criminalization of gold futures only exacerbated the gold premium, and banks successfully lobbied Congress for its repeal in early July 1864. In the wake of these failures, Chase resigned as Secretary before taking his seat as Chief Justice of the Supreme Court by the end of the year.[8]

When the last Confederate troops finally surrendered in the spring of 1865, the federal government faced two interrelated problems affecting the transition back to the peacetime economy. The first was the stabilization of the value of the greenback against gold, which served as an intermediate objective before resumption of specie payments. The second was providing for some means ensuring reduction of the national debt. The Treasury remained the single institution positioned to manage these problems, although war-related legislation had diluted the Independent Treasury of much of its Jacksonian orthodoxy. The establishment in 1863 of a new National Banking System in many ways negated the very need for an Independent Treasury, since now federal officials could rely on national banks to hold revenue instead of less reliable state institutions. Legislation in 1864 authorized the treasury secretary to select national banks to store federal revenue as long as the banks posted collateral in the form of "United States bonds and otherwise."[9] But the other major aspects of the Independent Treasury System remained intact, including the Treasury serving as the default monetary authority for open market operations.

Under legislation passed in 1862, Congress mandated a sinking fund pegged to 1 percent of the national debt. The Treasury drew on the fund to buy U.S. securities from the public. Though the Treasury canceled the securities that it had bought, interest on the purchased bonds was still added to the sinking fund to help finance continued purchases.[10] From June 1869 to June 1874, the Treasury purchased a total of $141 million in U.S. bonds to meet its requirements for the sinking fund while paying out a market premium of $16.6 million.[11] From June 1870 to June 1873, the Treasury purchased a total of $182.2 million in U.S. bonds in excess of its requirements for the sinking fund while paying out a market premium of $23 million.[12] The national debt fell from around $2.4 billion in 1865 to $1.7 billion by 1874.[13]

The Treasury operations were not entirely responsible for reducing the national debt. Another major factor lowering the federal debt burden was protectionist trade policy. In the years after the end of hostilities, Republican Congresses preserved the high wartime tariff rates, which protected growing industries and generated surplus revenue. Even in the depression year of 1874, the Treasury was left with a small surplus of $2.3 million.[14]

In 1866, Congress authorized the treasury secretary to retire greenbacks from circulation but limited this authority to no more than $10 million within six months of passage of the legislation and to no more than $4 million in any month afterwards. Under this legislation, the Treasury contracted the supply of greenbacks from $422.7 million in April 1866 to $356.2 million in February 1868.[15] In 1868, Congress suspended the Treasury's authority over contracting greenback circulation while also only authorizing the treasury secretary to issue new greenbacks to replace mutilated ones, leaving in place a supply of $356 million in greenbacks.[16] The Treasury acted within the parameters of this authority when it issued $1.5 million in greenbacks in 1871 to replace notes that had been destroyed during the Great Chicago Fire. More controversial was the Treasury's decision to issue $4.6 million in October 1872 for no obvious reason, which pushed the total supply back up to $360 million.[17] The Treasury had relied on bond purchases in order to issue the additional greenbacks.[18]

Because this action appeared to be unlawful, the House of Representatives passed a resolution demanding clarification from the Treasury. Secretary George Boutwell responded that the notes had been issued while he had been away from his office. The Assistant Secretary, William Richardson, apparently ordered their issuance to alleviate seasonal stringency in the money market because of the autumnal shipment of crops from the interior to the East. Boutwell claimed that the Civil War-era legislation mandating a circulation of $400 million in greenbacks provided a basis in law for the action. But he disregarded the Act of 1866, which authorized the reduction in circulation to $356 million, and the Act of 1868, which kept circulation at $356 million.[19] The question hinged on whether the Treasury still had legal authority to issue $44 million in greenbacks, the differential between the $356 million at the time of the 1868 Act and the 1864 cap of $400 million. After investigating the matter, the Senate Finance Committee concluded that the Treasury's action was unlawful.[20]

As the controversy subsided, the circulation of greenbacks declined from $360 million in November 1872 back to $356 million by March 1873.[21] While Richardson's decision to issue the $4.5 million had violated the statute, the deeper question, the extent to which the Treasury could actively manage conditions in the money market, remained unclear. The Treasury needed to find ways to expand the money supply in the autumn, when markets tightened as crops were shipped from the South and

West to the East Coast. Recognizing that the money supply should only be temporarily expanded to ease stringency, Boutwell admitted in his 1872 *Annual Report* that "[t]he problem is to find a way of increasing the currency for moving the crops and diminishing it at once when that work is done. This is a necessary work, and, inasmuch as it cannot be confided to the banks, where, but in the Treasury Department, can the power be reposed?" [22]

The Treasury's ability to serve as a competent monetary authority was critically tested during the Panic of 1873. The Panic occurred after nearly five years of solid real growth marked by a boom in railroad construction. The trigger came in the form of the collapse of Kenyon, Cox and Co. due to losses on the Canada Southern Railroad, as well as the suspension of the New York Warehouse and Security Co. because of its involvement with the Missouri, Kansas, and Texas Railroad.[23] After the New York Stock Exchange closed its doors in late September 1873, Richardson, now serving as Secretary, publicly committed the Treasury to buying $10 million in bonds, but it ended up only buying $2.5 million from the market. Richardson and President Grant then traveled to New York to meet with bankers to try to bring some calm to the situation. The bankers wanted the Treasury to re-issue the $44 million differential in greenbacks, but the two top representatives of the Administration squelched the idea. Richardson instead relied on more limited open market operations, purchasing nearly $7 million in bonds by the end of the month before calling a halt to any further easing.[24] These isolated actions failed to pacify markets, at least in part because under its operating procedures the Treasury only entered into transactions of this magnitude with savings banks instead of the more distressed commercial banks of the New York Clearinghouse. The purchases did not succeed in preventing commercial banks from suspending payments.[25]

As economic depression set in after the Panic, Congress passed a bill expanding greenback circulation back up to $400 million. The passage of this bill in 1874 was the high watermark, at least among mainstream political parties, for fiat monetary expansion during the greenback era. The bill for expansion was well timed in the face of deepening depression, but that did not prevent Grant from vetoing it. Grant's veto message emphasized the need for sound money tied to gold by asserting that paper currency "is valuable exactly in proportion to the amount of coin that it can be converted into."[26] While the bill for expansion might have helped to alleviate the economic contraction over the short-term, Grant's veto message raised the inevitable question of when Resumption was supposed to occur, unless the nation were truly expected to continue using what could best be characterized as a holdover of wartime finance. A lame-duck Republican majority in Congress passed the Resumption Act in January 1875 during the continuing depression. Scheduling Resumption for January 1, 1879, the Act contracted the supply of greenbacks to $300 million at a rate of 80 percent of national banknote issuance. Greenbacks would thereafter be maintained at $300 million.[27]

Lags had often occurred in Europe from the end of a wartime fiat standard to the reinstitution of convertibility. But nonetheless not until ten years after the end of the Civil War did Congress formally mandate Resumption, and this was done in a lame-duck session in which convertibility was still delayed another four years. The Treasury had also engaged in expansionary, countercyclical open market purchases, while Congress had successfully passed a bill for permanently increasing the supply of greenbacks to $400 million. Monetary affairs were not influenced along strict partisan lines, with both the Republican and Democratic Parties containing inflationist factions. The Greenback Party formed in 1876 on a platform of repealing the Resumption Act and replacing national banknotes with paper instruments accruing interest of 1 percent or less per $100.[28] The Greenback Party was only a marginal party in presidential and congressional elections, but even so the political climate of the time could not be described as one universally or automatically favoring hard money.

The undertaking of Resumption finally fell to the Administration of Rutherford B. Hayes. In 1877, Hayes appointed Senator John Sherman of Ohio as Treasury Secretary and tasked him with carrying out Resumption. Sherman held hard money views and thought that the experiment with peacetime fiat had only harmed the economy and delayed the inevitable restoration of convertibility. Responding to a call for repeal of Resumption, Sherman wrote in a journal article in late 1877, "The experiment of further inflation to cure inflation was fairly, though illegally tried, by throwing into the maelstrom $26,000,000 of United States notes that had been retired and cancelled."[29] Sherman was referring to the $26 million in bonds purchased by the Treasury in 1873 and early 1874, which pushed greenback circulation over the $356 million limit.[30]

The Treasury began selling government bonds for the purpose of stockpiling gold coin in its vaults in preparation for the scheduled date of convertibility on January 1, 1879. The Treasury needed to coordinate with New York banks prior to this date because the Resumption Act required the Treasury to receive only gold and not notes for the sale of bonds. Since coin was not held by the public at large, the Treasury would have to transact mainly with banks that held gold reserves.[31] Sherman further estimated that the Treasury needed a gold reserve equal to about 40 percent of circulating paper money, which came to $138 million. The Treasury continued selling bonds in order to stockpile gold coin, until the Treasury held $95 million as a result of market operations. Another roughly $38 million had accumulated in Treasury vaults due to budget surpluses, giving the Treasury a total reserve of $133 million at the time of Resumption.[32]

The Resumption Act mandated that the public could only convert legal tender notes into coin at the Assistant Treasurer's office in New York.[33] The decision to restrict redemptions of notes to the New York office aroused criticism that the Treasury was not intending to undertake Resumption on a national level.[34] Limiting gold conversion to a single office arguably functioned as a form of gold device, or a monetary authority's ability to regulate gold flows through institutional means. Had the Treasury offered conversion to gold at branch offices nationwide, the Treasury's reserve in coin might have been more rapidly depleted. The Act's provision limiting conversion to the New York office still failed to quell worry that banks were planning to rack up greenbacks and turn them in for gold on the day of Resumption. One banker had even offered to pay $50,000 for the right of first access at the gold window on January 1. But Sherman thought that any panicky actions taken by the banks would be commercially irrational. The end of the day of January 1, 1879 vindicated his attitude. The New York subtreasury had netted $265,000 in gold.[35]

A surge in agricultural exports during 1879–81 eased the transition to convertibility through the generation of gold inflows. The boom in these years followed the long economic contraction that had begun with the Panic of 1873. From the standpoint of price specie flow, U.S. exports might have gained a competitive advantage due to depression, but the more direct cause of the export boom can be traced to poor harvests abroad. The merchandise trade balance was negative through much of the first half of the 1870s. The trade balance then turned in a surplus of $91.7 million in 1876 before leaping to $163.6 million the following year. The surplus then reached $269.4 million in 1878, $276.4 million in 1879, and $263.9 million in 1881. These surpluses helped to offset gold outflows after Resumption. Indeed, gold movements netted outflows of $77 million in 1880 and $98 million in 1881.[36] A Wholesale Price Index (WPI) compiled by the Bureau of Labor Statistics (BLS) showed a price rise of 21 percent over the course of 1879–82. But the export boom ended when agricultural output recovered in Europe, and the gold inflows slowed. WPI fell 44 percent by 1894.[37]

Resumption also meant the restoration of fixed exchange rates. Unlike during the greenback era, when the dollar floated against other currencies, the gold standard necessitated fixed exchange rates between currencies linked to gold. The reason for this was that currencies contained different quantities of gold. The dollar contained 23.22 grains of fine gold. Because pound sterling contained substantially more gold, the exchange rate with sterling was $4.86. Currencies could also be valued in terms of troy ounces; $20.67 was worth 1 troy ounce of gold.[38] Even though exchange rates were nominally fixed, they might still shift because of fluctuations in the value of currencies in different markets. Under certain circumstances, traders financially gained from shipping and insuring gold across the ocean. When domestic currency depreciated against foreign currency, the exchange rate hit the export point, and importers shipped gold across the Atlantic instead of purchasing appreciated foreign exchange. When domestic currency appreciated against foreign currency and hit the import point, exporters found it worthwhile to ship home gold instead of depreciated foreign exchange.[39]

Central banks supposedly followed the so-called rules of the game, which in the narrowest sense meant that they avoided impeding adjustments to the balance of payments. The rules could also be meant to imply a forbearance of countercyclical actions.[40] Yet the notion of central banks following rules of the game should not be taken too far. The Bank of England periodically raised its discount rate simply in response to depletion in its gold reserves. A hike in the discount rate sparked gold outflows from the U.S. An extreme case of this occurred in the early 1880s when the Bank raised its discount rate by over three percentage points by January 1882, generating outflows from the U.S. and under some theories contributing to the Panic of May 1884.[41]

A second major issue overlapping with Resumption was whether to continue to recognize silver as full legal tender. Just before the start of the Civil War, the use of silver had been limited to fractional coinage, and it had become the undervalued metal at the Mint because of expanded gold production. Congress passed legislation in 1873 that ended silver coinage. This legislation would later come to be known as the "crime of 1873" among partisans of silver, but at the time the bill encountered little controversy.[42] Silver's market price fell after the U.S. and other nations demonetized the metal.[43] Largely in an attempt to placate farming and silver mining interests, Congress passed the Bland-Allison Act of 1878. The treasury secretary was required to purchase $2 to $4 million in silver bullion at the market price per month and coin this amount into dollars. The Treasury could also issue silver certificates to the public in exchange for silver coin. Taxes were payable in silver under the legislation.[44] Congress overrode Hayes's veto with a two-thirds majority.[45]

Bland-Allison operated conventionally in that bullion was brought to the Mint and coined, with the Treasury earning seigniorage. The Act was otherwise unconventional because the Treasury purchased a limited amount of silver bullion per month at the market price to expand the money supply without resorting to the free coinage of silver. Silver was touted by specific interests, but the Treasury wanted the public at large to accept silver as a legitimate means of exchange.

That all said, passage of Bland-Allison complicated Sherman's bond sales to creditors in Europe in the period leading up to Resumption by weakening European confidence in the U.S.'s commitment to gold.[46] There was also some initial fear that silver purchases would activate Gresham's Law and drive gold from circulation, since gold was of inherently higher market value and would be hoarded. In an 1878 Treasury report, Sherman warned that Bland-Allison could produce just such a result. He advised either that silver dollar coinage be capped at 50 million oz. or that the coinage ratio of gold to silver be pegged to the market ratio.[47] Sherman warned in his report that excessive silver coinage would cause silver to "become the sole coin standard of value. Gold will be either hoarded or exported. When two currencies, both legal, are authorized without limit, the cheaper alone will circulate." [48] Congress did not find Sherman's warning persuasive, and Bland-Allison remained on the books until 1890, after which it was replaced by an even more aggressive Silver Purchase Law.

Under Bland-Allison, the Treasury coined silver totaling roughly $308.2 million in value until 1890 while it earned $70 million from seigniorage.[49] Silver purchases carried out under Bland-Allison coincided with a decline in the market price of bar silver.[50] The legislation did not initially trigger Gresham's Law, and indeed the greater challenge initially was in trying to induce the public into accepting and using silver as a means of exchange, whether in the form of coin or certificate. Silver dollars earned the derisive nickname cart wheels because of their heavy weight.[51] Sherman reported that only a little over a third of the newly coined silver was kept in circulation, while New York banks entered into an informal agreement not to pay each other in silver. Congress eventually threatened to withhold their charters, but even then banks still apparently agreed not to deal in silver. To pump silver into circulation, the Treasury paid out certain expenditures in silver, such as federal salaries. Under the original legislation, silver coin could only be deposited for certificates at the Treasury in sums of $10 or more. Congress revised this provision in an effort to increase the circulation of silver certificates and allowed silver coin to be traded in for certificates of $1, $2, and $5. The Treasury even amassed gold convertible notes and held them in its vaults to drive up the demand for silver certificates under $10.[52]

Despite the public's reluctance to use silver, the deflation of the 1880s exacerbated silver agitation in agricultural and silver mining regions. This agitation, fed by silver purchases, possibly contributed to gold outflows of $30 million in the two months prior to the Panic of 1884.[53] Two years later, the House of Representatives narrowly averted passing a bill for the free coinage of silver by 37 votes, and silver partisans unsuccessfully challenged the Treasury to pay expenditures in silver without restriction.[54] A climate of labor unrest in the mid-1880s only worsened the silver agitation. Industrialization had led to the mobilization of workers into unions. The labor organizer Samuel Gompers helped found the Federation of Organized Trades and Labor Unions in Pittsburgh in 1881, which eventually became the American Federation of Labor (AFL).[55] The more radical Knights of Labor also formed during this time, with its membership spiking from 60,811 in 1884 to 702,924 in 1886.[56] The Knights rapidly admitted new members into their ranks while engaging in a series of strikes in the mid-1800s. But the preeminence of the Knights was only fleeting, and its membership quickly dropped off by the late 1880s.[57]

Against this backdrop of silver agitation and labor unrest, Grover Cleveland became the first Democrat elected president since before the Civil War. Although elected in the depths of deflation in 1884, Cleveland stood resolved in his hard money views, thinking that Bland-Allison had only aggravated the monetary problems facing the economy. Cleveland focused on the threat that silver would replace gold in the Treasury's reserve in his first message to Congress in December 1885. Cleveland wrote, "Every month two millions of gold in the public Treasury are paid out for two millions or more of silver dollars, to be added to the idle mass already accumulated. If continued long enough, this operation will result in the substitution of silver for all the gold the Government owns applicable to its general purposes." [58] He was implying that the Treasury purchased silver with gold under Bland-Allison, while the public increasingly paid taxes and other dues in silver instead of gold. If the Treasury were left with only silver in its reserve, then it would be forced into paying all expenditures in silver. Cleveland conceded that "[t]here is certainly not enough silver now in circulation to cause uneasiness," but he warned that "it is the ceaseless stream that threatens to overflow the land which causes fear and uncertainty," and which would presage the hoarding of gold and its replacement by silver in the money supply.[59]

Cleveland accurately emphasized the fact that international conferences aimed at remonetizing silver had utterly failed and that a roving ambassador of his had reported that European governments were uninterested in changing their position on silver.[60] He saw no choice but to recommend that Congress repeal the mandatory provisions of Bland-Allison before the situation became uncontrollable.[61] Cleveland's view, shared by John Sherman and other monetary conservatives, was that silver purchase legislation would activate Gresham's Law just as would official bimetallic standards. Consistent with these attitudes, Cleveland's Treasury Secretary, Daniel Manning, issued a report in 1885 finding that silver purchases should be discontinued.[62]

Congress did nothing to limit Bland-Allison, and in fact Cleveland's successor in office, the Republican Benjamin Harrison, held pro-silver leanings. In his message to Congress in 1889, Harrison stated, "I have always been an advocate of the use of silver in our currency. We are large producers of that metal, and should not discredit it." Harrison also noted, "As a coin it has not had general use, and the public Treasury has been compelled to store it. But this is manifestly owing to the fact that its paper representative is more convenient." [63] He reported that from 1878 to 1889 gold coin circulation had expanded by $293.4 million and silver certificates by $276.6 million. On the other hand, gold certificates expanded by only $72.3 million and silver dollars by a mere $57.5 million.[64]

Harrison viewed silver from a completely different angle than his political rival Cleveland. The underlying problem for Harrison was not Gresham's Law but inducing the public into using silver for transactional purposes. Harrison was not ignorant of the dangers of Gresham's Law and indicated that he would only tolerate the free coinage of silver if legislation could "secure the equality of the two coins in their commercial uses."[65] From Cleveland's vantage, gold was clearly the more valuable commodity and any attempt at the free coinage of silver would only lead to gold hoarding.

Harrison also recognized that silver's lack of easy mobility made the certificates all the more important and pointed to the fact that $277 million of the $283 million in silver coin in the Treasury reserve were held as certificates by members of the public.[66] Though Harrison's point was valid, it did not answer for the danger that taxes payable in silver could ultimately force the federal government to unconditionally pay out expenditures in silver and put the U.S. on a de facto silver standard. Harrison was in any case not a radical on the issue and clearly implied in his public rhetoric that he only sought a greater use for silver if it were consistent with an international agreement.[67] He also acknowledged that his Administration, like those of earlier Administrations, had refrained from purchasing the maximum allowable $4 million in silver per month.[68]

If both sides could muster plausible arguments to advance their respective cases, gold advocates like Cleveland still had reason to be worried about the state of government finances in the mid-1880s. Gold fell by $39 million in the Treasury reserve through much of 1884 in contrast to a $21.3 million rise in silver. The market price of gold hit a premium when a Treasury official implied that the New York office could be forced into paying out silver. Gold certificates had also fallen from 74 percent to 31 percent of customs dues in New York during 1883–84, while silver had risen over the same period from 17 percent to 36 percent.[69] These indicators begged the question of whether bimetallism, either formally mandated or informally implemented through Silver Purchase Laws, was truly more efficient than monometallism, even if in basic arithmetic terms it was capable of expanding the money supply.

After Harrison assumed office in 1889, his Treasury Secretary, William Windom, drafted a plan for new silver purchase legislation designed to supplement Bland-Allison. Windom's proposal called for freely coining silver dollars and purchasing silver at the cap of $4 million per month, but it never came to fruition.[70] Harrison instead signed into law in July 1890 the Sherman Silver Purchase Act, which replaced Bland-Allison. The Act mandated that the Treasury purchase 4.5 million oz. of silver bullion per month at the market price by using notes of full legal tender value. The statute granted the Treasury discretion to convert the notes into gold or silver coin.[71] John Sherman, again serving as Senator from Ohio and a member of the Finance Committee, did not per se support the legislation but saw it as a preferable alternative to a bill for the free coinage of silver.[72]

A crucial distinction between the 1890 Act and Bland-Allison was that the former denominated monthly Treasury purchases in terms of ounces of silver while the latter had done so in terms of dollars. The 1890 Act therefore did not serve as an unconditional price support mechanism. But the legislation did transmit a constant amount of silver into the money supply irrespective of fluctuations in silver's market price. By the time Congress repealed the Act three years later, the Treasury's purchase of silver amounted to 169 million ounces.[73]

The Bland-Allison Act in particular and the Sherman Silver Purchase Act to a lesser extent represented creative attempts to expand the money supply using the limited coinage of silver. Under Bland-Allison, the treasury secretary had discretion to purchase silver bullion in a range of $2 to $4 million per month, but otherwise the Act established an automated procedure to induce mild inflation. A falling market price for silver worked to expand silver coinage while a rising price slowed the rate of coinage. The Bland-Allison Act might have even represented a new step forward in the development of monetary policy because it was based on a controlled but discretionary process for monetizing silver without freely coining silver at the mint ratio. While the Sherman Silver Purchase Act was cruder in operational terms, it also embodied an attempt to target moderate inflation without freely minting silver. But from a more conservative perspective, the Silver Purchase Laws were not helpful. The Silver Purchase Laws did not cause two metals to optimally coexist. Bland-Allison may not have unleashed Gresham's Law in the 1880s, but it still fueled perceptions that the U.S. was not wholly committed to the gold standard.

Undeniably, however, international developments impeded the effectiveness of the Silver Purchase Laws as European nations shifted to gold monometallism during the 1870s. Most delegates at the 1867 International Monetary Conference in Paris opted for a uniform standard based on gold instead of silver. The U.K. had been on gold since 1821. Germany demonetized silver by imperial proclamation in 1871 after its victory in the Franco-Prussian War and started selling off silver the following year. Other European nations were then pressured into adopting gold standards partly out of fear that the German silver sales would convey devastating inflows of silver across their borders. Norway, Denmark, Sweden, Belgium, and the Netherlands soon joined the emerging gold bloc, followed by Russia in 1876 and France and Switzerland in 1877.[74] As Edward Leech, the former Director of the Mint, noted, by the time Bland-Allison was enacted into law in 1878, "not a single mint in Europe was open for the coinage of silver for individuals."[75]

Though the U.S. in part joined the ranks of the gold standard after Resumption in 1879, the Silver Purchase Laws clearly deviated from the European move to gold. While other countries continued to use silver, including China, India, and Mexico, some of the U.S.'s closest trading partners were now solely on gold. European perceptions that the U.S. was not fully anchored to gold were compounded by the fact that many inflationists who earlier supported the Greenback Party had now joined the silver movement. Unlike silver mining interests, these inflationists did not necessarily seek a bimetallic standard, but they did repudiate notions of gold monometallism.

As directed under the Bland-Allison Act, the U.S. sought to organize an international conference on the question of reviving the monetary use of silver. This diplomatic initiative led to the 1878 and 1881 Intentional Monetary Conferences held in Paris. A pattern emerged in which other nations pledged their support for the monetization of silver in principle but stopped short of agreeing to a restoration of bimetallic standards in their own economies. German delegates did not even attend the 1878 conference, but Germany did suspend silver sales the following year.[76] Unfazed by this diplomatic stalemate, Benjamin Harrison hoped that another international conference would resuscitate the use of silver. When accepting the Republican nomination in 1892, Harrison noted in a public message, "The monetary conditions in Europe within the last two years have, I think, tended very much to develop a sentiment in favor of a larger use of silver."[77]

The 1892 International Monetary Conference convened in Brussels in late November of that year. The silver question had reached an impasse by the time of the Brussels conference. Having already passed two Silver Purchase Laws with mixed results, the U.S. government wanted Europe to readopt silver coinage. Perhaps the continued secular deflation and economic downturn would convince the other delegates to accept silverist proposals. The U.S. delegation submitted a program during the Conference's second session that called for bimetallism.[78] But an attempt at a breakthrough in negotiations at Brussels leading to a multilateral return to silver coinage was doomed to fail. Serving as one of the delegates representing the U.K., the banker Alfred de Rothschild entered into the record remarks opposing the abandonment of the existing monometallic system.[79] But he also suggested a proposal similar to the U.S. Silver Purchase Laws that would be implemented in Europe. Rothschild tentatively offered that European nations purchase £5 million in sterling per year. These purchases would be carried out "over a period of five years at a price not exceeding 43 pence per ounce standard, but, if silver should rise above that price, the purchases for the time being to be immediately suspended."[80]

The U.S. delegation's position of aggressive re-monetization of silver and Rothschild's cautious proposal of a £5 million silver purchase plan stood at odds with each other. Rothschild's plan essentially served as a price support mechanism for silver, since purchases would be suspended after silver reached a designated price. Silver partisans in the U.S., on the other hand, wanted to persuade other nations to restore silver to its full legal tender status along with gold. In the session following Rothschild's address, Senator William Allison of the U.S., one of the co-sponsors of the Bland-Allison bill, attempted to center the discussion back on bimetallism.[81] A second U.S. delegate, James McCreary, objected to the Rothschild plan on the grounds that the U.S. would be forced into purchasing more silver per dollar under current legislation than would European governments.[82] McCreary also predicted the repeal of the Sherman Silver Purchase Act in either the current or a subsequent session of Congress, implying that the U.S. had helped organize the Conference in order to restore bimetallism and move on from silver purchase legislation in the first place.[83] Restoring bimetallism was never brought to a vote because the delegates from the major European powers were clearly opposed to any such a monetary regime.[84] After about a month of discussions, the delegates adjourned before Christmas.[85]

In the domestic sphere, while the increase of silver in the Treasury vaults in the mid-1880s portended the triggering of Gresham's Law, the Treasury's gold reserve held relatively stable over the longer span of time from Resumption until the early 1890s. From 1879–91, the gold reserve rose from $140 million to $300 million. Members of the public were not at this point panickily converting their notes into gold at the Treasury.[86] Bland-Allison had not single-handedly driven gold out of government vaults, Cleveland's forewarnings aside.

In the first half of the 1890s, however, the combined effects of gold outflows, banking distress, and a diminishing Treasury gold reserve produced crisis conditions. In mid-1890, $15 million in gold flowed out of the U.S. because of weakening exchange rates indirectly caused by souring British investments in South America.[87] Bank reserves dipped below their legal limits, and call loans were contracted, but no banks failed.[88] The Treasury publicly communicated that it would purchase $20 million in bonds in response to the turmoil. The announcement itself alleviated distress in the banking sector, with the subsequent purchases only coming to $9 million.[89] As monetary stringency set in during the autumn, the Treasury announced that it would purchase bonds worth $16 million through a syndicate. These purchases helped to ease the money market, and loans expanded back to over $400 million.[90] In early November, the Bank of England raised its discount rate from 5 percent to 6 percent, which caused New York bank reserves to fall by $4 million a day later.[91] The Baring crisis in London later in November fortunately did not spark all-out panic in New York.[92]

Gold outflows reached $53 million in the first half of 1891.[93] But a surge in agricultural exports induced by weak European production temporarily mitigated the outflows and triggered net inflows of $34 million.[94] Gold outflows netted $50 million the following year.[95] As foreign investors became increasingly skittish towards the American commitment to the gold standard, they started selling off U.S. securities, which ignited a gold outflow of $11 million in December 1892 and $60 million in early 1893.[96] The Panic of 1893 broke in early May with the collapse of the Philadelphia and Reading Railroad and the National Cordage Company. Banks called loans while stock prices fell, until the stock market crashed on May 4.[97] As was the case in other panics, calm would have been restored more quickly had the crisis only been confined to New York. But as panic spread around the country, New York banks were forced to suspend. Agitation on whether Congress would repeal the Silver Purchase Act accelerated gold outflows.

Grover Cleveland remained adamant in his support for gold as a private citizen in the early 1890s. In an 1891 letter to the Chairman of the Reform Club of New York, Cleveland wrote of the "dangerous and reckless experiment of free, unlimited, and independent silver coinage."[98] Cleveland's views were shared by Edward Leech, who wrote in July 1893 that "[t]his immense stock of uncoined silver [in the Treasury reserve] is a standing menace to the market for silver. If Congress should direct that it be sold, the very fact that this huge pile of silver was for sale would break the market and cause a serious fall in the price of the white metal." And if it should be coined, "it would still further unsettle confidence in the ability of our government to maintain the gold standard, and hasten our steps towards a silver basis for our currency."[99]

At the start of his second non-consecutive Administration in 1893, Cleveland picked up right where he left off with his anti-silver views. In June 1893, in the midst of financial crisis, he demanded that Congress decide the fate of the Sherman Silver Purchase Act. He then worked to push the process along by submitting his own message reiterating the call for repeal.[100] The Senate finally voted to repeal the Act in October, by which time the Panic had sent the economy into depression.

The Treasury's gold reserve began to fall in the wake of the Panic as federal revenue contracted and the public increasingly converted notes into gold at the Treasury.[101] In order to maintain its gold reserve, the Treasury sold bonds under the 1875 Resumption Act. The Treasury ended up selling $100 million in bonds during 1894, mainly in January and the following November. These bond sales failed to stabilize the gold reserve because the public kept converting notes into gold at the Treasury at the same rate. The Treasury then bought gold from banks in exchange for 30-year bonds at 4 percent interest.[102] But the reserve continued to fall and sat at around $90 million in mid-1896.[103]

The depression of the 1890s almost inevitably spurred new momentum for inflationism, even though the economy would have arguably been better served without the Sherman Silver Purchase Act, let alone the issuance of inconvertible greenbacks. Perhaps the most graphic example of radical inflationism was that of Coxey's army, in which the agitator Jacob Sechler Coxey led hundreds of people on a march to Washington, D.C. Coming from Massillon, Ohio, Coxey owned a stone quarry and was reasonably prosperous, but he identified with labor and appeared earnest in the promotion of his fringe views.[104] Coxey called for Congress to issue $500 million in fiat money not convertible into gold or silver while municipalities be authorized to sell bonds at no interest to the federal government in order to fund public works projects, particularly roads.[105] The march involving some 356 demonstrators ended anticlimactically when Coxey was tossed into jail after trespassing on the lawn of the Capitol.[106]

Coxey's views were a blend of fiat inflationism and attempts to increase employment through government sponsored public works. The enthusiasm generated by Coxey showed that economic stagnation had brought the inflationism of the old Greenback Party back into vogue. Coxey's movement also augured policies in the twentieth century that revved up public works projects to boost aggregate demand. In literature circulated among his supporters for a second march in 1912, Coxey asserted that "[f]ew people realize the waste to the nation by the loss of 5,000,000 unemployed men daily. Even at an average in purchasing power alone of $1.50 per day each, it means $7,500,000 each day, $195,000,000 each month, $2,340,000,000 each year, loss in wages. If this lost labor were employed in building roads at $15,000 per mile it would build 156,000 miles of 18 ft. brick roads a year which would in less than seven months complete the road system of Ohio."[107]

The political winds were shifting against gold. Perhaps not improbably, by 1896 the Democratic Party selected a presidential candidate whose views on monetary affairs were diametrically the opposite of Cleveland's. William Jennings Bryan had served as a two-term member of the House of Representatives from Nebraska in the early 1890s. He was well positioned in this office to call for more active steps in addressing deflation among his farming constituents. One of Bryan's planks during the 1890 congressional elections declared, "We demand the free coinage of silver on equal terms with gold and denounce the efforts of the Republican party to serve the interest of Wall Street as against the rights of the people." Bryan backed another plank championing free silver for the Nebraska Democratic Party the next year.[108] He vehemently opposed the repeal of the Sherman Silver Purchase Act in 1893. When attempts to delay a bill for repeal became futile, Bryan uttered on the floor of the House, "Silver will lay aside its grave clothes and its shroud. It will yet rise and in its rising and its reign will bless mankind."[109]

After losing a Senate race in 1894 and retiring from Congress in 1895, Bryan continued to lend support to the silver movement through speeches and editorials in the *Omaha World Tribune*. He helped to mobilize Silver Democrats in preparation for the 1896 Democratic convention in Chicago. At the convention, Bryan delivered his "cross of gold" speech that elevated him to the presidential nomination, culminating with the famous declaration that "you shall not crucify mankind upon a cross of gold."[110]

Bryan's 1896 candidacy brought the U.S. to within its closest reach of free silver. Bryan called for the free coinage of silver under a mint ratio of 16:1 gold to silver "without waiting for the aid or consent of any other nation."[111] The McKinley campaign by default opposed any monetary changes unsupported by international agreement. The Democratic platform of 1896 represented a departure from Harrison's refusal to unilaterally take further steps in remonetizing silver, let alone Cleveland's total opposition to the white metal. The Republican plank for silver, meanwhile, remained consistent with its earlier iteration under the Harrison Administration, but it appeared far more conservative when compared to the rhetoric of Bryan. In the November election, William McKinley won 61 percent in the Electoral College and 51 percent of the popular vote. In a rematch against Bryan in 1900, McKinley's victory in the Electoral College rose to 65 percent.[112] Bryan drew his support from the "Great Crescent" that incorporated the South and the West, while McKinley's stronghold was in the Northeast and Midwest and centered upon his native Ohio. After the 1900 election, one editorial opined that "this magnificent victory sounds the death knell of Bryanism, Demogogism, Populism, and Repudiation."[113] Although the Great Commoner ran unsuccessfully for a third time against William Howard Taft in 1908, the earlier defeats in 1896 and 1900 ended market tensions over the U.S.'s commitment to gold.

New production trends ultimately ensured the continuation of the international gold standard. The adoption of gold standards in Europe in the 1870s initially exacerbated the secular deflation because more nations demanded gold as their sole legal tender. The real value of gold rose as a result. But worldwide gold production did not expand significantly until the late 1880s due to gold discoveries and new technologies. Discoveries occurred in South Africa in 1886 and in Australia in 1889.[114] Prospecting in Alaska and Colorado eventually resulted in discoveries that, along with mines in other regions of the U.S., accounted for about a fifth of expanded gold supply around the world near the turn of the twentieth century.[115] Gold production also benefited from a new cyanide process. The commercial use of cyanide exploded during the 1890s.[116]

Global gold production per year rose from $203 million in 1896 to $408 million in 1914. U.S. wholesale prices vaulted by 46 percent and general prices by 41 percent over the same timespan.[117] Gold certificates in the U.S. reached $1 billion by 1914, having been only $131 million twenty-four years earlier.[118] The U.S. formally adopted gold monometallism with the passage of the Gold Standard Act of 1900, which set a parity of

$20.67 to 1 troy oz. gold. The production of silver, on the other hand, inevitably contracted after the repeal of the Sherman Silver Purchase Act, falling from 60 million oz. in 1893 to about 50 million oz. the following year but thereafter stabilizing at 55 million oz. in 1895.[119] The market value for silver also fell. Silver miners convened in Denver in June 1893 and agreed to temporarily close their mines.[120] For a period of time, silver mining only occurred at copper and lead sites.[121]

Rebounds in gold production stopped the secular deflation and reversed the shortfall in the money supply. Support for the free silver movement in the 1890s was understandable due to the U.S.'s silver ore resources in Western states and territories. But uncertainty remained whether bimetallic standards and Silver Purchase Laws were capable of efficiently generating a circulating medium. A restored bimetallic mint ratio or "doing something for silver" through purchase legislation could arithmetically expand the money supply, but the bimetallic standard had already proved futile in the antebellum era. There was no reason to believe that a bimetallic standard would have worked to a greater degree of efficiency after the Civil War, and the European de-monetization of silver certainly hindered any further efforts of this kind. The Silver Purchase Laws only raised the question of whether the U.S. was truly on gold.

At the same time, gold monometallism morphed into something resembling an effective regime in the late nineteenth century after fortuitous gold discoveries took place around the world and new extraction methods were introduced. Even if the assumption were to be made that the real value of gold regulated gold production over the long-term, a nearly four-decade lag occurred from the discovery of gold in eastern Australia in 1850 until a major new discovery in South Africa in 1886. Even then the discovery in western Australia did not follow until 1889, while the mainstream use of cyanide waited until the 1890s. During this four-decade lag, the nations of Europe uniformly switched to a gold standard. The need obviously existed for increased gold production by the early 1880s, which did compel the efforts of prospectors and metallurgists. Less clear was whether the supply of gold could continue to keep pace with a new process of economic globalization unfolding at the turn of the twentieth century. Fortunately, at least for that period, the answer was in the affirmative. But instead of representing an efficient monetary regime, the international gold standard became synonymous with timely discoveries and technologies that possibly saved it from political ruin.

NOTES

1. Wesley C. Mitchell, "The Suspension of Specie Payments, December 1861," *Journal of Political Economy* 7, no. 3 (1899): 307–9.
2. Mitchell, "Suspension of Specie Payments," 309–11.
3. Ibid., 319–320.

4. Ibid., 320–24.
5. O.P. Austin, "The Public Debt of the United States," *The North American Review* 175, no. 552 (1902): 704.
6. Eugene B. Patton, "Secretary Shaw and Precedents as to Treasury Control over the Money Market," *Journal of Political Economy* 15, no. 2 (1907): 67–68.
7. Wesley C. Mitchell, "The Circulating Medium During the Civil War," *Journal of Political Economy* 10, no. 4 (1902): 538–39.
8. Albert Bushnell Hart, *American Statesman: Salmon Portland Chase* (New York: Houghton, Mifflin, and Co., 1899), 284–87.
9. Milton E. Ailes, "National Banking System and Federal Bond Issues," *The Annals of the American Academy of Political and Social Science* 36, no. 3 (1910): 121.
10. Austin, "Public Debt," 715–16.
11. Secretary of the Treasury, *Annual Report of the Secretary of the Treasury on the State of the Finances for the Year 1874* (Washington, D.C.: Government Printing Office, 1874), 21–22.
12. Treasury Secretary, 1874 *Annual Report*, 23–24.
13. Austin, "Public Debt," 720.
14. Treasury Secretary, 1874 *Annual Report*, IV.
15. Patton, "Treasury Control," 70–71.
16. Ibid., 72.
17. Ibid., 73.
18. Ibid., 81.
19. Ibid., 73–75.
20. Ibid., 75–76.
21. Ibid., 81.
22. Secretary of the Treasury, *Annual Report of the Secretary of the Treasury on the State of the Finances for the Year 1872* (Washington, D.C.: Government Printing Office, 1872), XXI.
23. O.M.W. Sprague, *History of Crises under the National Banking System* (Washington, D.C.: Government Printing Office, 1910), 35.
24. Patton, "Treasury Control," 82–83.
25. Sprague, *History of Crises*, 42.
26. Dewey, *Financial History*, 361.
27. Ibid., 372–73.
28. Ibid., 378–79.
29. S.A. Bronson, *John Sherman: What He Has Said and Done, Being a History of the Life and Public Services of the Hon. John Sherman, Secretary of the Treasury of the United States* (Columbus, OH: H.W. Derby & Co., 1880), 212–13.
30. Dewey, *Financial History*, 361.
31. Ibid., 374.
32. Ibid., 375.
33. Kemmerer, *Gold and the Gold Standard*, 86.
34. Winfield S. Kerr, *John Sherman: His Life and Public Service*, vol. II (Akron, OH: Werner Co., 1907), 32.
35. Kerr, *John Sherman*, 30–31.
36. Matthew Simon, "The United States Balance of Payments, 1861–1900," in *Trends in the American Economy in the Nineteenth Century*, ed. Conference on Research in Income and Wealth (Princeton: Princeton University Press, 1960), 700–03.
37. Kemmerer, *Gold and the Gold Standard*, 89.
38. Anna J. Schwartz, "Alternative Monetary Regimes: The Gold Standard," in *Money in Historical Perspective*, ed. Anna J. Schwartz (Chicago: University of Chicago Press, 1987), 365.
39. Ibid., 366.
40. John Dutton, "The Bank of England and the Rules of the Game under the International Gold Standard: New Evidence," in *A Retrospective of the Classical Gold Stan-*

dard, 1821–1931, ed. Michael D. Bordo and Anna J. Schwartz (Chicago: University of Chicago Press, 1984), 174–75.

41. Huffman and Lothian, "The Gold Standard," 474.
42. Dewey, *Financial History*, 404–405.
43. Ibid., 405–06.
44. Kemmerer, *Gold and the Gold Standard*, 94.
45. Dewey, *Financial History*, 407.
46. Ibid., 375.
47. Kerr, *John Sherman*, 26.
48. Ibid., 27.
49. Dewey, *Financial History*, 407.
50. Ibid., 406.
51. Kemmerer, *Gold and the Gold Standard*, 95.
52. Dewey, *Financial History*, 407–08.
53. Sprague, *History of Crises*, 109.
54. Dewey, *Financial History*, 410.
55. Leo Wolman, "Changes in Union Membership, 1889–1923," in *The Growth of American Trade Unions, 1880–1923* (New York: National Bureau of Economic Research, 1924), 30.
56. Wolman, "Changes in Union Membership," 32.
57. Ibid., 29.
58. Grover Cleveland, *The Public Papers of Grover Cleveland: Twenty-Second President of the United States, March 4 1885 to March 4, 1889* (Washington, D.C.: Government Printing Office, 1889), 32.
59. Cleveland, *Public Papers*, 34.
60. Ibid., 34–35.
61. Ibid., 36.
62. Dewey, *Financial History*, 409.
63. Benjamin Harrison, *The Public Papers and Addresses of Benjamin Harrison: Twenty-Third President of the United States, March 4, 1889 to March 4 1893* (Washington, D.C.: Government Printing Office, 1893), 45.
64. Ibid., 44.
65. Ibid., 45.
66. Ibid., 44–45.
67. Ibid., 139–40.
68. Ibid., 45.
69. Alexander D. Noyes, "The Treasury Reserve and the Bond Syndicate," *Political Science Quarterly* 10, no. 4 (1895): 578.
70. Dewey, *Financial History*, 436–37.
71. Kemmerer, *Gold and the Gold Standard*, 96–97.
72. Kerr, *John Sherman*, 239–40.
73. Kemmerer, *Gold and the Gold Standard*, 97.
74. E. Benjamin Andrews, "The Monetary Conference of 1892," *Political Science Quarterly* 8, no. 2 (1893): 197–98.
75. Edward O. Leech, "Silver Legislation and Its Results," *North American Review* 157, no. 440 (1893): 44.
76. Andrews, "Monetary Conference," 198–99.
77. Harrison, *Public Papers*, 19.
78. American Delegates to the International Monetary Conference, *Report of the Commissioners on Behalf of the United States, and Journal of the Sessions of November 22, 1892, to December 17, 1892* (Washington, D.C.: Government Printing Office, 1893), 54.
79. 1892 *Report*, 61.
80. Ibid., 71.
81. Ibid., 98–99.
82. Ibid., 115.
83. Ibid., 118.

84. Andrews, *Monetary Conference*, 214.
85. Ibid., 216.
86. Dewey, *Financial History*, 442.
87. Sprague, *History of Crises*, 131–32.
88. Ibid., 134.
89. Ibid., 137.
90. Ibid., 139–40.
91. Ibid., 141.
92. Ibid., 144.
93. Ibid., 154.
94. Ibid., 156.
95. Ibid., 157.
96. Ibid., 158.
97. Ibid., 163–67.
98. Grover Cleveland, *Grover Cleveland: Addresses, State Papers, and Letters*, ed. Albert Ellery Bergh (New York: The Sun Dial Classics Co., 1909), 204.
99. Leech, "Silver Legislation and Its Results," 46.
100. Kemmerer, *Gold and the Gold Standard*, 99.
101. Dewey, *Financial History*, 447.
102. Ibid., 448–50.
103. Ibid., 454.
104. Oliver Otis Howard, Thomas Byrnes, and Alvah H. Doty, "The Menace of 'Coxeyism,'" *The North American Review* 158, no. 451 (1894): 688.
105. Howard, Byrnes, and Doty, "The Menace of 'Coxeyism,'" 690.
106. William H. Cordell and Kathryn Coe Cordell, "Unions among the Unemployed," *The North American Review* 240, no. 3 (1935): 500–501.
107. Jacob S. Coxey, *The Coxey Plan: Medium of Exchange Without Cost, Public Bonds Without Interest, Common Carriers Without Private Profit* (Massilon, OH: Jacob. S. Coxey, 1914), 14.
108. Harvey E. Newbach, *William Jennings Bryan: A Concise But Complete Story of His Life and Services* (Lincoln, NE: The University Publishing Co., 1900), 42.
109. Newbach, *Bryan*, 47–48.
110. Ibid., 60–61.
111. William J. Bryan, *The First Battle: A Story of the Campaign of 1896* (Chicago: W.B. Conkey Co., 1896), 148.
112. William H. Allen, "The Election of 1900," *The Annals of the American Academy of Political and Social Science* 17 (1901): 53.
113. Allen, "The Election of 1900," 54.
114. Rockoff, "Real Price of Gold," 623.
115. Ibid., 626.
116. Ibid., 628–29.
117. Kemmerer, *Gold and the Gold Standard*, 101.
118. Ibid., 103.
119. Edward Sherwood Meade, "The Recent Production of Silver and Its Probable Future," *Annals of the American Academy of Political and Social Science* 14 (1899): 43.
120. Meade, "Recent Production of Silver," 45.
121. Ibid., 46.

FIVE

The National Banking System

The money supply was not only affected by changes in the available stock of specie but also by Civil War-era legislation relating to the banking sector. In his *Annual Report* submitted in mid-1862, Treasury Secretary Chase elaborated on his proposal for the establishment of a new national banking association. Chase wanted to increase the demand for U.S. securities, and one way of doing so was to require that national banks post bonds with the Treasury as collateral in order to issue banknotes. Chase predicted that the new system of banks "would require within a very few years, for deposit as security for circulation, bonds of the United States to an amount not less than $250,000,000." Chase went on to note that "[a] steady market for the bonds would thus be established and the negotiation of them greatly facilitated."[1]

The impetus behind the proposal was undoubtedly the need to drive up the demand for Treasurys to help fund the war effort. But Chase foresaw the new banking system continuing into the peacetime economy. If this were the case, then banknote circulation would be regulated by fluctuations in the national debt. Chase admitted that if hypothetically speaking the federal government steadily paid off its debt, then "some other security for circulation may be devised, or, possibly, the vast supplies of our rich mines may render all circulation unadvisable except gold. . . . But these considerations may be for another generation."[2]

Chase turned what might have been a wartime expedient into a colossal reorganization of American banking, including the creation of a new currency in the form of national banknotes. Congress passed the National Banking Act in 1863 along with revisions in 1864. Congress imposed a 10 percent tax on state banknotes in 1865 in order to drive them from circulation. By 1909, 6,893 national banks held in the aggregate a capital stock of $934 million compared to 15,598 state banks with capital of $866 million. Total national bank deposits ranged at around $4.9 billion versus $9.2 billion for state banks.[3] Of huge importance, the National Banking System incorporated Chase's idea of pegging the national banknotes to Treasury bonds. With restrictions on bank branching remaining in effect, the Act capped a national bank's note circulation at 90 percent of its capital stock and 90 percent of the lower of the market or par value of the bonds it posted with the Treasury.[4]

Banks were discouraged from issuing banknotes when bonds sold at a premium in the open market. A rising premium meant that the price for the bond had risen and its yield had fallen. Because the law tied banknote circulation to the lower of the market or par value of bonds, banks that purchased bonds at a premium in the market could still only issue banknotes against the lower par value of the bonds instead of the higher market value. A differential would open up between the cost to banks of purchasing bonds in the market and the issuance of banknotes. In fact, as premiums on bonds rose, banks were forgoing substantial profit by holding bonds as collateral to back banknote circulation instead of selling the bonds in the market. The rise in premiums incentivized banks to retire banknotes, redeem bonds that the banks had posted as collateral with the Treasury, and then sell the bonds at the higher market prices. The retirement of banknotes caused a contraction in currency. Moreover, bonds sold at a premium when real interest rates fell, and real interest rates fell in periods of deflation, such as during the 1880s. The National Banking System was procyclical by reinforcing the contraction of banknotes at exactly the times when an expansion in their circulation was needed. The premium on government bonds only declined when the Treasury sold bonds on a large scale, such as just prior to Resumption and in the mid-1890s. But for the most part, the premium on U.S. bonds held steady through the 1880s and well into the 1890s.[5]

As an example of these dynamics, in 1875 banks posted bonds with a par value of $361 million. The market value of these bonds reached $426 million, which meant a premium of about $65 million. At the same time, the banks had issued $325.3 million in banknotes, resulting in a loss of about $100 million. Many banks unsurprisingly decided to exchange banknotes for bonds originally posted as collateral to sell them in the market.[6] Because of rising premiums and bank bond redemptions, banknote circulation contracted by $56.6 million in 1886, more than in any prior year.[7] A more general problem was the connection between banknote circulation and the national debt, in that Treasury purchases or redemptions of its bonds reduced the supply of bonds available to secure banknotes.

The National Banking System seemed to work reasonably well from 1866 to 1874. National banknote circulation rose from $280 million to $333 million. Legislation in 1870 authorized circulation to expand by $54 million, permitting banknotes to exceed the previously mandated cap of

$300 million.[8] Banknote circulation then contracted from $344.5 million to $167.9 million during 1880–91.[9] The decline in banknote circulation did not coincide with a downsizing of the national banking sector. National banks netted 248 in 1890.[10] The contraction was purely in currency. However, higher growth rates in the U.S. gold stock beginning in the second half of the 1890s created a more inflationary environment amenable to expanded banknote circulation. The 1900 Gold Standard Act also loosened up requirements by pegging banknotes to the higher of the market or par value of posted bonds.[11] Banknotes in the aggregate expanded from $254 million in 1900 to $759 million in 1911.[12]

The National Banking System distorted the money supply by linking what was intended as a uniform currency to the market price of Treasury bonds. The contraction in banknote circulation in the 1880s possibly even offset the inflationary effects of Bland-Allison. The National Banking System further distorted the money supply by causing national bank reserves to flow into the New York call loan market. National banks in small cities or towns were bound to a 15 percent legal reserve ratio against deposits. Sixty percent of these reserves could be held as deposits with national banks of reserve or central reserve status. Banks in reserve cities were bound to a 25 percent legal reserve ratio against deposits. Fifty percent of these reserves could be held as deposits with central reserve banks. Banks in central reserve cities were bound to a 25 percent legal reserve ratio. One hundred percent of these reserves needed to be held as cash.[13] Legal reserves were counted against both deposits and banknotes until 1874, but beginning that year reserves were only counted against deposits.[14] Because interbank deposits paid out interest, national banks put as much of their reserves as possible in correspondent balances, particularly in the central reserve city of New York. These reserves were mainly invested in the call loan market secured by equities. By 1909, call loans comprised about 45 percent of total loans made out by New York central reserve banks.[15]

Because New York initially served as the only central reserve city, national banks from around the country transferred a part of their cash reserves to the New York central reserve banks. The central reserve banks used these deposits to fund investments in the call loan market. The money supply was thereby directed into the speculative trading in equities. To relieve the concentration of interbank deposits in New York, Congress made changes in 1887 to allow cities whose population was at least 200,000 to elect central reserve status. Chicago and St. Louis met the population threshold and chose to be central reserve cities.[16] But Chicago and St. Louis banks held only $34 million in interbank deposits while the interbank deposits of their counterparts in New York were over four times as large at $145 million. Chicago and St. Louis banks also continued to hold substantial amounts of cash in New York, despite the fact that this money did not count as part of their legal reserves.[17]

The National Banking System set up the central reserve city banks as de facto central banking institutions, but these banks could not fulfill such a quasi governmental role. They were private banks organized for profit that used the reserve balances of other banks for speculative investments.

The Panics of 1873, 1893, and 1907, in addition to distress in 1890 and the briefer Panic of 1884 characterized the National Banking era. The Panics of 1873 and 1907 occurred in the autumn. Country banks in the interior pulled out money from New York deposits in order to accommodate crop shipments. The contraction in call loans and sales of stock drove down stock prices and sometimes caused panic on the floor of the New York Stock Exchange. The Treasury had the potential to serve as a lender of last resort through bond purchases to savings and commercial banks, but the clearinghouse associations of local commercial banks functioned as the more direct safeguard against financial chaos. Clearinghouse associations issued loan certificates to member banks during panics. These loan certificates substituted for cash reserves and allowed banks to use their on-hand cash for meeting payments with depositors. Associations also occasionally equalized member reserves. When equalizing reserves, the association pooled the clearinghouse's reserves and directly controlled the allocation of cash to distressed institutions.

In September 1873, suspensions and failures of financial institutions forced the Stock Exchange to shut down for well over a week, after which two trust companies suspended operations and a national bank collapsed.[18] The New York Clearinghouse Association swiftly responded by issuing loan certificates and equalizing reserves.[19] Loan contraction was heavy, but runs died down the following week. The New York banks were unfortunately still forced to suspend payments because of their liabilities to reserve and country banks in other regions.[20] The suspension was only partial, and the Clearinghouse was able to make most payments. The Clearinghouse directly controlled member reserves, allowing it to continue to make payments to calm the market, even if this meant a reduction in reserves. It avoided stringent policies that might have tightened the money market.[21] Government reports subsequently identified interest bearing interbank deposits as a major flaw in the System, but Congress took no action on the matter.[22] In 1893, the New York banks again coordinated to pacify the local market, but their liabilities to other national banks forced them to suspend payments. The New York Clearinghouse refrained from equalizing reserves in 1893, and it probably did not serve as decisive and effective an unofficial lender of last resort as it had in 1873.[23]

The years leading up to the Panic of 1907 were marked by robust monetary and real growth but also by an interventionist Treasury Department. Leslie Shaw, the former Governor of Iowa, served as Treasury Secretary from 1902 to 1907. Under his control the Treasury increasingly acted like a central bank. The Treasury had maintained its network of depository banks since passage of the National Banking Act, but barring some exceptions it had avoided interfering in the money market. The actions of Boutwell and Richardson served as one exception, as had also the decision of Secretary Charles Fairchild in the late 1880s to allow the Treasury's public deposits at banks to grow after revenue brought in a surplus of $300 million. In addition to purchasing bonds, Fairchild raised the limit on how much revenue individual banks could hold from $500,000 to $1 million, causing public deposits to eventually rise to $61.5 million by February 1888.[24]

Shaw took the Treasury in a new direction by attempting to manipulate the money supply on a regular basis through its contacts with national banks. In response to financial stringency in the autumn of 1902, Shaw expanded public deposits up to $150.2 million at 577 national banks around the country. In addition, Shaw widened the eligibility of collateral for public deposits by accepting not only U.S. bonds but state and municipal debt as well. State and municipal bonds eventually reached $20 million in posted collateral by the end of the year. Although Shaw later reverted to the earlier definition of eligible collateral, he relaxed his policy again in 1904 by accepting railroad bonds. By easing the limitations on eligible collateral, banks could instead post their U.S. bonds with the Treasury in order to issue more banknotes.[25]

Shaw also declared in 1902 that banks were not required to hold cash reserves against government deposits. This new policy released an aggregate of $130 million. Members of the press roundly criticized the action (as they had the liberalized collateral requirements), and the New York banks did not change their practices as a result of the announcement. But the action still affected bank reserves in other parts of the country.[26]

Shaw further asserted that national banks holding public deposits were incorporated into the Treasury. This action served as a workaround to the statutory and constitutional limitations placed on the Treasury, which prohibited the transfer of money from Treasury vaults except pursuant to congressional appropriations. In the past, the Treasury eased the money market through more passive means. Treasury officials simply stopped bringing in revenue from the public deposits at depository banks into the Treasury's vaults. Revenue continued to collect in the public deposits and increase the money available to banks.[27] Shaw plainly wanted the Treasury to operate as a regulator of the money market. As he stated in his 1906 *Annual Report*, "If the Secretary of the Treasury were given $100,000,000 to be deposited with the banks or withdrawn as he might deem expedient, and if in addition he were clothed with authority over the reserves of the several banks, with power to contract the national-bank circulation at pleasure, in my judgment no panic as distinguished from industrial stagnation could threaten either the United States or Europe that he could not avert."[28]

Lastly, Shaw announced in April 1906 that the Treasury would lend money to banks to incentivize the importing of gold. While this action might have temporarily alleviated financial tightness in the money markets by inducing the import of $50 million in gold through New York, it could not serve as part of a sustainable regime. When Shaw attempted to renew this policy in September, the Bank of England and the Reichsbank raised their discount rates, forcing Shaw to abandon the effort.[29] Shaw stepped down as Treasury Secretary before the Panic of 1907, but his unilateral actions could have never permanently compensated for the inadequacies of the Treasury as a pseudo central bank. At least two of Shaw's rulings were probably unlawful, while attempting to accelerate the import of gold threatened to set off a mercantilist tug-of-war between the U.S. and Europe.

Shaw tried to stave off tight markets through exotic measures. An alarming aspect of his policies was that the Treasury worked to hold down short-term interest rates even in the face of monetary expansion, conditions under which real interest rates should have risen. Shaw attempted to delay the inevitable correction to markets.[30]

In the build-up to the Panic of 1907, the economy had expanded for nearly three years. The business cycle reached a trough in August 1904 and then a peak in May 1907, soon after Shaw resigned from his office.[31] The Bank of England had hiked its discount rate to 6 percent by late October 1906.[32] In January 1907, the Interstate Commerce Commission (ICC) commenced an anti-trust related investigation of E.H. Harriman, Chairman of the Union Pacific Railroad.[33] Though the ICC ultimately advised President Theodore Roosevelt against taking legal action, Union Pacific's stock came under heavy selling pressure in late February. While the ICC investigation had fed market worries of an anti-trust action, the catalyst for the selloff included talk of Harriman's impending resignation and of a supposed emergency meeting between Harriman and Roosevelt at the White House.[34] Whatever the causes, by early March the stock selloff produced a so-called rich man's panic that appeared to affect only a handful of magnates holding Union Pacific stock.[35]

Trust company speculation in copper sparked the main panic in October. Most of the trust companies had resisted inclusion into the bank clearinghouses. The Knickerbocker Trust in New York suspended operations, and runs occurred on the Trust Company of America and Lincoln Trust.[36] Even though a trust committee was organized to manage the trusts, runs on trusts continued, and the New York Clearinghouse delayed action. J.P. Morgan helped to set up a money pool worth $25 million in subscriptions as stock prices rapidly fell.[37] Clearinghouse banks also faced runs while having to transfer currency to country and reserve city banks for crop shipments. As in 1893, the Clearinghouse issued loan certificates but did not equalize reserves. After a few troubled banks suspended, the contagion of panic spread, with most banks giving in to suspension.[38] Payments would not fully resume until early in the new year in the longest period of suspension in the National Banking era.[39] In addition to forgoing the equalization of reserves, the Clearinghouse waited longer than in 1873 before issuing loan certificates.[40] The Panic ignited with the trusts before the Clearinghouse took active steps to stabilize the situation.

The Treasury's actions before and during the Panic failed to restore calm to markets. Shaw's successor, George Cortelyou, ordered the transfer of additional sums of money to national banks beginning in early September, bringing total deposits up to $176 million after a little over a month. Cortelyou then ordered the transfer of another $31 million at the height of the crisis in late October, but this did not prevent the Clearinghouse banks from suspending payments a few days later. In the following weeks, Cortelyou continued to transfer large sums to the banks that brought the total in public deposits to $242 million.[41] Though the Treasury attempted to manage the money market, it still did not enjoy the mandate of a central bank, and the Panic of 1907 only paved the way for banking reform.

Yet the series of panics in the late 1800s and early 1900s did not prevent the real economy from undergoing a period of unparalleled growth and technological development, despite the shortfall in gold and currency. The settlement of the Great Plains expanded agricultural output, with the production of cereals rising from 1.2 billion bushels in 1860 to 4.4 billion in 1900. As railroads and Great Lakes shipping linked farms in the interior to the East Coast, exports became the means to selling off excess output and fomenting gold inflows. The U.S. exported over 66 percent of its cotton in the late 1800s.[42] Total merchandise exports rose from $228.5 million in 1861 to $1.4 billion in 1900.[43] Aided by the high tariffs that Congress maintained after the war, the monetary value of manufacturing output increased from $1.8 billion in 1860 to $13 billion by 1900. Capital investment in manufacturing increased during the same period from $1 billion to $9.8 billion. Industrialization at home, along with the export gains in agriculture, sharply contrasted with the deterioration of the merchant marine, a lucrative sector earlier in the century.[44]

Simon Kuznets computed high percentage expansion in national income in the late 1800s.[45] Robert Gallman similarly estimated high percentage real GNP growth under constant prices.[46] Population more than doubled from 43.5 million persons in 1869–78 to 89.6 million in 1904–13, which had a direct effect on GNP.[47]

NOTES

1. Secretary of the Treasury, *Report of the Secretary of the Treasury on the State of the Finances for the Year Ending June 30, 1862* (Washington, D.C.: Government Printing Office, 1863), 18.

2. Treasury Secretary, 1862 *Annual Report*, 20.
3. Ailes, "National Banking System," 119.
4. Philip Cagan, "High-Powered Money," in *Determinants and Effects of Changes in the Stock of Money*, 1875–1960, ed. Philip Cagan (New York: NBER, 1965), 86.
5. Charles A. Conant, "Fluctuations in the Secured Circulation of the National Banks and Their Relations to the Prices and Investment Values of Bonds," *Publications of the American Statistical Association* 3, no. 24 (1893): 472.
6. Knox, *History*, 150.
7. Ibid., 189.
8. Dewey, *Financial History*, 385–86.
9. Ibid., 412.
10. Conant, "Secured Circulation," 473–74.
11. Dewey, *Financial History*, 479.
12. Ibid., 480.
13. Edward S. Meade, "The Deposit-Reserve System of the National-Bank Law," *Journal of Political Economy* 6, no. 2 (1898): 210.
14. Meade, "Deposit-Reserve System," 216.
15. O.M.W. Sprague, "Proposals for Strengthening the National Banking System," *The Quarterly Journal of Economics* 24, no. 2 (1910): 211.
16. Sprague, *History of Crises*, 124.
17. Ibid., 125.
18. Ibid., 38–43.
19. Ibid., 46–48.
20. Ibid., 50–52.
21. Ibid., 54–55.
22. Ibid., 105.
23. Ibid., 183–86.
24. A. Piatt Andrew, "The Treasury and the Banks Under Secretary Shaw," *The Quarterly Journal of Economics* 21, no. 4 (1907): 525–27.
25. Andrew, "Treasury," 531–34.
26. Ibid., 536–39.
27. Ibid., 540–41.
28. Secretary of the Treasury, *Annual Report of the Secretary of the Treasury on the State of the Finances for the Fiscal Year Ended June 30, 1906* (Washington, D.C.: Government Printing Office, 1906), 49.
29. Andrew, "Treasury," 543–48.
30. A. Piatt Andrew, "The United States Treasury and the Money Market. The Partial Responsibilities of Gage and Shaw for the Crisis of 1907," *American Economic Association Quarterly* 9, no. 1 (1908): 228.
31. NBER, "U.S. Business Cycle."
32. Huffman and Lothian, "The Gold Standard," 475.
33. Elgin Groseclose, *America's Money Machine: The Story of the Federal Reserve* (1966, reprint, Auburn, AL: Ludwig von Mises Institute, 2009), 17.
34. Groseclose, *America's Money Machine*, 18–19.
35. Ibid., 20.
36. Sprague, *History of Crises*, 251–54.
37. Ibid., 254–56.
38. Ibid., 258–61.
39. Ibid., 277–78.
40. Ibid., 257.
41. Andrew, "Treasury and the Money Market," 229–30.
42. Emory R. Johnson, T.W. Van Metre, G.G. Huebner, and D.S. Hanchett, *History of Domestic and Foreign Commerce of the United States* (Washington, D.C.: Carnegie Institution, 1915), 259.
43. Simon, "Balance of Payments," 699–704.
44. Johnson, Van Metre, Huebner, and Hanchett, *History*, 264–65.

45. Simon Kuznets, "Long-Term Changes, 1869–1938," in *National Income: A Summary of Findings*, ed. Simon Kuznets (New York: National Bureau of Economic Research, 1946), 32.
46. Robert E. Gallman, "Gross National Product in the United States, 1834–1909," in *Output, Employment, and Productivity in the United States after 1800*, ed. Dorothy S. Brady (New York: National Bureau of Economic Research, 1966), 9.
47. Kuznets, "Long-Term Changes," 32.

SIX

Reform Proposals and Legislation

The Panic of 1893 and the blatant deficiencies of the National Banking System energized the reform movement for banking. Reform-minded politicians and academics pointed to the need for an elastic currency, or one that was more responsive to changing business conditions. At a convention of the American Bankers' Association in October 1894, the Baltimore Clearinghouse submitted its own proposal, which came to be dubbed the Baltimore Plan. Under the Baltimore Plan, banks were no longer required to post U.S. bonds as collateral to back banknote circulation. Banks were authorized to issue notes against 50 percent of their capital stock, in addition to an Emergency Circulation against 25 percent of their capital. Banks were further required to contribute to a Guarantee Fund for insolvent institutions, paid for through taxes on the regular and Emergency Circulation at rates of .5 percent.[1]

If the Baltimore Plan served as one example of reform ideas, the overall goal was to foster a more elastic currency that replaced the Treasury bond-backed banknotes with an asset-backed circulation that collateralized short-dated paper arising out of commercial and agricultural transactions. The reformers wanted a currency tied to the market for commercial paper and not government debt. Basing currency circulation on real bills instead of U.S. bonds might have looked like it was founded on the wisdom of laissez-faire. But the real bills doctrine became a more meaningful concept when understood as a criterion for central banking policy and not simply as a guide for how to change the laws governing the clearinghouses.

Not until after the Panic of 1907 was Congress seriously committed to investigating and resolving problems associated with the banking system. The Aldrich-Vreeland Act of 1908 formalized the use of the clearinghouse system among banks. Small groups of national banks were authorized to form associations for the purpose of issuing emergency currency against their holdings of securities and commercial paper. The Act capped currency circulation at 75 percent of the securities and paper held by the associations. The emergency currency was taxable to incentivize its retirement after the end of a crisis, with the total circulation of the currency contained at $500 million.[2] The Act also permitted national banks to under certain conditions deposit non-U.S. government bonds with the Treasury in exchange for currency.[3] The Act was intended as a provisional measure until permanent reforms could be implemented, and it was put into effect only once at the outbreak of World War I after which it expired in 1915.

The Aldrich-Vreeland Act also ordered a National Monetary Commission to begin an investigation into possible banking reform measures. Nelson Aldrich, the long-time Republican Senator from Rhode Island and Chairman of the Finance Committee, oversaw the investigation. He was advised by Paul Warburg, a prominent banker and German emigre to the U.S. who had already written a series of newspaper editorials that outlined his recommendations for changing the banking system. While various other writers had also proposed turning the U.S.'s bond-backed currency into an asset-backed one, Warburg contributed to the discussion by focusing on the institutional shortcomings of U.S. banking from a European vantage.

In "Defects and Needs of Our Banking System," published in the *New York Times* in January 1907 before the Panic of that year, Warburg's point of departure was in suggesting revisions to the medium of short-dated paper. Under the National Banking System, U.S. banks were prohibited from dealing in bankers' acceptances, or bank indorsed bills of exchange that financed international trade. Because trade acceptances for funding domestic transactions had fallen out of use since the Civil War, banks were left to hold only illiquid, single-name notes that could not be bought or sold in the money market. As Warburg noted, U.S. banks mainly relied on un-indorsed promissory notes that were rarely traded and rediscounted, while in Europe indorsed paper increased the liquidity of banks because the paper could be readily traded in the open market. Warburg considered the American reliance on un-indorsed paper to be nothing short of primitive.[4]

Bank indorsements for commercial paper would turn promissory notes into acceptances and thereby render short paper more liquid. The indorsing of bills would infuse liquidity into money markets. Indorsements would allow banks to sell their bills to private dealers or a hypothetical central bank with relative ease. In describing European money markets, Warburg impliedly characterized indorsed paper as a money-like instrument and certainly the closest possible substitute to currency, to the point where only market interest rates conceivably prevented indorsed paper from being sold by banks in the open markets.[5] By contrast,

U.S. national banks invested in stock loans, which for Warburg disastrously meant that "the overflow of money of the entire country, from the Atlantic to the Pacific, is thrown into the stock exchange. . . . Our whole elasticity is built up on the bond and stock market."[6]

Warburg could look to European practices as a model for everything that he was proposing. He advocated an autonomous central bank that served as a middle ground between the opposing extremes of an interventionist Treasury and private banking associations.[7] Warburg never assumed that revising the National Banking System alone could foster changes in the money market. Yet he still implied that by lifting the restriction on bankers' acceptances, along with other regulatory changes, national banks would switch from investing in call loans to acceptances and commercial paper. According to this view, under the right conditions U.S. financial markets would operate in the same way as European markets.

But there was no guarantee that banks would suddenly start investing in short paper, especially if they considered call loans to be more lucrative assets during a bull market. The structure of the U.S. banking sector also differed significantly from European banking systems, in that state and federal laws regulated against branching. These restrictions created a decentralized banking system that greatly contrasted with the powerful and sophisticated universal banks of Germany, the nation of Warburg's birth. What had become clear was that a redirection of money flows into real bills and away from the stock market could only be accomplished through an overhaul of federal banking law. Fortunately for Warburg, his January 1907 article appeared several months before the Panic in October, which validated the view that hot money needed to be prevented from entering the stock market.

In "A Plan for a Modified Central Bank," published in November 1907 after the outbreak of the Panic, Warburg proposed a Government Bank that combined features of European central banks with those of the First and Second U.S. Banks. The plan relied on a rediscount facility. The proposed central bank would exchange its notes for eligible collateral submitted by private banks. A discount rate indicated the rate at which the central bank would purchase the paper submitted at its window. Among European central banks, eligible collateral could be discounted on an anonymous basis. A rediscount facility would be used to build a market in bankers' and trade acceptances because the Government Bank would only accept multiply indorsed short paper as an eligible form of collateral, in addition to government and railroad bonds. Warburg intended for the clearinghouse associations to regulate the collateral of the member banks and certify its eligibility with the Government Bank. Warburg hoped that "[t]he clearinghouse would thus be able, to a certain degree, to prevent the moneys so received from Washington from being used for any but strictly legitimate purposes."[8]

Warburg had earlier emphasized the need for banks to invest in acceptances instead of stock market loans. A limitation on the eligibility of collateral at the discount window to certain forms of acceptances and bonds could do much to incentivize the holding of short paper on the part of banks. But in the end nothing could prevent banks from using currency received from the central bank for speculative investments. Warburg appeared to hold out the belief that the clearinghouses might serve as an additional buffer in preventing Government Bank notes from entering the stock market, though a clearinghouse could not entirely control how national banks would use the notes that they received through the discount window.

In "A United Reserve Bank of the United States," initially delivered as an address in 1910, Warburg expanded on his plan by introducing a new United Reserve Bank (URB). Warburg emphasized the regular discounting of eligible paper between the URB and private banks instead of incorporating an oversight role for clearinghouses. As with the Government Bank, the URB would purchase and sell foreign exchange and debt of the U.S. government. Warburg also implied a decentralized structure for the URB. The URB would consist of branches located around the country, while local banking associations would be partly responsible for hiring personnel to manage the branches.[9] Warburg's concession of a decentralized reserve reflected the fact that this structure was more politically feasible than an actual central bank.

The immediate objective of the URB would be to ease the annual contraction of currency and credit during the autumn when crops were being shipped for sale. Warburg considered a URB-like system capable of augmenting the liquidity of money markets simply by ensuring a stable reserve of credit. Bills would be so liquid that banks would not even be motivated into hoarding non-interest bearing cash during a panic.[10] In other respects, Warburg intended for the URB to serve as a typical central bank. Warburg envisioned the URB adhering to Bagehot's rule, responding to an external drain of gold by raising its discount rate, responding to an internal drain by lending freely, and responding to an external and internal drain by lending freely at a high rate. Warburg thought that the URB should serve as a lender of last resort that could also manipulate gold flows through changes in its discount rate.[11]

The one major distinction from European central banking practices in these articles was Warburg's newfound incorporation of a decentralized structure in the form of the URB. While Warburg's ideas might have appeared novel to an American audience, they were otherwise intended to advocate as quintessentially a central bank as possible.

Even when accounting for ingrained aversions to centralization, the defects of the National Banking System strengthened the case for a new regulatory structure in some ways resembling a central bank. An asset-backed currency also offered the opportunity to separate currency from the national debt. The national debt had fallen to $931 million by 1902 after having temporarily risen above $1 billion to accommodate funding for the Spanish-American War.[12] For various reasons, then, Warburg's proposals around the time of the Panic of 1907 were extremely timely, and a bill introduced by Carter Glass, Democratic Chairman of the House Banking Committee after the 1912 elections, included components of the Warburg plan, among other proposals for an asset-backed currency, into its major provisions. However, if the Warburg plan can be distilled to four objectives—eliminating the seasonal contraction in currency, restricting the function of the central bank to a lender of last resort, keeping central bank notes out of the stock market, and establishing a national market in bankers' acceptances—only the first of these objectives would be fulfilled as the 1920s progressed.

Nelson Aldrich contended with these same political realities when proposing a National Reserve Association to the National Monetary Commission in 1911. Aldrich agreed with Warburg and other bankers that the U.S. needed to establish a central bank, and his proposal reflected these views. Under the Aldrich plan, national and state banks gaining membership to the National Reserve Association posted the equivalent of 20 percent of their capital with the Association's capital stock.[13] Aldrich allowed for some element of decentralization, in that member banks entered into local associations of at least ten banks with their own corporate functions.[14] But Aldrich foremost conceived of a centralized institution run by a board of directors and an executive committee, with a network of branches stretching around the country. Aldrich planned for the Association to be overseen by 45 directors, including a chairman, the secretaries of the treasury, labor, and commerce, and the comptroller of the currency serving as ex officio members. The president appointed the chairman of a smaller executive committee to manage the Association's operations.[15] The plan authorized the Association to rediscount commercial paper of 28 days' maturity with banks that held deposits with the Association, as well as commercial paper with a maturity of up to 4 months if guaranteed by a local banking association. The Association was further authorized to deal in bankers' acceptances, government securities, gold, and bills of exchange denominated in foreign currencies.[16]

Aldrich reincorporated aspects of the old U.S. Banks into the plan. The Association held the non-interest bearing deposits of the federal government and all banks that had subscribed to the Association's capital stock. The plan required the federal government to transfer all of its revenue to its deposits with the Association. The government was also to direct expenditures from these deposits.[17] The Aldrich plan intended to change the money supply by steadily replacing the national banknotes with new Association notes. Banks were no longer required to post U.S. bonds as collateral in order to issue banknotes. The Association was then authorized to purchase the bonds of member banks using new Association notes. The banks were also permitted to redeem the bonds with their banknotes, which the Association then retired. The circulation in banknotes would be steadily eliminated. In its place, the Reserve Association issued new notes to the member banks against the value of their deposits. These notes were receivable for all federal dues. The Association was required to hold gold against a third of the note circulation and to hold commercial paper against the remainder. Currency circulation of over $900 million not adequately backed by gold and commercial paper under these requirements triggered special taxes to expedite their partial retirement. A holder of the notes could convert them into gold with the Association.[18]

One glaring problem with Aldrich's proposal was that national and state banks were not apparently required to join the Association. Because of the costs of subscribing to the Association's capital stock, some of these banks might have been deterred from doing so. As a result, the Association might not have held much sway in the banking sector. Aldrich otherwise proposed an institution that could have taken decisive action during a crisis while still coordinating with the local associations. The Aldrich plan was unfortunately unable to overcome political opposition to any centralized institution that looked like it might have been a stooge for Eastern bankers. The chances of passing the Aldrich plan into law became impossible after the Democrats won the House of Representatives in 1910 and the Senate and White House in 1912. Under the guidance of Carter Glass, Congress fashioned a new bill setting up a more decentralized Federal Reserve.

Congress passed the Federal Reserve Act in December 1913. The preamble read that the Act's intent was to "furnish an elastic currency, to afford means of rediscounting commercial paper, to establish a more effective supervision of banking in the United States, and for other purposes." The Act established a range of 8 to 12 Federal Reserve Banks to operate under the supervision of the Federal Reserve Board located in Washington, D.C. The Reserve Banks were owned and operated by local banks, while regional planning boards appointed personnel to the Reserve Banks. The president was responsible for appointments to the Federal Reserve Board, which also included the treasury secretary and comptroller of the currency as ex officio members.[19] Reserve Banks were granted authority to issue Federal Reserve notes or reserve deposits against the rediscount of eligible collateral. Eligible collateral included commercial paper with a maturity of up to 90 days, bankers' acceptances of up to 3 months, bills of exchange used to finance imports or exports of up to 6 months, and agricultural loans of up to 6 months.[20]

The Act further authorized Reserve Banks to buy and sell bankers' acceptances, bills of exchange, government securities, and gold coin and bullion in the open market.[21] Running a portfolio in Treasurys was assumed to allow Reserve Banks to more effectively manage their earnings, but open market operations were not yet envisioned as a major tool of monetary policy. A 1916 amendment to the 1913 Act authorized Reserve Banks to directly make advances to member banks on member banks' own 15-day promissory notes backed by eligible paper or U.S. bonds or notes.[22] The 1916 amendment thereby expanded the rediscount facility to a lending one. Finally, a 1920 amendment authorized the Reserve Banks to alter discount rates subject to the Board's approval.[23]

Each Reserve Bank was required to hold gold reserves equal to at least 40 percent of its notes and 35 percent of its deposit liabilities, the latter of which functioned as reserve balances of member banks.[24] Under the Act as amended in 1917, Reserve Banks were permitted to issue Federal Reserve notes against the security of gold and eligible paper, specifically commercial paper and acceptances purchased in the open market. Such security was required to equal the value of Federal Reserve notes for which it was submitted.[25] Because gold needed to back at least 40 percent of Federal Reserve note circulation, the remainder, if not backed by gold, needed to be backed by eligible paper. The Act did not sanction the use of Treasurys in directly serving as security against notes. Reserve Banks were of course authorized to purchase and sell Treasurys in the open market, but the security provision remained bound to gold and short-term eligible paper. Such a restriction reflected the influence that the real bills doctrine bore over policymaking at this stage. However, Reserve Banks were authorized to rediscount paper secured by U.S. bonds and notes. A 1918 amendment expanded this provision to include bonds issued by the War Finance Corporation.[26]

Federal Reserve notes created a new class of currency that was receivable for all public dues.[27] Federal Reserve notes were positioned to drive national banknotes out of circulation, in that national banks were under the Act permitted to retire all or part of their banknotes by selling U.S. bonds that secured banknote circulation to the federal government. The provision requiring national banks to deposit U.S. government bonds with the Treasury was repealed.[28] National banks were required to join the Federal Reserve System by subscribing to the capital stock of their local Reserve Banks.[29] State banks, on the other hand, were eligible to apply for inclusion, provided they fulfilled the same requirements pertaining to capital stock as national banks.[30] As amended in 1917, the Act required that member banks exclusively hold their legal reserves at Reserve Banks in the form of deposits.[31] This requirement superseded those provisions of the National Banking System that transferred legal reserves from country and reserve city banks to the central reserve cities, which had helped to fuel speculation in stock loans. While the actions of the Federal Reserve since its inception have frequently invited criticism, the Act of 1913 should still be credited with eliminating destabilizing features of the National Banking System.

NOTES

1. J. Laurence Laughlin, "The 'Baltimore Plan' of Bank-Issues," *Journal of Political Economy* 3, no. 1 (1894): 101–02.
2. J. Laurence Laughlin, "The Aldrich-Vreeland Act," *Journal of Political Economy* 16, no. 8 (1908): 497–98.
3. Laughlin, "Aldrich-Vreeland Act," 500.
4. Paul M. Warburg, "Defects and Needs of Our Banking System," in *Essays on Bank Reform in the United States* (New York: Academy of Political Science, Columbia University, 1914), 7.
5. Warburg, "Defects and Needs," 8.
6. Ibid., 11.
7. Ibid., 17–18.
8. Paul M. Warburg, "A Plan for a Modified Central Bank," in *Essays on Bank Reform in the United States* (New York: Academy of Political Science, Columbia University, 1914), 25–26.
9. Paul M. Warburg, "A United Reserve Bank of the United States," in *Essays on Bank Reform in the United States* (New York: Academy of Political Science, Columbia University, 1914), 78–80.
10. Warburg, "United Reserve Bank," 82.
11. Ibid., 84.
12. Austin, "Public Debt," 720.
13. Nelson W. Aldrich, *Suggested Plan for Monetary Legislation: Submitted to the National Monetary Commission, Revised Edition* (Washington, D.C.: National Monetary Commission, 1911), 5.
14. Aldrich, *Suggested Plan*, 7–8.
15. Ibid., 10–11.
16. Ibid., 15–16.
17. Ibid., 14.
18. Ibid., 21–23.
19. *Federal Reserve Act: As Amended to December 24, 1919* (New York: National Bank of Commerce in New York, 1920), 24–25.
20. *Federal Reserve Act*, 34–35.
21. Ibid., 38–39.
22. Ibid., 36.
23. Ibid., 38–39.
24. Ibid., 42.
25. Ibid., 41–42.
26. Ibid., 34.
27. Ibid., 41.
28. Ibid., 49–50.
29. Ibid., 6–7.
30. Ibid., 20–21.
31. Ibid., 52–53.

SEVEN

The Early Federal Reserve

The early Federal Reserve faced the crisis of World War I and then the postwar effort to rebuild the international monetary and economic system. The Reserve Banks initially met these challenges with central banking tools that had been developed during the relative tranquility of the late nineteenth century.

In their daily practices, the Reserve Banks rediscounted commercial paper and purchased bankers' acceptances. Bill buying rates regulated how much money Reserve Banks paid member banks for their acceptances. Cutting the bill buying rate meant that Reserve Banks paid out more for acceptances, just as cutting the discount rate meant that Reserve Banks paid out more for commercial paper. The Reserve Banks were committed to a policy of bolstering the market for bankers' acceptances by buying acceptances at preferential rates. Because the market for bankers' acceptances remained largely confined to New York, the New York Bank played an especially critical role in these operations.[1] Setting preferential rates meant that Reserve Banks would be operating as absorber and facilitator of the acceptance market instead of as a more specialized lender of last resort during critical times. Banks regularly made use of the bill buying window in the 1920s with no associated stigma. Nor was stigma initially attached to the discount window, whether for rediscounts or borrowings on eligible paper. Borrowings among member banks continued to rise even after the end of World War I, increasing from $1.8 billion when the fighting stopped to $3.1 billion two years later. By comparison, Reserve Banks had purchased acceptances to the amount of $400 million by war's end.[2]

When the U.S. entered World War I, Reserve Banks began offering preferential rates on loans secured by Treasury bonds to member banks. The Treasury sold over $18 billion in bonds to the public to finance the war effort.[3] At the end of the war, Federal Reserve credit continued to expand, even with the outbreak of hyperinflation and the overheating of the stock market. The economist E.W. Kemmerer cited various factors for causing the inflation, among them secular growth in the U.S.'s gold stock after 1900.[4] These trends were exacerbated by heavy gold inflows at the outbreak of the war. During the phase of the war preceding the U.S.'s participation, $1.1 billion in gold flowed into the U.S., after which gold inflows temporarily subsided. Even though the U.S. posted robust export surpluses in these years, most of the goods sold abroad were not paid for in gold.[5]

The wartime restriction on gold exports was removed in 1919 and helped set in motion an outflow of $322 million in gold.[6] But the lifting of the embargo did not alone neutralize a building inflation, in large part because of a decline in production after the outbreak of war in Europe. Kemmerer estimated that business expansion only averaged 1.6 percent during 1913–19.[7] A lowering of reserve requirements in order to facilitate looser credit only added to inflationary pressures.[8]

By the time the war ended, multiple factors were sending the money supply into the realm of hyperinflation. Wartime or postwar economic conditions often breed inflation, but the postwar hyperinflation also came at the tail end of long-term growth in the gold stock and a gold inflow before the U.S. declared war. A wage and price spiral had been avoided during the war through the use of controls implemented by the War Industries Board, War Trade Board, and other regulatory bodies that ensured the flow of credit into war-related production. But these controls were inevitably removed after the Armistice, and inflation and credit expansion began in earnest in early 1919. The price rise was initially set off by increased consumer demand and spiking prices for merchantable wares.[9]

The Reserve Banks stood poised to choke off the inflation through hikes in their discount rates subject to approval from the Board. But the Treasury needed the Federal Reserve to maintain preferential rates to help it float a final Victory Loan in the spring of 1919, which was intended to end war-related funding.[10] When the Reserve Banks eventually began to raise their discount rates in early 1920, they were responding partly to a loss in their gold reserves and partly to inflation. Reserve Bank gold reserves had fallen by $253 million from May 1919 to March 1920.[11] Gold reserves had remained strong prior to 1919 because of the embargo on gold exports and the Federal Reserve's intention of concentrating gold in its own vaults to help finance the war.

Reserve authorities were equally concerned with the unsustainable credit expansion. The Reserve's *Annual Report* for 1919 stated that "[t]he expansion of credit set in motion by the war must be checked" and even proposed the triggering of increased discount rates if banks began borrowing in excess of a "normal maximum rediscount line."[12] But the following year, the System's Advisory Council, a consultative body drawn from the Federal Reserve districts, criticized the idea of a "normal maximum rediscount line" because "due regard must be given to the nature of the business of each member bank." Under this thinking, a maximum rediscount line should not apply to member banks that advance credit to legitimate business.[13]

The Board approved discount rate hikes in November 1919, and the Reserve Banks began stepping up their rates in January 1920, when most Banks raised their key rates from 4 ¾ percent to 6 percent. After these actions looked to be inadequate at midyear, some Banks raised them again to 7 percent.[14] Reserve Banks did not reduce their rates until mid-1921, when Reserve authorities determined that their gold reserves had stabilized. The economy had entered a deep recession in the interim, and the Reserve Banks were criticized for having waited too long to stop inflation before a massive correction was necessary. Even Benjamin Strong of the New York Bank conceded that, "if it had been possible, it would have been desirable for the Federal Reserve System to have advanced its rates at some point in the period between January and March, 1919" rather than delaying action until late in the year.[15] The Federal Reserve's responsibility over inflation had unfortunately conflicted with the Treasury's goal of expediting financing for the Victory Loan.

The contraction in Federal Reserve notes reflected the emerging deflation. In 1920, total Federal Reserve note circulation expanded from $3.1 billion to $3.7 billion, and it also expanded in every month that year except for November.[16] In 1921, note circulation contracted uninterrupted from $3.5 billion at the end of January to $2.7 billion on November 30.[17] The economy had entered a recession, but a contagion of panic did not break out as it had periodically during the National Banking era. Reserve Banks were situated as lenders of last resort to advance credit and discount the paper of member banks. R.M. Gidney, Controller at Large for the New York Bank, pointed out that Reserve Banks managed "to conduct their relations with member banks along much the same lines as those by which the larger banking institutions of the country have in the past so successfully conducted their relations with out-of-town correspondents."[18]

Gidney's assertion implied that the Reserve Banks were not functioning collectively as a true central bank and that they continued to resemble in some ways the New York central reserve banks from the National Banking era. Federal Reserve Banks could still forge coalitions and coordinate their policies, but ultimately the Banks were granted large autonomy over their discount and bill buying rates. The desire for that kind of decentralization had of course been the very motivation behind creating the Federal Reserve System in the first place. But the lurking question remained whether Reserve Banks could be counted upon to coordinate their policies during every recession and financial crisis.

Reserve authorities were also beginning to consider qualitative ways in which to influence bank behavior. The Reserve's *Annual Report* for 1920 stated "the necessity of the curtailment of general credits and especially for non-essential uses," "continuing to discourage loans for capital and speculative purposes," and "checking excessive borrowings through the application of higher rates."[19] Reserve authorities could always hike their discount rates to combat excessive borrowing, but their ability to directly pressure member banks into only using Federal Reserve credit for legitimate purposes and not for speculative investments was far from certain.

The Federal Reserve arguably mishandled the postwar economy not only by assisting the Treasury in its Victory Loan campaign in 1919 but by also relying on the blunt instrument of stepped-up discount rates in 1920–21. The discount rate had served as the most obvious policy tool for the Reserve Banks since the establishment of the System. Yet in the aftermath of the recession Reserve authorities began to consider new ways of using open market operations. Reserve Banks had originally purchased Treasury securities only with the idea of increasing their earnings. Under the leadership of New York Bank Governor Benjamin Strong, the Banks established an Open Market Investment Committee (OMIC) to coordinate open market operations in order to manipulate conditions in the money market. Beginning in 1923, the OMIC consisted of representatives from the Reserve Banks of New York, Chicago, Cleveland, and Philadelphia. In the recovery year of 1922, the New York Bank purchased $796.3 million in Treasury notes and bonds, while System purchases overall came to $1.2 billion. This latter figure far exceeded that for 1921, which was only $104.4 million in System-wide purchases.[20]

Open market policy had the potential of making monetary policy more efficient by rapidly eliminating seasonal tightness in money markets. The New York Bank's routine purchase of bankers' acceptances under Strong's leadership possibly gave it the direction and experience to pursue an open market policy in Treasurys. But the parallel between acceptances and Treasurys cannot be taken too far because the Bank was obligated to purchase all eligible bankers' acceptances brought to its window, albeit at discretionary rates, while market operations in Treasurys implied a more active posture of setting targets. An increasingly activist open market policy based on Treasury securities was also fundamentally inconsistent with the real bills doctrine. The two opposing agendas could even be characterized as mutually exclusive. The real bills doctrine only relied upon self-liquidating short paper as a means for expanding liquidity and not government securities.

The shift from the real bills doctrine to open market policy had the potential of completely altering the ways in which the Reserve Banks managed the money supply. Reserve authorities distinguished between borrowed and non-borrowed reserves of member banks. Reserve Banks increased the non-borrowed reserves of member banks by purchasing securities from them. Strong indicated in 1926 that Reserve officials could now base operating procedures on the rate of borrowing through the discount window. Reserve Banks needed to increase their purchases when member banks were borrowing in larger amounts. But if bank borrowing declined, then Reserve Banks could taper their purchases.[21]

Reserve Banks could make use of both open market policy and the discount window in order to target borrowed and non-borrowed bank reserves. Although orthodox believers in the real bills doctrine contended that the discount window and open market policy canceled each other out if they worked to opposite effect, the use of both in a coherent targeting regime came to be known as the scissor's effect. Because the targeting of bank reserves through open market policy affected interbank rates and other short rates, the sudden change in the discount rate could be conceivably confined more or less to situations when Reserve Banks deliberately wanted to send a signal to markets of a general policy shift. Purchases and sales of securities at this early juncture also mainly implied the dealing in shorter-dated securities. Not until the 1930s would the Federal Reserve begin to expand its operations into longer-dated securities, and even well after that there occurred a reversion to a bills-only protocol.

The New York Bank pursued expansionary policies in 1924 and 1927. The domestic counter-recessionary aims of these policies dovetailed with attempts to help European nations restore convertibility to gold. In 1924, the New York Bank lowered its discount rate from 4 ½ percent to 4 percent in May, to 3 ½ percent in June, and then to 3 percent in August.[22] This discount rate reduction was part of an effort to assist the Bank of England reestablish its prewar parity to gold by helping to foment gold flows to the U.K. as a result of interest rate differentials. The New York Bank also purchased in the open market a total of $426.1 million in government securities in 1924, making it by far the largest Reserve Bank purchaser of Treasurys. The next largest purchaser was the Chicago Bank at $194.7 million. Other than that, of the twelve Reserve Banks, only Minneapolis and Cleveland made purchases of securities of over $100 million that year.[23] The New York Bank also purchased in the open market in 1924 $1 billion in bankers' acceptances, which dwarfed the next largest purchaser, Boston, at $259.5 million.[24]

In 1927, Strong agreed with his British, French, and German counterparts to defend sterling against selling pressure in the foreign exchange markets. In pursuit of this goal, the New York Bank cut its discount rate from 4 percent to 3 ½ percent in August.[25] Yet open market policy was not necessarily the privileged domain of the New York Bank. Reserve Banks were also able to coordinate monetary policy through OMIC's Special Investment Account. Total holdings for the Special Investment

Account reached $449 million in 1924 before falling to $212.3 million by 1926, but then rose again to $423.2 million in 1927.[26]

Strong fully adhered to the gold standard, and from his point of view a major objective during the 1920s was restoration of convertibility abroad, which explains the credit lines and other packages put together by the New York Bank for European monetary authorities. The use of monetary easing for purposes of shoring up the interwar gold standard cannot therefore be ignored. In 1924, Strong cut his policy rate in coordination with a rate hike on the part of the Bank of England, while in 1927 Strong acted pursuant to an international conference that intended to take pressure off sterling. Such a concern for the gold standard on Strong's part conformed to the reality that New York was more closely intertwined with trans-Atlantic trade than any other Reserve city. George Harrison, Strong's successor at the Bank, fully shared that adherence to gold.

Strong's commitment to the gold standard also filled in the void left by an absence of institutional machinery to coordinate the activities of central banks. The Financial Commission of the 1922 Genoa Conference had recommended that central banks cooperate to maintain stable price levels, which went hand-in-hand with preventing against a mutually destructive race to accumulate gold bullion. In the spirit of this recommendation, the Bank of England would organize an international conference to foster cooperation. The Commission further indicated that the U.S. needed to be included in these negotiations.[27] The proposed conference never materialized due to differences of whether to include war reparations in the negotiations and France's takeover of the Ruhr.[28] As a result, Strong worked without the aegis of a formal international framework.

But if restoration of the gold standard influenced Strong's policy, the commitment to domestic stability also cannot be disregarded. The business cycle reached a trough in July 1924, so that expansion at that time did work countercyclically against domestic business trends. A trough was again reached in November 1927, roughly four months after his meeting with foreign counterparts. Strong thus acted during a slowing economy.[29] The New York Bank pursued greater ease when it appeared to suit both its international and domestic objectives.

Reserve Banks faced the problem of gold inflows in the early 1920s, which netted $294 million in 1923.[30] After a temporary outflow of gold during 1920, Federal Reserve gold reserves rose by $1 billion over the next three years.[31] Europeans were parking their gold holdings in U.S. banks, which could dangerously fuel inflation if no countermeasures were taken. Reserve officials assumed that the inflows were temporary and that the gold would be repatriated upon restoration of convertibility abroad. Reserve Banks attempted to sterilize gold inflows by paying out gold certificates to member banks instead of Federal Reserve notes. The amount of gold in the money supply rose while Federal Reserve notes contracted.[32] The gold inflows also meant that reserve ratios could no longer serve as a reliable indicator for policy, since the inflows were causing gold to accumulate in member bank reserves irrespective of trends in the money market.[33]

Through the 1920s, the Federal Reserve was forced to address problems specific to the postwar transition, whether it was assisting in the return to parity abroad or attempting to negate the effects of transitory gold inflows. The Federal Reserve's overall aim was to help restore the monetary system that had collapsed in 1914. While the New York Bank successfully assisted in these efforts in the short-term, a restored international gold standard gave rise to fears of long-term deflationary instabilities beyond the control of any one institution. The Financial Commission at the Genoa Conference drew on an earlier committee's idea of gold bullion standards. Such a system would restrict the private holding of gold and keep bullion stockpiled in official institutions at the center of the world economy.[34] European nations adopted bullion standards when they restored convertibility, but the U.S. maintained a coinage system through the 1920s.

In more immediate terms, the Reserve Banks encountered the ever-present threat of their credit flowing into speculative trading. Now that reserve ratios had been thrown out of whack because of the gold inflows, Reserve authorities contemplated new criteria for managing the flow of credit. The *Annual Report* for 1923 flatly stated that "[t]he Federal reserve system is a system of productive credit. It is not a system of credit for either investment or speculative purposes." A new guideline was necessary to ensure that credit was channeled into productive credit for "agricultural, industrial, or commercial purposes."[35]

Reserve Banks were still unsuccessful at preventing abuse of the discount window and dissuading banks from using borrowings for speculative purposes. Any attempt at dissuasion was bound to fail absent a concrete rule, such as the earlier proposal for a "normal maximum rediscount line." The 1928 *Annual Report* indicated that "[i]n cases where individual banks have been guilty of such abuse, the Federal reserve authorities have taken up the matter with officers of the offending banks and have made clear to them that their reserve position should be adjusted by liquidating a part of their loan or investment account rather than through borrowing." But this effort at direct pressure was futile, and Federal Reserve credit continued to flow into the stock market right up until the crash of October 1929. As the 1928 *Annual Report* conceded, "There is no way of earmarking for special purposes the credit extended by the Federal reserve banks," and from 1925 to 1928 member bank stock loans rose from $6.7 billion to $9 billion.[36] Total System-wide discounted paper rose from $661 million in April 1928 to over $1 billion from June through September 1928. Total discounts again rose above $1 billion in July and August 1929. Total discounts stayed over $800 million in every month after April 1928 until the stock market crash, and indeed until the end of 1929.[37]

The Federal Reserve's diversion into moral suasion might have eventually attached stigma to use of the discount window, which became enormously consequential during the Great Contraction. If banks only used the discount window under genuinely emergency conditions, then their very access to the window would put markets and the public on notice of their distressed condition. As this restricted access to the discount window became more widely understood, banks would be deterred from using the discount window or else they would possibly trigger a run on their deposits.

NOTES

1. E.E. Agger, "The Development of an Open Market for Commercial Paper," *The Annals of the American Academy for Political and Social Science* 99 (1922): 213–14.
2. O.M.W. Sprague, "The Discount Policy of the Federal Reserve Banks," *The American Economic Review* 11, no. 1 (1921): 21.
3. A.C. Miller, "Federal Reserve Policy," *The American Economic Review* 11, no. 2 (1921): 185.
4. E.W. Kemmerer, "Causes and Progress of Inflation," *Proceedings of the Academy of Political Science in the City of New York* 9, no. 1 (1920): 1.
5. Kemmerer, "Causes and Progress of Inflation," 7.
6. Miller, "Federal Reserve Policy," 181–82.
7. Kemmerer, "Causes and Progress of Inflation," 11.
8. Ibid., 8.
9. Miller, "Federal Reserve Policy," 186–87.
10. Ibid., 188–89.
11. Ibid., 181.
12. Federal Reserve Board, *Sixth Annual Report of the Federal Reserve Board: Covering Operations for the Year 1919* (Washington, D.C.: Government Printing Office, 1920), 71.
13. Federal Reserve Board, *Seventh Annual Report of the Federal Reserve Board: Covering Operations for the Year 1920* (Washington, D.C.: Government Printing Office, 1921), 601.
14. Miller, "Federal Reserve Policy," 190.
15. Wesley C. Mitchell, "The Crisis of 1920 and the Problem of Controlling Business Cycles," *The American Economic Review* 12, no. 1 (1922): 23.
16. FRB, *Seventh Annual Report*, 108.
17. Federal Reserve Board, *Eighth Annual Report of the Federal Reserve Board: Covering Operations for the Year 1921* (Washington, D.C.: Government Printing Office, 1922), 112.
18. R.M. Gidney, "Relations of Reserve Banks to Member Banks and Inter-Relations of Federal Reserve Banks," *The Annals of the American Academy of Political and Social Science* 99 (1922): 91.
19. FRB, *Seventh Annual Report*, 603.
20. Federal Reserve Board, *Ninth Annual Report of the Federal Reserve Board: Covering Operations for the Year 1922* (Washington, D.C.: Government Printing Office, 1923), 140.
21. Charles Calomiris and David Wheelock, "Was the Great Depression a Watershed for American Monetary Policy?," in *The Defining Moment: The Great Depression and the American Economy in the Twentieth Century*, ed. Michael D. Bordo, Claudia Goldin, and Eugene N. White (Chicago: University of Chicago Press, 1998), 34.

22. Federal Reserve Board, *Eleventh Annual Report of the Federal Reserve Board: Covering Operations for the Year 1924* (Washington, D.C.: Government Printing Office, 1925), 33.

23. FRB, *Eleventh Annual Report*, 94.

24. Ibid., 89.

25. Federal Reserve Board, *Fourteenth Annual Report of the Federal Reserve Board: Covering Operations for the Year 1927* (Washington, D.C.: Government Printing Office, 1928), 89.

26. FRB, *Fourteenth Annual Report*, 71.

27. Barry Eichengreen, "International Policy Coordination in Historical Perspective: A View from the Interwar Years," in *International Economic Policy Coordination*, ed. William H. Buiter and Richard C. Marston (Cambridge: Cambridge University Press, 1985), 151–52.

28. Ibid., 152–53.

29. NBER, "U.S. Business Cycle."

30. Federal Reserve Board, *Tenth Annual Report of the Federal Reserve Board: Covering Operations for the Year 1923* (Washington, D.C.: Government Printing Office, 1924), 16.

31. FRB, *Tenth Annual Report*, 17.

32. Ibid., 23–24.

33. Ibid., 29–30.

34. Eichengreen, "International Policy Coordination," 150–51.

35. FRB, *Tenth Annual Report*, 33.

36. Federal Reserve Board, *Fifteenth Annual Report of the Federal Reserve Board: Covering Operations for the Year 1928* (Washington, D.C.: Government Printing Office, 1929), 8.

37. Federal Reserve Board, *Seventeenth Annual Report of the Federal Reserve Board: Covering Operations for the Year 1930* (Washington, D.C.: Government Printing Office, 1931), 39.

EIGHT

The Great Depression

The Great Contraction of 1929–33 tested not only the Federal Reserve but the viability of an independent monetary policy that prioritized domestic economic goals over concerns for the survival of the gold standard. Since the last deep recession in the early 1920s, Reserve authorities had experimented with open market policy as a more fine-tuned approach to managing the money market than the rigid reliance on discount rates. This foray into open market policy, however, did not mean that in another contraction Reserve authorities would coalesce around the idea of an aggressive open market policy committed to easing the economy beyond short-term horizons. Reserve authorities relied on the same operating procedures implemented in the 1920s, in which borrowing through the discount window served as a guide for the appropriate intensity of open market purchases.

Preservation of the gold standard was still of overriding importance. Classical central banking rules for regulating gold flows remained highly relevant to Reserve officials into the early 1930s. Although the Reserve Banks did not per se revert to the sterilization protocol of the 1920s, from an abstract standpoint gold inflows expanded member bank reserves and in effect negated the need for a proportional amount of Federal Reserve credit. Reserve Banks were also still required to hold at least 40 percent gold against note circulation and 35 percent gold against deposit liabilities to member banks. Even if Reserve officials were hypothetically motivated to purchase securities or acceptances on a large scale, the gold reserve requirements would ultimately constrain their actions.

Reserve policies from 1920–22 provide an inescapable context for the response to the stock market crash of 1929. The recession at the beginning of the decade was the last deep contraction before the crash, putting aside business cycle troughs occurring in the intervening decade. In 1920–21, monetary policy was not associated with centralized, proactive approaches to easing the economy but with allowing the Reserve Banks to function as regional pillars of stability for their local money markets. The Reserve Banks were intended to automatically discount eligible paper or purchase acceptances at reduced rates to tide over markets. The cycle reached its peak in January 1920 and its trough in July 1921.[1] Through much of 1920, the primary goal was to stop inflation and overheating credit conditions. In 1920 and 1921, the Reserve Banks discounted a total volume of $85 million and $58 million respectively, with discounts falling further to $22 million in the recovery of 1922. Purchases of total U.S. securities in 1920 came to $8 million. Almost all of these purchases were of Treasury certificates of indebtedness and not notes. Purchases of Treasury notes then rose from $66 million in 1921 to $845 million in 1922, an overwhelming chunk purchased by the New York Bank. The New York Bank also purchased $2.1 billion in Treasury certificates of indebtedness in 1922. New York in fact purchased $2.9 billion in U.S. securities in 1922, whether classified as Treasury certificates of indebtedness, notes, Victory notes, or bonds. Total purchases of acceptances in the open market, on the other hand, fell from $3.2 billion in 1920 to $2 billion in 1922.[2]

The fall in discounts in 1922 could probably be attributed to the rising volume of securities purchases, with one form of credit replacing another. The Reserve Banks had worked to wring out inflation and excessive ease from the economy. Although the stepped-up discount rates in late 1919 and 1920 set into motion a process of contraction and liquidation, these adjustments were undertaken without triggering widespread panics and suspensions because of the presence of Reserve Banks as lenders of last resort. Also of crucial importance, European nations had not yet restored convertibility, so that only the U.S. was on gold at the time. The U.S. netted gold imports of $667 million in 1921 and $238 million in 1922.[3] These timely gold inflows stabilized the money supply and allowed the Reserve Banks to pursue expansionary open market policies, at least in the sense that Reserve officials did not need to worry about open market purchases triggering outflows.

By the end of the 1920s, however, this abnormal situation had been corrected, with the international gold standard restored. Reserve Banks bought $350 million in securities from the crash in October 1929 until the end of the year.[4] The average amount of securities held by Reserve Banks in the System Investment Account rose from $29 million in October 1929 to $107 million in November before jumping further to $272 million by the end of the year.[5] Average daily figures for discounted paper rose from $885 million in October 1929 to $953 million in November before falling back to $803 million in December.[6] The Reserve Banks also implemented a round of discount rate reductions in late 1929, with the New York Bank cutting its rate from 6 percent to 5 percent in early November and then to 4 ½ percent in the middle of the month.[7] Borrowing then fell off in the new year. System-wide discounts fell from an average daily figure of $702 million on January 4, 1930 to $230 million on March 29.[8]

Under the operating procedures then in place, which Strong had articulated back in the 1920s, reduced borrowing signified less need for expansionary open market policy. Moreover, because of instability abroad, the U.S. netted gold imports of nearly $60 million in February 1930, $55.7 million in March, and $65.7 million in April. The U.S. in fact netted $280 million in gold for all of 1930.[9] Because of the gold inflows, total Federal Reserve credit sat at $1 billion from May until October. At this same time the year before, total credit had been $1.4 billion.[10] The movement of currency from public circulation back into bank deposits also greatly contributed to the reduction in Federal Reserve credit.[11] Despite these indicators, the economy was clearly entering a state of deep contraction. In addition to a precipitous fall in industrial production and employment since the crash, the loans and investments of member banks decreased by $1 billion from early October 1929 to December 1930.[12] Wholesale prices fell by 15 percent during 1930.[13]

In the first half of 1930, George Harrison of the New York Bank waged an unsuccessful campaign to persuade other Reserve Bank governors and the Board into pursuing a coherent, expansionary policy. Other Reserve officials objected to the idea of expanded purchases because they would only cause member banks to replace one form of Federal Reserve credit with another and because the economy needed to proceed through a natural and unimpeded process of liquidation before recovery was possible. At its January 28–29, 1930 meeting, the OMIC reached a series of findings, including that "[t]he panicky feeling has subsided," "[a] business recession has taken place, the extent or duration of which is not yet possible to determine," "[m]oney has been made available to commerce and industry at more reasonable rates," and [l]iquidation is progressing in an orderly fashion."[14]

Harrison did not attend a March 24–25 meeting because he was in Europe. The other members of the OMIC discussed the New York Bank's authorization to purchase $50 million in securities earlier in the month. Many of them were not "in sympathy with this purchase of Governments and felt that money rates had been eased more rapidly than was desirable." [15] The OMIC then issued a policy minute stating that "the steps already taken by the Federal Reserve System in easing the money market through open market operations have gone as far in providing the stimulus of easy money for business use as seems desirable at this time." [16] The committee members also voted to discontinue the OMIC and replace it with a new Open Market Policy Conference (OMPC) made up of representatives from all of the Reserve Banks and vested with authority for formulating open market policy subject to the Board's approval.[17]

At the first OMPC meeting on May 21–22, Harrison noted the global aspects of the contraction and that, in addition to overcapacity, reduced income and tight liquidity were causes for the economic collapse.[18] Though the OMPC acknowledged a state of depression in both domestic and foreign commerce, it refrained from recommending any open market operations at the present time.[19] The OMPC's executive committee, responsible for implementing monetary policy and made up of representatives from New York, Chicago, Philadelphia, Boston, and Cleveland, met on June 23. Harrison made clear that the economy was not recovering from contraction and advised the use of open market purchases to support the bond market. He also thought that a fall in the buying of acceptances had neutralized the effectiveness of the recent purchase of $50 million in securities.[20] The committee then voted 4 to 1, Harrison's the single dissenting vote, that the OMPC would not make any more purchases under the System Account.[21]

Harrison failed to persuade his colleagues to implement aggressive and expanded purchases, but his proposal to actively back the bond market was notable in its departure from the real bills doctrine. While other Reserve Bank officials still adhered to relatively laissez-faire views that liquidation and contraction were inevitable and should not be interfered with, Harrison proposed an apparently long-term program intended to promote economic recovery into the foreseeable future. Not entirely clear in the first half of 1930 was whether this should be the function of the Federal Reserve. Harrison lost the debate, and monetary policy continued to be marked by indecision during the remaining years of the Great Contraction.

Conditions worsened when bank panics broke out in late 1930, culminating in the failure of New York's Bank of United States in December. The bank's official sounding name might have only aggravated the sense of panic. Currency in circulation rose from $4.5 billion in October to $4.9 billion in December as the public withdrew cash from bank deposits.[22] A total of 1,345 banks with $865 million in deposits suspended in all of 1930. These were overwhelmingly state banks outside the Federal Reserve System.[23] By the end of the year, the New York Bank had cut its discount rate to 2 percent.[24] A net $19.6 million in gold flowed out of the country in both July and August, but these outflows turned into robust inflows in the autumn.[25]

The economy continued its path through contraction as new bank panics hit in the spring of 1931. Domestic distress coincided with continuing gold inflows, mainly from Asia and other parts of the Americas, which drove a $230 million gain in the U.S.'s gold stock by June. The U.S. received another $190 million in gold during the summer largely due to the implosion of the Credit Anstalt, one of the major banks in Central Europe.[26] The gold inflows absorbed currency demand, so that the monthly average of daily Reserve Bank credit increased by only $40 million until September.[27] When the U.K. suspended its gold standard in September, panic spread that the U.S. would follow. European investors with gold in the U.S. began transferring their holdings back to other nations still on the gold standard, especially France, causing $725 million in gold to flow out of the U.S. during the autumn.[28] An internal drain matched the external drain, with the public increasingly withdrawing currency from deposits and hoarding it. End of month figures for currency in circulation rose by $595 million from the end of August to the end of December.[29]

Facing an external and internal drain, the Reserve Banks followed Bagehot's rule of lending freely at a high rate. The monthly average of daily Reserve Bank credit ballooned from $40 million earlier in the year to $637 million from September through December.[30] At the same time, the Reserve Banks hiked their discount rates. New York raised its discount rate from 1 ½ percent to 2 ½ percent on October 9 and then again to 3 ½ percent on October 16.[31] The crisis represented nothing short of a convulsion in the market for bankers' acceptances. Outstanding bankers' acceptances had contracted from $1.7 billion in December 1929 to $996 million by September 1931.[32] With the onset of the crisis, System-wide holdings of acceptances rose from $259.3 million in September to $691.7 million a month later.[33] By late October, the Reserve Banks held well over two-thirds of all bankers' acceptances then outstanding. The gold outflows to Europe largely stopped during the rest of the year and were replaced by inflows from Japan. But in the year-end tally, the U.S.'s gold stock sustained a loss of $135 million.[34] The epidemic of bank panics had also worsened from a year ago. In 1931, 2,298 banks suspended, but again over three quarters of these banks were outside the Federal Reserve System.[35]

The U.S. netted gold outflows of $73 million in January and $90.6 million in February 1932.[36] With the loss of gold obstructing the already bleak prospects of carrying out purchases on a large scale, President Hoover called for a robust package of proposals to rescue the economy, among them the creation of a Reconstruction Finance Corporation (RFC). Hoover also supported expanding the definition of "eligible paper" against Federal Reserve notes. He noted in his memoirs that as bank runs and withdrawals drove up Federal Reserve notes in circulation, the expanded currency needed to be increasingly covered by gold instead of eligible paper since the latter was in short supply. Hoover estimated that gold coverage for currency had risen from the statutory minimum of 40 percent to roughly 70 percent. The gold reserve needed to be again contained to 40 percent of currency in order to release gold to accommodate outflows. Free gold had indeed fallen to only $300 million.[37]

During a meeting at the White House in early February 1932, Harrison and Eugene Meyer, the chair of the Federal Reserve Board, agreed to widen the definition of eligibility to include certain types of Treasury securities. Hoover then met with Senate leaders the following day to discuss the plan. Treasury Secretary Ogden Mills spoke in favor of the idea to the senators. Carter Glass, now in the Senate, reluctantly came around to supporting it. One strong selling point for expanding eligibility was that it would save the gold standard. Hoover met with House members later that day, and Henry Steagall, Democratic Chairman of the House Banking Committee, agreed to move forward with a bill. Hoover had successfully reached out to the Democrats controlling the House of Representatives while retaining the support of fellow Republicans. Passage of the bill into law on February 27 was a bipartisan success.[38]

The Glass-Steagall Act of 1932 permitted the Federal Reserve to count Treasury bonds purchased in the open market as part of the 60 percent eligible paper requirement held against note circulation until March 1933. Glass-Steagall did not alter the original provision mandating a 40 percent gold requirement.[39] The legislation was primarily intended to help keep the U.S. on the gold standard. But it still in effect relaxed the constraints of the gold standard on domestic monetary policy. Congress granted Reserve Banks the authority to replace their holdings of commercial and agricultural paper with U.S. securities purchased in the open market against notes in circulation. Congress made the legislation permanent the next year.

Passage of Glass-Steagall initially prodded the Reserve Banks into engaging in large-scale purchases that pushed Reserve Bank holdings of U.S. securities up to $1.9 billion by early August. But holdings did not significantly increase during the latter part of 1932.[40] Gold outflows possibly inhibited the Banks from continuing these more aggressive efforts. During May and June, when Reserve Banks were carrying out the purchases, gold outflows netted respectively $195.5 million and $206 million. After the Banks scaled down the purchases, net outflows turned into net inflows. Outflows fell dramatically in gross terms to $18 million in August and only $60,000 in September. By December, net inflows reached over $100 million.[41] Another factor was that the purchases might only have been replacing one form of Reserve Bank credit with another. From March to August, the average daily holdings of government securities among Reserve Banks rose from $809 million to $1.9 billion. The corresponding figure for discounts fell from $714 million to $451 million over the same period. The average daily figure for total Reserve Bank credit still rose during this time from $1.7 billion to $2.4 billion.[42]

At a July 14 joint meeting of the OMPC and the Board, Harrison proposed targeting excess bank reserves in the range of $200 to $250 million. He also thought that the ebbing in gold outflows meant that large scale purchases were no longer necessary.[43] The OMPC voted 9 to 3 to target excess bank reserves at about $200 million and to purchase securities in a range of $5 to $15 million per week.[44] The implication of the meeting was clear. Passage of Glass-Steagall had pushed the OMPC into organizing some semblance of a large-scale purchase program. After the purchase of around $1 billion in securities that coincided with heavy gold outflows, the Reserve authorities were finished with the experiment. Any hope of recovery now lay with the executive and legislative branches of government.

The Reserve Banks had sought to accommodate the market after the crash in 1929 and during the crises in late 1930 and 1931. The New York Bank held its discount rate at 1 ½ percent for all of 1931 until October 9.[45] Total end of the year securities holdings of the Federal Reserve had risen from $510.6 million in 1929 to $729.5 million in 1930, to $817 million in 1931, to $1.9 billion in 1932.[46] But these actions did not form a coherent policy. In 1930 and through most of 1931 the Reserve Banks failed to execute a unified and ongoing response to deteriorating conditions. This failure prevented them from sending a clear signal to markets and boosting business confidence.

Putting aside the institutional flaws of the Federal Reserve, the gold standard still dominated the world economy in 1929. With the U.S.'s assistance, European nations had struggled to restore convertibility. Governments did not want to bear responsibility for tearing apart all that they had worked for unless no alternative availed itself. Even had the Federal Reserve functioned more coherently, the gold standard would have still impeded an expansionary domestic policy by 1931, when major European economies were forced off gold. Glass-Steagall might have relaxed collateral requirements, but large-scale purchases apparently triggered gold outflows. That all said, if the Reserve Banks should have acted more decisively, then the time to do it was undoubtedly the first half of 1930, when the U.S. robustly imported gold and the contraction was still in its early stages.

The 1935 Banking Act centralized the Federal Reserve by transferring more policymaking power from the Reserve Banks to the Federal Open Market Committee (FOMC) sitting in Washington, D.C. The Act further mandated that all seven members of the Board of Governors, a renaming of the Federal Reserve Board, be included within the FOMC, while the Act limited Reserve Banks to only five seats on the Committee. Because of its numerical weight in the FOMC, the Board of Governors gained greater power in managing open market policy. The treasury secretary and comptroller of the currency were also eliminated as ex officio members of the Board of Governors.[47] The heads of Reserve Banks were even renamed presidents instead of the supposedly more exalted title of governor. The plan for the 1935 Act was influenced by Marriner Eccles, who chaired the reorganized Fed.[48]

Only with the 1935 Act was the Federal Reserve consolidated into something like a central bank. Unfortunately, by the time Congress passed the legislation the Federal Reserve had missed its opportunity to respond to the contraction. The sinking economy had now become a full-blown political issue and was of central importance in the 1932 presidential election. The Democratic candidate, Franklin Roosevelt, relied on an eclectic group of advisers during the campaign that came to be known as the Brain Trust, none of whom were experts in monetary policy. Roosevelt held no dogmatic views regarding gold, and he appeared receptive to any proposals that might push the economy out of depression.

Among the range of options for generating inflation, one included tapping into the nation's silver resources. A silverist faction in Congress favored remonetizing silver to boost farm prices. Silver purchases in the early 1930s offered a more practical inflationary countermeasure than the purchases carried out in the late 1800s. Congress had passed the Bland-Allison and Sherman Silver Purchase Acts when other nations were moving onto the international gold standard. But in 1933 the situation was reversed, with the U.S. remaining on gold and most of the other large economies having abandoned convertibility. The argument for renewed silver purchases was strengthened by the fact that silver purchase legislation from over a decade earlier had not triggered gold outflows. Congress passed the Pittman Act in 1918, which authorized the Treasury to purchase silver to offset silver outflows. The Mint had converted $10 million in silver bullion into coin by 1920, while the Treasury sold $260 million in bullion. Because of these operations, Reserve Banks were authorized to issue up to $270 million in Federal Reserve notes.[49]

Contrary to setting off gold outflows, Congress passed the legislation just before historically large gold inflows. At the time of course, only the U.S. remained on gold in the aftermath of World War I. Now that many European nations had again gone off gold, silver purchases could be viewed as a legitimate means to producing inflation. Devaluation offered another potential avenue to inflation. One theory propounded by Professor George Warren of Cornell University was that devaluation would automatically trigger a rise in farm prices. Warren's theory was of great practical relevance to Roosevelt because Warren promoted a ready-made policy that perfectly suited the conditions of 1932–33.

But in more immediate terms, the new Administration confronted the severe banking panic that had swept the nation beginning in February shortly before Roosevelt came into office. Bank runs and conversions of deposits into currency were severe. Worried about gold outflows, the New York Bank raised its discount and bill buying rates while also expanding its volume of loans and purchases of acceptances. Reserve Bank holdings of bankers' acceptances reached $307 million in February 1933 before dipping to $280 million in March.[50] At the same time, currency in circulation rose to as high as $7.5 billion.[51] On March 6, just a little after twenty-four hours upon assuming office, Roosevelt issued an executive order implementing a national bank holiday that temporarily closed all banks. Roosevelt simultaneously prohibited the export of gold during the course of the holiday under authority of the Trading with the Enemy Act. Congress sanctioned this action by passing the Emergency Banking Act on March 9, which authorized the treasury secretary to order the public to transfer its gold holdings to the Treasury.[52] The national bank holiday was unprecedented in its complete closure of all banks. During the National Banking era, clearinghouse banks might have individually suspended payments to depositors, but that did not mean that they would entirely shut down their operations.

Even as the crisis and holiday were unfolding, Roosevelt began to take steps that would culminate in the nationalization of the gold stock and the devaluation of the dollar. On April 5, under authority of the Emergency Banking Act, Roosevelt issued an executive order prohibiting private parties from holding gold worth more than $100 and directing the public to send all gold over this amount to the Federal Reserve by May 1. By the end of the year, the Treasury ordered the transfer of gold holdings $100 or less to Reserve Banks, bringing virtually the entire gold stock into the vaults of the Federal Reserve.[53] The executive order on April 5 contained an authorization for the treasury secretary to grant licenses to individual banks for the export of gold. These licenses led to the outflow of $600,000 in gold to the Netherlands and $9 million in gold to France. With dollar exchange rates hitting the export point, the Administration was not going to tolerate any more outflows. Roosevelt issued an executive order on April 20 formally prohibiting gold exports except for official settlements. The Administration's prohibition of gold exports neutralized the effects of the dollar's fall against other currencies. Congress formalized the suspension of gold convertibility on June 5 by passing legislation that abrogated gold payment clauses in all government and private contracts.[54] The Supreme Court upheld the legality of abrogation in a ruling two years later.

Roosevelt's executive orders prohibiting the export of gold were extraordinary in their power and scope. Roosevelt could be thought of as having imposed a massive gold device on the entire country. Legal means were being taken to literally block the export of gold and fully prevent against any possible gold outflows. Roosevelt's additional step of ordering the public to transfer most of its gold holdings to the Federal Reserve initiated a new era of nationalization of the gold stock and the creation of a gold bullion standard. Roosevelt's efforts in 1933–34 followed from what European nations had done when restoring convertibility in the 1920s, which was to restrict the private holding of gold coin while retaining the currency's peg to gold. Though Roosevelt's first steps in nationalizing gold were extreme, they had already been taken in other parts of the world and enjoyed wide public support. J.P. Morgan declared his full support for the blockade on the export of gold. Republican Senator Arthur Vandenberg of Michigan noted that the dollar's falling exchange rate would finally help exports.[55] The Committee for the Nation, formed by members of the business and academic communities, called for dollar reflation.[56]

The focus now shifted to reflating the dollar and raising prices. Under the Thomas Amendment to the Agricultural Adjustment Act of 1933, the president was granted a series of options for reflation. The most critical provision of the Thomas Amendment authorized the president to reduce the gold content of the dollar by up to 50 percent. The Act additionally authorized the president to direct the Federal Reserve to engage in open market purchases of up to $3 billion. If the Fed failed to carry out these operations, the Act authorized the president to instruct the Treasury to issue $3 billion in fiduciary currency through purchases of U.S. securities.[57]

While Roosevelt was imposing drastic changes upon the domestic economy, he faced possible international constraints after the World Economic Conference convened in London on June 12. The conference had been planned with the goal of stabilizing exchange rates and preventing further efforts towards competitive devaluation. Roosevelt met with foreign leaders in the months before the conference and generally committed the U.S. to the ultimate stabilization of exchange rates. Roosevelt sent a handful of individuals with pro-gold views to the conference, including Harrison of the New York Bank, James Warburg, an economist and son of the German-born banker, and the economist Oliver Sprague. Whether Roosevelt would allow any agreement reached at the conference to affect his domestic agenda was unclear.[58]

When the conference began in June, the U.S. delegation reached an agreement with its British and French counterparts to temporarily peg sterling at $4.00 at least until they adjourned. Sterling had been floating against the dollar since the U.K. went off gold. Even though his advisers strongly supported the agreement, Roosevelt sent a message stating that he opposed any parity with sterling under $4.25. He further mentioned that such a provisional exchange rate regime would hinder his ability to act in the domestic sphere.[59] The tentative agreement had also committed signatory governments to forgoing domestic policies inconsistent with international goals aimed at reestablishing fixed exchange rates. Such a declaration clearly applied to the Thomas Amendment, and indeed in his response Roosevelt added that he would not relinquish the authority granted to him pursuant to the Thomas Amendment.[60]

Now that Roosevelt had shunted aside concrete proposals, the parties negotiated a declaration for restoring convertibility and fixed exchange rates at some future point at the discretion of each government. The dollar had by now depreciated to $4.40 against sterling, and many advisers and associates of Roosevelt lent their support to the planned communique, but Roosevelt disagreed. After receiving a draft on June 30, he repudiated it the following day.[61] Roosevelt then sent a telegram to the conference declaring that "old fetishes of so-called international bankers are being replaced by efforts to plan national currencies with the objective of giving to those currencies a continuing purchasing power which does not greatly vary in terms of the commodities and need of modern civilization."[62]

Roosevelt's "bombshell" message indicated that he would in no way allow gold pegs and fixed exchange rates to interfere with his domestic agenda. His pejorative reference to "international bankers" reinforced the point that currency should be made national because the gold standard had been historically shaped by international linkages of trade and finance. At the heart of the telegram, Roosevelt communicated both to the conference and to the public that, as the American president, he would not allow an international rule such as a fixed exchange rate to distract him from the needs and goals that he deemed necessary for the country.

Upon news of Roosevelt's bombshell, the dollar inevitably plunged against sterling and the franc in the open markets. Yet as the World Economic Conference wound down after having achieved nothing substantive, Roosevelt did not make an immediate decision regarding devaluation. With deflation still a problem, Roosevelt decided to first pursue a gold purchasing program that had been supported by George Warren, which would push up the price of gold and facilitate the eventual devaluation of the dollar. The RFC purchased domestic gold fresh out of the mines or foreign gold each day at fluctuating market prices beginning in October. The program's domestic purchases were limited to gold that had been recently mined, since the Administration had already ordered most of the existing gold stockpiled at the Federal Reserve. The price of gold rose about three dollars until reaching $34.45 per oz. at the beginning of 1934.[63]

Roosevelt then asked for greater power to devalue the dollar. Congress responded by passing the Gold Reserve Act on January 30, 1934, which authorized the president to devalue the dollar by up to 60 percent of its current value. Acting under this legislation, Roosevelt fixed the price of gold at $35 per oz. The legislation also eliminated the private holding of gold coin.[64] Bullion reserves in government vaults would instead fund international transactions with other nations still on the gold standard. The gold stock became fully nationalized when the Treasury took control of it. The process that had begun almost a year ago was now completed, with a new gold bullion standard established and the dollar permanently devalued. Reflationary policies worked to remove the gold standard as an obstacle to economic recovery.

Having restored the dollar to its gold peg, the Treasury briefly relied on interventions intended to keep the dollar within the gold points, but it soon abandoned these interventions in favor of multilateral initiatives. Developments in the 1930s served as a departure from the practices of the New York Bank in the 1920s, which had mainly used credit lines and monetary policy to strengthen European pegs to gold. The Exchange Stabilization Fund (ESF) was established in 1934 partly in response to fears of competitive devaluation abroad. The ESF came to be known chiefly for its loans to Latin American governments, culminating in a $20 billion loan to Mexico in 1995. But it also made isolated interventions in the foreign exchange markets in the 1930s and later assisted in attempts to stabilize dollar exchange rates in the 1960s. The ESF initially received $2 billion in gold. In order to accumulate dollars to finance forex operations, the Treasury exchanged $200 million in gold for dollars at the New York Bank to serve as an operating fund.[65]

The ESF was committed to preventing gold from flowing out of the country because of a breach in the export point. The Treasury also collaborated with other nations still on gold, particularly France, in maintaining exchange rates within their bands. Gold inflows into the U.S. after 1933 tended to strengthen the dollar and weaken European currencies. As a daily practice, the Treasury used dollars to purchase foreign exchange in the market before trading the foreign exchange for gold to protect itself from exchange rate movements.[66] If the dollar weakened against the franc, the Treasury sold foreign exchange for dollars. This scenario occurred in August 1934 as false reports circulated of impending U.S. devaluation. Twenty-eight million dollars in gold flowed from the U.S. to France over a two week period, while speculators sold dollars and drove down its value against the franc. The ESF successfully responded by borrowing francs and selling them in the spot market.[67]

After the depreciation of the franc, the U.S., France, and the U.K. entered into the Tripartite Agreement in September 1936. The Agreement formally committed the three nations to stabilizing exchange rates and renouncing competitive devaluation of their currencies. Because cheaper currencies enhance the competitiveness of a nation's exports, this issue had become paramount during the protracted Depression. A few months later, the three nations agreed to more specific arrangements intended to facilitate the stabilization of exchange rates. The three governments sold gold to one another at prices that changed daily. The parties assigned a gold price for each twenty-four hour period, which protected the monetary authorities from losses due to exchange rate movements sustained during this period. The gold could then be used to fund currency operations in the local market.[68]

When the dollar weakened in 1937 amid new rumors of U.S. devaluation, the Treasury deposited its overseas earmarked gold into French and British hands while also shipping $50 million in gold across the Atlantic, most going to France. The French and British used this gold to purchase dollars in their local markets and stabilize the dollar exchange rates. The Treasury had delegated the carrying out of exchange rate interventions to its counterparts in Europe, but it had spent $250 million in the process.[69] The Tripartite governments terminated these arrangements at the outbreak of World War II.

As the economy improved in the mid-1930s and market perceptions of the commitment to gold at the devalued rate stabilized, the U.S. became subject to large gold inflows that disrupted the money supply and bank reserves. The inflows followed shortly after devaluation when in 1934 the net outflow reversed to a net inflow. Net gold inflows came to $1.2 billion in 1934, $1.7 billion in 1935, and $1.1 billion in 1936.[70] The gold inflows exacerbated excess bank reserves, which rose from about $800 million at the end of 1933 to a peak of over $3 billion in August 1936.[71]

The gold inflows and the modified peg to gold allowed greater opportunity for silver purchases. Though the Thomas Amendment granted the president the option of purchasing silver, the 1934 Silver Purchase Act expanded these powers by giving the Treasury authority to enter into domestic and foreign purchases of silver at a market price not over $1.29 per oz.[72] During 1933–38, Treasury issued silver certificates caused bank reserves to rise by $1.2 billion, compared to $7.4 billion in bank reserves attributable to gold.[73] Silver purchases therefore aggravated excess bank reserves. Silver purchases also in no way weakened confidence in the U.S.'s adherence to gold, even as these purchases were carried out after Roosevelt had devalued the dollar and nationalized the gold stock. Devaluation and the establishment of a bullion standard might actually have stabilized market attitudes towards the U.S.'s commitment to gold, in that the Roosevelt Administration had taken whatever radical steps it thought necessary to produce reflation and now affirmatively abided by the new parity. Like its predecessors in the nineteenth century, the 1934 Silver Purchase Act represented a bold effort at expanding the money supply, but unlike the prior legislation it did so without triggering debilitating gold outflows. Unfortunately, the Act only led banks to increase their already sizeable excess reserves.

The excess bank reserves distorted the Federal Reserve's operating procedures because they created free reserves in excess of both legal requirements and borrowed reserves. Nor did the Federal Reserve hold enough securities in its portfolio to sell to banks to reduce excess reserves. Conventional policies were now neutralized. The Thomas Amendment granted the Federal Reserve authority to lower or raise reserve requirements under presidential supervision. This provision was later superseded by the 1935 Banking Act, which gave the Board of Governors more autonomy in this area.[74]

Under this legislation, the Board raised reserve requirements to soak up the excess member reserves. "In order to eliminate the possibility of these excess reserves becoming the basis of an injurious credit expansion," as the 1936 *Annual Report* explained, the Board decided to raise reserve requirements by 50 percent on July 14, 1936 and again by 50 percent on January 30, 1937.[75] In addressing the decision to further raise requirements in January 1937, the 1937 *Annual Report* noted that in spite of the hike, "the banking system would still have the basis of a potential expansion of more than $5,000,000,000 without recourse to the Federal Reserve banks."[76] From the standpoint of the Board of Governors, the reserve requirements were necessary to preempt an impending credit expansion and inflation, a danger rooted in abnormal gold inflows. But regardless of the motivation behind the hikes, the economy entered a deep recession starting in 1937.

Despite the Board's new authority over reserve requirements in the mid-1930s, major components of monetary policy came to be subordinated to the Treasury's agenda of debt management. As nominal interest rates rose simultaneous to stronger GDP growth, the Treasury wanted to conscript the Fed into an effort to strengthen the demand for government securities. A stable market in Treasurys required the Fed to purchase securities to boost their market prices and reduce their yields. Yet the Treasury's goal to support the market for government debt directly conflicted with the Fed's own objective of containing excess reserves, since purchases would have only further added to excess reserves.[77]

By the early spring of 1937, Treasury Secretary Henry Morgenthau was pressuring the FOMC to stop a fall in the price of government securities. At an April 3 meeting of the FOMC, Marriner Eccles, who as Chairman of the Board of Governors also presided over the Committee, submitted a draft resolution from Morgenthau for the Federal Reserve to receive $500 million in gold certificates from the Treasury to be used for open market purchases. According to Eccles, Morgenthau had related to him that Morgenthau "proposed the action for the purpose of letting the market know that the Treasury intended to do what it could to prevent a disorderly market" and "that if joint action could not be agreed upon by the Federal Reserve System and the Treasury the latter would take independent action."[78] Eccles also clarified that Morgenthau did not insist that the FOMC make purchases of a specific amount.[79] Because purchases conflicted with a reserve requirements hike proposed for May, Eccles rationalized purchases on the grounds that banks had already been more intensively selling Treasurys than expected since the Board raised requirements.[80] The following day, the FOMC voted on a resolution authorizing purchases of at least $25 million but capping operations at $250 million until the next Committee meeting.[81] The monthly average of daily figures of Reserve Bank securities holdings rose by only about $95 million by May.[82]

Monetary policy was deemphasized after the Reserve Banks' $1 billion purchase program in 1932. Open market operations now served the Treasury's goal of managing the market in government debt. When the U.S. entered World War II, the Fed initiated the more formal policy of pegging Treasury yields. By 1945, the Fed pegged the yields of Treasury bills at 7/8 percent and long-term bonds at 2 ½ percent.[83]

NOTES

1. NBER, "U.S. Business Cycle."
2. FRB, *Ninth Annual Report*, 116.
3. Ibid., 13.
4. FRB, *Seventeenth Annual Report*, 1–2.
5. Ibid., 53.
6. Federal Reserve Board, *Eighteenth Annual Report of the Federal Reserve Board: Covering Operations for the Year 1931* (Washington, D.C.: Government Printing Office, 1932), 30.
7. FRB, *Seventeenth Annual Report*, 76.
8. Ibid., 35.
9. Ibid., 69.
10. Ibid., 4–5.
11. Ibid., 8.
12. Ibid., 9.
13. Ibid., 224.
14. OMIC Minutes, January 28–29, 1930, Minutes of the Meetings of the Open Market Investment Committee, Federal Reserve Archival System for Economic Research, St. Louis Federal Reserve, 6.
15. OMIC Minutes, March 24–25, 1930, Minutes of the Meetings of the Open Market Investment Committee, Federal Reserve Archival System for Economic Research, St. Louis Federal Reserve, 1.
16. March 24–25 Minutes, 2.
17. Ibid., 4.
18. OMPC Minutes, May 21–22, 1930, Minutes of the Meetings of the Open Market Policy Conference, Federal Reserve Archival System for Economic Research, St. Louis Federal Reserve, 3–4.
19. May 21–22 Minutes, 7.
20. OMPC Executive Committee Minutes, June 23, 1930, Minutes of the Meetings of the Open Market Policy Conference, Federal Reserve Archival System for Economic Research, St. Louis Federal Reserve, 1–2.
21. June 23, 1930 Minutes, 3.
22. FRB, *Seventeenth Annual Report*, 70.
23. Ibid., 17–18.
24. Ibid., 76.
25. Ibid., 69.
26. FRB, *Eighteenth Annual Report*, 10.
27. Ibid., 2–3.
28. Ibid., 11.
29. Ibid., 69.
30. Ibid., 3.
31. Ibid., 75.
32. Ibid., 122.
33. Ibid., 39.
34. Ibid., 11.
35. Ibid., 18.
36. Federal Reserve Board, *Nineteenth Annual Report of the Federal Reserve Board: Covering Operations for the Year 1932* (Washington, D.C.: Government Printing Office, 1933), 98.
37. Herbert Hoover, *The Memoirs of Herbert Hoover: The Great Depression, 1929–1941* (New York: The Macmillan Company, 1952), 116.
38. Hoover, *Memoirs*, 116–17.
39. FRB, *Nineteenth Annual Report*, 16.
40. Ibid., 11.
41. Ibid., 98.

42. Ibid., 46.
43. OMPC Meeting Minutes, July 14, 1932, Minutes of the Meetings of the Open Market Policy Conference, Federal Reserve Archival System for Economic Research, St. Louis Federal Reserve, 2.
44. July 14 1932 Minutes, 3.
45. FRB, *Eighteenth Annual Report*, 75.
46. FRB, *Nineteenth Annual Report*, 72.
47. Board of Governors, *Twenty-Second Annual Report of the Board of Governors of the Federal Reserve System: Covering Operations for the Year 1935* (Washington, D.C.: Government Printing Office, 1936), 6.
48. Calomiris and Wheelock, "The Great Depression," 31–32.
49. FRB, *Seventh Annual Report*, 386.
50. Federal Reserve Board, *Twentieth Annual Report of the Federal Reserve Board: Covering Operations for the Year 1933* (Washington, D.C.: Government Printing Office, 1934), 112.
51. Ibid., 14.
52. Ibid., 26–27.
53. Ibid., 27.
54. Ibid., 27–28.
55. Murray N. Rothbard, *A History of Money and Banking in the United States: The Colonial Era to World War II* (Auburn, AL: Ludwig von Mises Institute, 2002), 457.
56. Rothbard, *History*, 454–55.
57. FRB, *Twentieth Annual Report*, 267–68.
58. Rothbard, *History*, 459–60.
59. Ibid., 460–61.
60. Rodney J. Morrison, "The London Monetary and Economic Conference of 1933: A Public Goods Analysis," *The American Journal of Economics and Sociology* 52, no. 3 (1993): 311.
61. Rothbard, *History*, 464–65.
62. Franklin Roosevelt, "Wireless to the London Conference: July 3, 1933," University of California-Santa Barbara, http://www.presidency.ucsb.edu/ws/?pid=14679, accessed August 2017.
63. Kenneth W. Dam, "From the Gold Clause Cases to the Gold Commission: A Half Century of American Monetary Law," *University of Chicago Law Review* 504, no. 50 (1983): 512–13.
64. Dam, "Monetary Law," 513–14.
65. Arthur I. Bloomfield, "Operations of the American Exchange Stabilization Fund," *The Review of Economics and Statistics* 26, no. 2 (1944): 70.
66. Bloomfield, "Exchange Stabilization Fund," 71.
67. Ibid., 74–75.
68. Ibid., 75–76.
69. Ibid., 79.
70. Board of Governors, *Twenty-Third Annual Report of the Board of Governors of the Federal Reserve System: Covering Operations for the Year 1936* (Washington, D.C.: Federal Reserve System, 1937), 105.
71. BoG, *Twenty-Third Annual Report*, 11.
72. Federal Reserve Board, *Twenty-First Annual Report of the Federal Reserve Board: Covering Operations for the Year 1934* (Washington, D.C.: Government Printing Office, 1935), 11.
73. Board of Governors, *Twenty-Fifth Annual Report of the Board of Governors of the Federal Reserve System: Covering Operations for the Year 1938* (Washington, D.C.: Federal Reserve System, 1939), 20.
74. Calomiris and Wheelock, "The Great Depression," 32–34.
75. BoG, *Twenty-Third Annual Report*, 10.

76. Board of Governors, *Twenty-Fourth Annual Report of the Board of Governors of the Federal Reserve System: Covering Operations for the Year 1937* (Washington, D.C.: Federal Reserve System, 1938), 4.
77. Barry Eichengreen and Peter M. Garber, "Before the Accord: U.S. Monetary-Financial Policy, 1945–51," in *Financial Markets and Financial Crises*, ed. R. Glenn Hubbard (Chicago: University of Chicago Press, 1991), 178–79.
78. FOMC Minutes, April 3, 1937, Federal Open Market Committee, Federal Reserve Transcripts and other historical materials, Board of Governors, 3–4.
79. April 3, 1937 Minutes, 8.
80. Ibid., 7.
81. FOMC Minutes, April 4, 1937, Federal Open Market Committee, Federal Reserve Transcripts and other historical materials, Board of Governors, 11.
82. BoG, *Twenty-Fourth Annual Report*, 43.
83. Board of Governors, *Thirty-Second Annual Report of the Board of Governors of the Federal Reserve System: Covering Operations for the Year 1945* (Washington, D.C.: Federal Reserve System, 1946), 7.

NINE

Postwar Adjustments

The new monetary system planned at the international conference in Bretton Woods, New Hampshire in 1944 pegged only the dollar to gold. Other currencies were pegged to the dollar through adjustable bands. Convertibility of currencies at the pegged rates for current account transactions was not restored until late 1958. From the end of World War II through most of the 1950s, the international economic situation could best be described as abnormal, with European and Asian economies recovering from the war and the flow of currency still subject to controls. Necessary adjustments in the world economy occurred during the lag from the end of the war until the activation of exchange rates for current account transactions in 1958. Some of these adjustments reflected the inevitable erosion of the U.S.'s artificial position at the end of the war. Well over half of the world's gold was located in the U.S. in the late 1940s, but foreign aid transfers were bound to correct this artificial position, as former trading partners devastated by war rebuilt their economies and export capabilities. Similarly, U.S. manufactured output constituted about 60 percent of the world's total after the war, but this figure would fall to 40 percent by 1963.[1] These adjustments were considered necessary at the time to foster recovery in Europe and Asia.

The emergence of the dollar as the world's reserve asset in the 1950s appeared to further facilitate macroeconomic adjustments and inject added liquidity into the world economy. But an ulterior problem was the secular decline in the world's gold stock. The economist Robert Triffin concluded that gold reserves would not be large enough into the near future as represented in International Monetary Fund (IMF) reports. Triffin contended that the global gold supply would contract because of the declining real price of gold. True to Triffin's theory, by the 1960s the gold supply did not appear to be keeping pace with global economic growth.

Triffin predicted that the U.S. balance of payments deficit would mitigate the gold shortage. The transfer of dollars from the U.S. to Europe for investment would keep the world awash in liquidity. The repercussion of this was that claims on U.S. gold would increase as dollars accumulated abroad. The U.S. would eventually be forced into tightening its policies in order to stop and reverse the outflow of dollars, but this might lead to depression in the U.S. and around the world. The Triffin dilemma pitted two crucial interests against one another: preservation of the nation's gold reserve versus dollar liquidity.[2]

From the standpoint of 1946, concerns related to the Triffin dilemma were still at least over a decade away. European demand for U.S. exports caused wholesale commodity prices to spike by 15 percent and consumer prices by 9 percent in 1947.[3] In July 1947, the Federal Reserve and the Treasury agreed to abandon the peg for Treasury bills. Bill yields increased from the pegged 3/8 percent to almost 1 percent by the end of the year.[4] With inflation becoming more visible, the Board of Governors decided to raise reserve requirements from 20 percent to 22 percent against net demand deposits in central reserve cities in January 1948. The Board then raised this requirement to 24 percent in June.[5] In September, after a special session of Congress convened by President Truman had authorized the Board to raise reserve requirements temporarily beyond their legal limits, the Board increased requirements by 2 percent against net demand deposits and 1 ½ percent against time deposits in non-reserve cities. The Board later extended the increase to other cities.[6] Open market policy was not entirely consistent with the increases in reserve requirements. System-wide holdings of securities rose by $800 million.[7]

As the economy entered into recession by early 1949, the FOMC ended up selling government bonds in large volume because of increased market demand. In the first half of 1949, the FOMC sold $3 billion in bonds.[8] The FOMC was still formally committed to providing for an orderly market in Treasury bonds, and the bond sales were crowding out private investment during a recession. In bowing to these concerns, the FOMC issued a press release on June 28 indicating that it would resume policies aimed at pegging Treasury bond yields and fostering economic recovery.[9] System holdings of Treasury bonds again approached $5 billion by the end of 1949 after having dipped below $4 billion earlier in the year.[10]

Inflation reemerged in mid-1950, but the outbreak of the Korean War only further pressured the FOMC into using monetary policy for debt management. Reserve authorities wanted to raise interest rates in the face of worsening inflation, but Treasury officials initially stonewalled any efforts in this direction. The Treasury and Fed finally reached the so-called Accord in February 1951. Under the agreement, the Fed pledged to purchase another $400 million in Treasury bonds in order to peg yields at 2 ½ percent, after which the regime in pegged yields would end, if not the

Fed's attention to the market in government debt. When the Fed finished buying up the $400 million, Treasury yields increased to 2 ¾ percent.[11]

Under the new chairmanship of William McChesney Martin, the Fed pursued an autonomous monetary policy that was both cautious and focused on stopping inflation before it became a major threat. The FOMC voted in a March 4, 1953 meeting for a resolution directing that "[u]nder present conditions, operations for the System account should be confined to the short end of the market."[12] Martin stated his personal view that engaging in operations in "the long-term market was entirely inconsistent with having a good Government securities market."[13] The FOMC began to implement a bills-only open market policy that returned to the operating procedures used by Strong of the New York Bank in the 1920s. The FOMC targeted the free reserves of banks through bill-based open market operations. The FOMC purchased bills and created or strengthened free reserves in a recession, while in an expansion it did the opposite, selling bills and eliminating free reserves. The FOMC influenced interest rates by targeting free reserves, since lower interest rates were correlated with large free reserves and higher interest rates were correlated with contracted reserves.

Members of the FOMC were focused on price stability as a precondition to the successful maintaining of the new system of adjustable exchange rates. Their views comported with the balanced budgets promoted by the Eisenhower Administration. The pursuit of disinflationary policies led the Fed to, according to one adage, lean against the wind, with tightening occurring in 1955 and 1958 relatively not long after troughs in the business cycle.[14] Detractors of the Martin Fed of the 1950s derided these policies as stop-go, in that the Fed became supposedly chained to a pattern of tightening in expansions and easing in contractions because of a misplaced fear of inflation.

But members of the FOMC were concerned with maintaining stability in the money supply and business cycle, even if such a concern led to unpopular actions. Nor could the Fed entirely manage the business cycle through a perfectly calibrated open market policy. The blunt visibility of the discount rate was also used to slow down an accelerating economy, such as in 1955. At an August 2, 1955 meeting, Martin worried that "[w]e are faced with a wage cost push at a time of virtually full employment, consumer and mortgage credit are 'running out of our ears,' . . . Inventory accumulation is already under way."[15] Martin used a metaphor and symbolism back-to-back to illustrate the perils of inflation; "Inflation is a thief in the night and if we don't act promptly and decisively we will always be behind. All of us know that it sometimes takes a long time for seeds to germinate, but when they flower, they do so with explosive force."[16] Members of the FOMC spoke of reducing free reserves in August 1958. Alarmed by a growing budget deficit, Martin said that the Fed needed to seize the opportunity for stopping the threat of inflation in its tracks before the Treasury sought financing in the fall.[17]

The concerns raised by Reserve officials in meetings from 1955 and 1958 translated into concrete countercyclical policies undertaken by the FOMC and the Board of Governors, which, if not wholly popular with the public, were at least serious attempts at managing the business cycle. In August 1955, the Board approved discount rate hikes from 1 ¾ percent to 2 percent at the Reserve Banks of Atlanta, Boston, and Chicago and from 1 ¾ percent to 2 ¼ percent at Cleveland.[18] Discount rates were incrementally raised to 2 ½ percent at the Reserve Banks of Atlanta, Chicago, Cleveland, New York, Philadelphia, and San Francisco from September to November.[19] At an August 19, 1958 meeting, the FOMC reached the view that free reserves could be eliminated without dramatic policy changes over the near term.[20] The Board of Governors authorized several Reserve Banks to increase their discount rates to 2 percent after first sanctioning the San Francisco Bank to do so in mid-August.[21]

Domestic concerns were bound to dominate in a partially closed system while other nations were still in the process of rebuilding their economies. Through most of the 1950s, the U.S. had not yet encountered competitiveness problems, capital flows remained contained, and exchange rates were not yet fully operational. But once current accounts were fully activated, the balance of payments and exchange rates swung into focus. The Martin Fed's preoccupation with inflation was also justified simply on the basis of bouts of inflation in the late 1940s and early 1950s.

In the area of fiscal policy, the Eisenhower Administration was ideologically committed to balanced budgets, but it allowed the budget to go into deficit during the two recessions in the 1950s. When the economy slipped into recession in 1953 after the end of the Korean War, the Administration backed looser tax policy once the danger of inflation receded. The Treasury announced that it supported a 10 percent personal income tax cut and the expiration of a war-related excess profits tax.[22] After recession reoccurred in 1957, the Administration used fiscal expediency to grease the wheels of the economy. It accelerated Defense Department contracts and expanded construction for military-related infrastructure.[23] Congress temporarily extended unemployment insurance the next year while also paying out grants to states to fund airports, hospitals, and interstate highways.[24] The federal budget alternated between deficit and surplus due to trends in the business cycle from 1953–58. The budget registered a deficit of $10 billion that coincided with the trough of the recession in mid-1954. The deficit turned to surplus during the subsequent expansion, which peaked around August 1957. The budget again posted a deficit after a trough was reached in April 1958 because of relatively expansionary fiscal policy.[25] In contrast to these two earlier recessions, the Eisenhower Administration sought to tighten the budget during the 1960 recession out of fear of inflation, which resulted in a budget surplus.

Leaning against the wind in coordination with tight fiscal policy represented a cautious but effective approach to managing the money supply at a time when the Federal Reserve had at last won back its independence. Yet more activist ideas were beginning to hold greater sway in postwar political and academic circles. The Employment Act of 1946 mandated that "it is the continuing policy and responsibility of the Federal Government to use all practical means . . . to promote maximum employment, production, and purchasing power."[26] While it did not contain specific provisions for meeting these goals, the Employment Act reflected a Keynesian, demand side mentality aimed at achieving full employment. The Act had been moderated from an earlier proposal mandating that the president prepare a budget gauged to a level of national production that was consistent with full employment.[27] Unlike this form of budget, which would have directly connected the budget sheet to attempts at achieving full employment, normal fiscal policy is inherently countercyclical since diminished revenue during a recession will trigger budget deficits.[28] Even during the Eisenhower Administration, the budget turned in deficits during the recessions of 1953–54 and 1957–58, although in the latter case fiscal policy was more discretionary.

The Employment Act also established the Council of Economic Advisers (CEA), which developed into an academic bastion in the White House. After coming into office, Dwight Eisenhower sought as highly esteemed a figure as he could to chair his CEA and so appointed Arthur Burns, who had taught at Columbia University and been a researcher at the National Bureau of Economic Research (NBER). John Kennedy similarly tapped into academia when making appointments to the CEA, including Walter Heller of the University of Minnesota as chair. Indeed in 1961 the incoming Kennedy Administration brought with it a CEA characterized by a distinctive policy activism that journalists dubbed the New Economics, even though the Kennedy CEA economists were influenced by demand side theories that had been formulated at the tail end of the Great Depression. The New Economics focused on more deliberately raising GNP while generating full employment. Arthur Okun, who later chaired the CEA under President Johnson, noted that the New Economics sought to eliminate the so-called output gap. Okun even thought that efforts to plug the output gap would supplant orthodox assumptions about the economy.[29]

The New Economics was presented in more cautious terms in official documents. The CEA's *Annual Report* for 1962, which was joined to the *Economic Report of the President* transmitted to Congress, articulated a demand side approach by indicating that "[t]he proper degree of general 'tightness' or 'easiness' of monetary policy, and the techniques by which the various governmental authorities can appropriately seek to achieve it, depend on the state of the domestic economy, on the fiscal policies of the Government, and on the international economic position."[30] The 1962 *Annual Report* in some respects conventionally laid out the case for countercyclical policies, but it did so in the context of demand side theory. It assumed that monetary policy decisions would be based on, among other factors, the fiscal policies taking shape. The 1962 *Annual Report* implied that fiscal policy could be used to target aggregate demand and hopefully keep the economy in a permanent expansion, with monetary policy only intended to safeguard against demand heating up in advance of production.[31]

The influence of the New Economics over Kennedy can be observed in Kennedy's commencement address at Yale University in June 1962. Kennedy espoused the need for the practical management of the modern economy and the informed discussion of technical issues among policymakers. Kennedy affirmed that "the national interest lies in high employment and steady expansion of output, in stable prices, and a strong dollar." Kennedy further noted that only subtle, technocratic means could be used to resolve contemporary economic issues facing the country. In a revealing part of the address, Kennedy asked rhetorically, how "can we make our free economy work at full capacity – that is, provide adequate profits for enterprise, adequate wages for labor, adequate utilization of plant and opportunity for all?"[32]

The New Economics sought to increase government expenditures and generate multipliers in consumption and income. The Kennedy Administration could move on from the built-in deficits of the Eisenhower era. But the goal of devising a discretionary fiscal policy confronted the reality that specially tailoring the budget sheet per fiscal year lagged business conditions on the ground. These unavoidable lags impeded the ability of the budget sheet to serve as a hyper-efficient mechanism.[33]

Upon taking office, Kennedy responded to the 1960 recession in ways like those of Eisenhower during the 1957–58 recession. Kennedy asked for the temporary extension of unemployment insurance and the acceleration of government contracts. The Administration also worked to expand Social Security benefits and other transfers to farmers and local governments.[34] Kennedy further called for an investment tax credit, which was legislated by Congress in October 1962.[35] Increased spending and diminished, post-recession tax revenue turned the budget from a $3.6 billion surplus when Kennedy was elected to a $6.8 billion deficit by his first year in office. Yet at least officially, Kennedy at this stage wanted to avoid a permanent deficit and proposed a budget surplus in early 1962.[36]

Recovery from the recession was comparatively weak. Writing later in the 1960s, Arthur Burns cited weakened business confidence as the source of the subpar recovery, due in part to the perception that trade unions had inordinate clout in the Democratic Party, but also because of

Kennedy's actions in dealing with the steel companies.[37] In order to avoid a strike among steel workers similar to the one that had lasted for four months in 1959, the Kennedy Administration helped to negotiate an agreement between organized labor and the steel companies that expanded fringe benefits without increasing wages. But U.S. Steel Co. decided to raise the price of steel by $6 per ton in April 1962, with the other major steel companies expected to follow suit. Kennedy worried that the price increases would cause inflation, especially since the Administration had already attempted to ease the economy. In a press conference, Kennedy denounced the price increase as a "wholly unjustifiable and irresponsible defiance of the public interest."[38] The Administration eventually forced U.S. Steel to cancel its price increase. Kennedy's involvement in labor disputes followed a pattern of presidential conduct reaching back into the nineteenth century. More recently, Truman wanted to draft striking railroad workers into the military in 1946, and in 1952 he ordered the government to seize control of the steel mills, an action that the Supreme Court ruled unconstitutional.

Burns suggested that Kennedy proposed across-the-board income tax cuts for individuals and corporations later in 1962 to placate companies and boost market confidence. At the beginning of 1963, Kennedy advanced an agenda of $4.5 billion in new spending and $10 billion in tax cuts, which combined would have sent the budget into deficit.[39] Congress eventually legislated on tax cuts for individuals and corporations in 1964, with the top personal income tax rate falling from 91 percent to 70 percent. A retrospective debate centers on whether Kennedy intended for the proposed tax cuts to strengthen corporate income on the supply side or expand aggregate consumption on the demand side. Kennedy's remarks to the Economic Club of New York in December 1962 appeared to corroborate the view that he held supply sider instincts, but on the other hand his CEA consisted of academics steeped in theories of demand management. Of course Kennedy's Economic Club remarks might simply have been motivated by the larger public relations effort to improve business confidence after his imbroglio with the steel companies. The most that can be said is that the Kennedy CEA wanted to organize a budget deficit ahead of time through income tax cuts.

The Kennedy Administration radically deviated from the Eisenhower Administration not in terms of spending but because of historic income tax reductions, which served as all the more of a departure given that the economy had already recovered from recession by the summer of 1962 when Kennedy first proposed them. Theoretical New Economics never translated into a revolutionary form of discretionary fiscal policy during the Kennedy Administration. Walter Heller admitted that, besides the 1964 tax cuts, the Kennedy and Johnson Administrations did not implement any major discretionary fiscal policies.[40] However, the New Economics was positioned to bestow theoretical legitimacy upon rising defense and social welfare spending under the Johnson Administration, even though this spending was intended to meet larger goals than simply increasing aggregate demand.

Regarding monetary policy, the FOMC adapted to the new policy climate by carrying out what became known as Operation Twist from 1961 to 1964. The first sign of this occurred during the 1960 campaign when Kennedy pledged to "get America moving again." This statement was understood by markets as a call to devalue. It was magnified by the fact that Franklin Roosevelt had been the last president to devalue the dollar, and he had also been the only other Democrat in the past thirty years elected into office at the start of his term. Although Kennedy subsequently clarified that he did not support devaluation, the dollar still came under selling pressure in October in the London market. In response to the crisis, the FOMC relaxed its bills-only protocol and agreed to purchase securities of longer maturity.[41]

Through Twist, the Treasury sold bills to halt capital outflows and strengthen the balance of payments, while the Fed purchased longer-dated securities to boost private investment and foment economic growth. The Treasury and Fed worked in concert to twist the yield curve by pushing up short interest rates and bringing down long rates. The plan assumed that capital flows responded to short interest rates, while business investment was more sensitive to longer rates. The supply of bonds would contract not only because of the Fed purchases but because of the Treasury's switch to issuing bills instead of bonds. The CEA's 1962 *Annual Report* stated that "[t]he ability of monetary policy to support economic expansion at home without stimulating outflows of short-term funds was simultaneously enhanced by new Federal Reserve open market techniques and by Treasurey [sic] debt management policies."[42]

The FOMC officially adopted these techniques at its meeting on February 7, 1961. Members of an ad hoc subcommittee of the FOMC determined that "[t]here had to be evidence accumulated from actual experiment or testing to enable the System to escape from the charge of doctrinaire commitment to a laissez-faire, free private market position in confining operations to short-term securities."[43] After subsequent discussion, the FOMC agreed to a directive that "should provide adequate latitude for an effective testing."[44] As a result of Twist, System holdings of Treasury bonds rose from $2.5 billion in 1960 to $4.1 billion in 1962. Holdings of shorter maturity Treasury notes increased from $12.5 billion in 1960 to $20 billion in 1961 before falling to $10.7 billion in 1962.[45] By the end of 1964, Treasury bond holdings had risen to $5.3 billion while note holdings came to $25.2 billion.[46]

Twist produced mixed results in terms of twisting the yield curve. While the yield on 3-month Treasury bills rose from just over 2 percent to about 3.5 percent by 1963, the yield on long-term government bonds did not fall substantially or consistently below 4 percent.[47] One issue with

Twist was that Treasury bills, notes, and bonds were functionally similar for investors, regardless of differences in maturity and yield. But the Fed might have more effectively driven down long rates had it decisively switched its holdings of notes with bonds after 1962. In any case, Twist at the very least kept long rates from rising and otherwise hurting the prospects for economic growth. Twist foremost represented a departure from leaning against the wind in that it aggressively utilized open market policy to strengthen business investment over a longer period of time. The easing accomplished through Twist assisted economic expansion, but GDP grew at a higher rate after Twist was phased out late in 1964. The expansion during the 1960s is in fact one of the longest on record.[48]

The goal of expanding the economy coincided with problems relating to the balance of payments, which the Treasury component of Twist was designed to address. The U.S. maintained a positive current account during most of the period of convertibility, but capital outflows to Europe produced a negative balance of payments. Net private outflows, in addition to marginal government payments, rose from $.9 billion on average around 1955 to $3.2 billion in 1957.[49] Some of these outflows were rooted in movements in short-term capital, which responded to interest rate differentials, but they increasingly took the form of long-term Foreign Direct Investment (FDI) in Europe. As the CEA's 1962 *Annual Report* noted, "Private long-term investment averaged $2.6 billion a year in the last five years, substantially higher than in the early 1950's. In addition, re-invested earnings of U.S. subsidiaries abroad averaged $1.1 billion annually."[50] As a result of these capital outflows, the total U.S. gold stock dropped from $22.9 billion in 1957 to $17.8 billion in 1960.[51]

The balance of payments deficit had become a serious issue when current accounts turned convertible in 1958. The U.S. could have closed some of its military bases in Europe to slow down capital outflows.[52] Shutting down infrastructure would have saved money and negated the need for payments tied to the presence of military personnel overseas. Eisenhower supported a drawdown because he thought that the U.S. had only deployed forces to Europe until non-communist bloc allies rebuilt their militaries. But he also viewed the payments deficit as its own problem that warranted a drawdown in Europe if the government was drained of its gold stock.[53] After the dollar crisis of October 1960, Eisenhower at one point even wondered about replacing the gold standard with a commodity standard based on plutonium or uranium.[54]

The payments deficit continued to burden the Kennedy, Johnson, and Nixon Administrations. Kennedy was reportedly about as concerned with the balance of payments deficit as he was the threat of nuclear war. As central banks accumulated dollars abroad, they could conceivably convert these dollars into gold at the Treasury. The federal government faced the prospect of losing all of its gold in a giant crisis by 1964, when foreign central banks were carrying more dollars than the U.S. owned gold.[55] The U.S. might have avoided this threat by devaluing the dollar, but devaluation would have unsteadied the global economy. Markets would have feared a second U.S. devaluation or devaluation by other governments, which could have created financial panic and a run on gold by central banks. Tighter monetary policy represented an alternative answer, and the Triffin dilemma was based on the assumption that the U.S. would probably need to contract its money supply to reel in dollars. But policymakers hoped to avoid the need for tighter monetary policy by adopting Twist, in which only the Treasury worked to reverse capital flows by selling bills at higher interest rates.

Rising inflation later in the 1960s threatened to worsen the capital outflows, but global economic adjustments caused the dollar outflows regardless of inflation. The outflows actually reached their greatest intensity in 1963–64 before inflation became a problem. The outflows would for a time be partly mitigated through tighter monetary policy in the later 1960s. While dollar overhang preceded inflation chronologically speaking, inflation could still exacerbate overhang and depletion in the gold stock because the dollar would not be devalued.

Under certain assumptions and conditions, the payments deficit was not necessarily problematic. The U.S. functioned as a lender by transmitting investment dollars to Europe against the Treasury's gold reserve.[56] This hypothesis is indirectly validated by the fact that the economy was in danger of overheating by 1965. Capital flows to Europe did not therefore represent a total redirection of investable resources that would have otherwise been used to ramp up the domestic economy. More at stake was that dollars held by foreign central banks represented claims on the U.S. gold stock. For the banking analogy to hold up, the U.S. needed to continue to post robust current account surpluses to shore up its gold reserve. This scenario was not playing out by the end of the 1960s. Even the U.S.'s renewed strength as an exporter would still not have resolved the underlying problem of stagnant growth in the world's gold stock. Another distortionary factor was that the dollar continued to serve as the world's primary reserve asset, and this would not change unless other currencies were made convertible to gold.

In the near term, the dollar glut threatened the functioning of Bretton Wood because any crisis could cause a run on the Treasury's gold window by foreign central banks. Restraining capital outflows appeared to represent the clearest way to contract the supply of dollars abroad short of domestic monetary tightening. To counter the payments deficit, the U.S. devised a number of remedial measures to try to rein in capital flows, possibly because policymakers had the erroneous impression that the deficit was only temporary and would correct itself by the end of the 1960s. The remedial measures pursued by the Kennedy and Johnson Administrations were all largely unsuccessful in reversing the payments imbalance. Among the first of these was Twist, with the Treasury selling bills at higher interest rates. Twist was designed foremost to contend with short-term capital outflows because these outflows were more elastic to interest rate differentials than FDI flows. Twist failed to stem short- or long-term capital outflows, and in fact outflows intensified in the years immediately following the start of the program. Total net capital outflows reached $3.9 billion in 1960, $4.2 billion in 1961, and $3.4 billion in 1962. Outflows then rose to $5.5 billion in the first half of 1963, receded to $3 billion in the second half, rose again to $5.7 billion in the first half of 1964, and were $4.9 billion in the third quarter of 1964.[57]

In July 1963, the Kennedy Administration submitted to Congress a package of proposals for stabilizing the payments imbalance. These proposals included linking foreign aid to U.S. exports, reducing $300 million in defense spending related to commitments abroad, and a "See America Now" initiative to encourage tourism into the U.S. The most important part of the package was a form of capital control called the Interest Equalization Tax (IET). The IET served as an excise tax on purchases of foreign securities in the U.S. and, according to the CEA's *Annual Report* for 1964, "was designed to impose on foreign sellers the equivalent of 1 percentage point of additional interest cost."[58] As an excise tax, the IET was levied on American investors, while its effect was felt by foreign companies trying to sell stocks and bonds in the U.S. But foreign companies could easily evade the IET by offering other types of credits instead of the ones covered under the tax.

The Johnson Administration implemented another package of proposals, among them an additional $500 million in funding for the Export-Import Bank, a $200 million program run by the Commerce Department to encourage exports, a voluntary restriction on "all nonessential travel outside the Western Hemisphere for two years," and an extension of the IET. The Administration also attempted to shut down the IET's loopholes through mandatory restrictions on FDI and reinvested earnings. The Fed Board of Governors was granted authority to issue regulations limiting the credit supplied by U.S. banks to foreign borrowers.[59] Finally, the IMF increased liquidity through General Arrangements to Borrow (GAB) in 1962 and Special Drawing Rights (SDR) in 1970 for official settlements.

The Treasury formulated and promoted the IET, while the Federal Reserve fulfilled an auxiliary role in dealing with the payments imbalance. As the imbalance worsened, the Board of Governors periodically raised Regulation Q, which capped interest on certain types of deposits. Discount rate hikes in the 1960s were also partly motivated by concerns with the payments imbalance. The Fed's secondary but active role in dealing with the payments deficit was consistent with Martin's support for the gold standard, in that dollar overhang could ultimately endanger convertibility. To that end, the Board approved discount rate hikes from 3 percent to 3 ½ percent at several Reserve Banks in July 1963, even as the FOMC continued to aggressively purchase Treasurys as part of Twist.[60]

The balance of payments deficit worked to press down on the value of the dollar. The ESF had not engaged in any exchange market interventions since the 1930s, and most of its resources had been used to pay for the U.S.'s initial subscription to the IMF. Nonetheless, by the early 1960s, the Treasury and the Fed employed new means for buttressing the dollar and keeping the dollar exchange rates intact. The Fed maintained short-term swap lines with foreign central banks. The Fed received foreign exchange through the swaps and used it to buy dollars in the international markets. The Treasury simultaneously sold Roosa bonds in exchange for foreign currency in order to fund the Fed swaps over the long-term. The Fed and Treasury could also have coordinated by selling gold for foreign exchange, but they wanted to avoid gold losses and therefore resorted to swaps and bond sales.[61]

Policymakers bided their time in the 1960s and waited for the capital outflows to subside and the payments imbalance to improve. The measures undertaken by the Kennedy and Johnson Administrations implied that the U.S. remained fully committed to the dollar's peg at $35 during the lag until the payments balance would be hopefully restored. Unfortunately, however, the U.S.'s competitive position had begun to erode. Almost from the beginning of convertibility until 1971, the U.S. posted a positive current account. However, the merchandise trade balance deteriorated through the 1960s. The balance actually rose from $5.1 billion in 1963 to $6.6 billion in 1964 but then fell to $4.7 billion in 1965, $3.6 billion in 1966, $3.5 billion in 1967, and $.4 billion in the first 3 quarters of 1968.[62]

Fundamental shifts in trade affected these trends. U.S. manufactured output as a percentage of the bloc of major First World national economies declined from 62 percent to 44 percent during 1950–77.[63] Exports in manufactured output fell from 29.4 percent in 1953 to 18.7 percent in 1959, before declining further to 13.2 percent in 1974.[64] U.S. corporations became increasingly specialized in sectors consistent with the country's comparative advantage, particularly advanced, capital-intensive industries like aircraft production. The trade deficit in raw iron and steel continued to expand after the war. Trade in intermediate iron and steel output went into deficit starting in 1963.[65] Trade in consumer goods similarly went into deficit in 1959, which eventually topped $18 billion by the late 1970s.[66] While the current account remained positive, due in part to earnings on FDI and overseas portfolio investment, a declining merchandise trade surplus worsened the payments imbalance and proved that the imbalance was not of transitory duration. Unless the merchandise trade balance began posting major surpluses, convertibility was bound to come to an end one way or another. The deteriorating trade surplus also implied that the dollar was becoming overvalued, which only further hurt competitiveness.

The dollar glut coincided with a contraction in the U.S.'s gold stock. The government's gold stock fell from $17.8 billion in 1960 to $12 billion by the end of 1967.[67] France began concertedly buying gold from the U.S. in 1962, which did much to force a contraction in the Treasury's gold reserve in the mid-1960s.[68] U.S. officials wanted to keep the market price for gold pegged to the official price. If the market price rose above the official price, foreign central banks could take advantage of the price differential and earn trading profits by buying gold with dollars from the Treasury and then selling it to the market. A higher market price could also be destabilizing and set off a run among central banks, regardless of their interest in selling gold to the market. After the dollar crisis of October 1960, central banks set up the London Gold Pool to maintain parity between the official and market price at $35 per oz. The central banks were committed to directly entering the private market to keep the market price pegged. The U.S. supplied over half of the gold for these transactions.[69]

The participating central banks managed the Gold Pool through the mid-1960s. But they sold more gold than they purchased after 1965 in large part due to rising international demand and a diminishing supply of gold.[70] The central banks could not sustain this regime after the U.K. devalued sterling in November 1967. With fears that the U.S. would devalue next, a run on gold followed in the private market. Central banks sold a total of $3 billion in gold to the market. The U.S. alone sold off over $2 billion. The Gold Pool was finally shut down in March 1968.[71] A two-tiered system replaced the Gold Pool. Under the two-tiered system, monetary authorities were in principle obligated to sell one another gold at the official price while avoiding any interaction with the private market. Now that governments no longer manipulated the market price, it soon rose to $42 before falling back to the official price.[72] The two-tiered system was in reality backed by a so-called gentlemen's agreement whereby European central banks agreed not to turn in their dollars for Treasury gold under certain conditions. The two-tiered system and gentlemen's agreement effectively took the world off the gold standard. In the same year that the Gold Pool was closed, Congress terminated the Federal Reserve's gold cover requirement against currency. The Fed had been holding gold certificates instead of actual gold ever since the Gold Reserve Act of 1934, but these certificates meant that the Fed obtained rights in gold held by the Treasury. The termination of this requirement was intended to free up gold for international settlements if necessary.

The inevitable transition to fiat standards began in 1968, though convertibility would not be suspended until 1971, and even then adjustable exchange rates would be continued for another two years. Dollars could still be redeemed for gold to meet official settlements through the Treasury's gold window, but these conversions would breach the gentlemen's agreement. Beyond that, the last official link to gold was the dollar's peg at $35 per oz. The transition to fiat took place at the end of a process of recovery, adjustment, and growth and at the beginning of a new period of relative economic saturation and inflation. The point had been reached for an American president to deliver the coup de grace by severing the final link to gold for any number of reasons.

The basic balance, made up of long-term capital flows and the current account, showed no signs of a permanent return to surplus. Swings in short-term capital flows were more dramatic because of their sensitivity to interest rates and Regulation Q ceilings. If Regulation Q ceilings did not keep pace with inflation, then investors would transfer their funds into the Eurodollar market of dollar denominated foreign bank accounts. Foreign capital flows also resulted from exchange rate shifts, such as when the devaluation of the franc in 1969 caused over $6 billion to flow into German markets and forced the authorities there into revaluing the mark.[73] But the basic balance continued to serve as the primary indicator of the U.S.'s international transactions. The basic balance remained negative in the 1960s and early 1970s. The merchandise trade surplus briefly rose from around $700 million in 1969 to $2.1 billion in 1970. But the deficit in private direct investment increased over the same period from $2.4 billion to $3.5 billion. In the first 3 quarters of 1971, the merchandise trade balance turned in a deficit of $1.7 billion, while the deficit in private direct investment rose further to $5.9 billion. The overall deficit in the basic balance reached 10.2 percent. Imports increased at a rate of 147 percent during 1964–71 in contrast to a 74 percent rise in exports. Moreover, the rise in imports could not be attributed to overall growth in the economy.[74]

The weak merchandise trade balance was now actively factoring into the payments imbalance, and it had gained the attention of Congress by 1970. The House of Representatives passed a bill that placed restrictions on selected merchandise imported from Japan, and the following year another bill was sponsored in the House and Senate to cap imports at their then-existing levels in the 1960s.[75] Members of Congress may have wanted a return to protectionism, but an overvalued dollar also clearly impeded U.S. competitiveness. The Treasury reported dollar overvaluation at over 10 percent in mid-1971.[76] At the time serving as a high ranking Treasury official in the Administration, Paul Volcker began to formulate plans for dealing with an overvalued dollar. In one scenario, the U.S. temporarily stopped converting dollars into gold at the Treasury to compel other governments into revaluing their currencies.[77] Revaluation of the Japanese yen and the German mark was an especially important goal. Japan and Germany were some of the strongest exporters in the world and earned large trade surpluses against the U.S. Having revalued the mark in 1969, Germany let its currency appreciate in May 1971.[78] Allowing the mark to appreciate against the dollar relieved the Bundesbank of purchasing billions of dollars in the open market to maintain the adjustable peg. News that summer of U.S. current account and merchandise trade deficits fueled dollar selloffs in the foreign exchange markets. This was the first time the U.S. posted a current account deficit almost since the beginning of the adjustable exchange rate system in the late 1950s.

In February 1971, President Nixon appointed former Texas governor John Connolly as Treasury Secretary. Connolly did not immediately support devaluation of the dollar because from a political vantage this could have looked like a national disgrace. But no one scrutinized the political implications of the economy more than Nixon. While the picture for inflation had not improved, Nixon thought that unemployment outweighed inflation in political significance. Even as Nixon had supported easing the economy after the recession early in his Administration, the unemployment rate still sat at 7 percent in 1971.[79] Any policy intended to strengthen the merchandise trade balance would work to drive down unemployment. The need for more competitive exports meshed with Nixon's overall strategy. It also implied the need for action against the overvalued dollar.

Nixon met with congressional leaders in July mainly to discuss his diplomatic opening to China, but he was surprised that many of them voiced concern over economic issues and wanted to know how the Administration intended to respond. Nixon saw that he needed to take action. Connolly advised him that if the Administration did not come up with its own package soon, the Democratic Congress would propose a far less palatable alternative.[80] Connolly had a discussion with Nixon at the White House on August 2 over handling the trade deficit and the dollar. Connolly recommended temporarily refusing to pay out gold and imposing a 10 percent import surcharge to pressure other nations, but especially Germany and Japan, into revaluing their currencies. To contend with inflation, Connolly proposed wage and price controls. Nixon responded positively to these recommendations, and they agreed to delay the announcement until September.[81] They thought that conditions should be allowed to worsen before the announcement, especially since the imposition of wage and price controls contradicted their earlier statements dismissing any notion of interfering with the free market. Connolly admitted to Nixon that he was uncertain whether the program would succeed, but he was certain that a less decisive package would fail to improve the current situation.[82] Four days later, a House subcommittee returned a report finding the dollar overvalued and responsible for the trade deficit. News also spread that France was asking for $200 million in gold from the Treasury, feeding a dollar selloff around the world and forcing central banks into purchasing some $3.7 billion in the open markets.[83]

The French request for gold threatened to set off a chain reaction among other central banks now holding billions more in dollars. In the analogy of the U.S. as a bank supplying liquidity to overseas markets, it at last faced the run that it had dreaded for years. The Administration needed to go into immediate action, especially after the British asked for cover if the U.S. devalued. This message was misinterpreted to mean a request for $3 billion in gold.[84] Nixon reflected on the dilemma. The Treasury might trigger a run on the U.S.'s gold reserve if it honored the supposed British request, and the Administration was conceding that it probably could no longer convert dollars into gold if the Treasury refused the request.[85]

Nixon assembled his top economic advisers for a covert weekend conference at Camp David starting that Friday. As Paul McCracken, Nixon's chair of the CEA, recounted, they were all required to observe strict secrecy. They could not let family members know of their location or make telephone calls.[86] Nixon was so worried about leaks that he instructed his advisers to maintain complete silence with the press over the weekend.[87] During the meeting, the advisers supported the decision to impose wage and price controls and the import surcharge. But Arthur Burns, now serving as Fed chair, vociferously opposed shutting the gold window. Burns claimed that suspending gold payments was unnecessary because the other policies would do enough to bolster market confidence on their own.[88] He even thought that it would allow the Soviets to gloat on the failures of the capitalist system.[89] As the meeting wound down, what to do with gold remained the final, lingering dilemma. Nixon pondered the issue in solitude for the rest of the night before deciding to shut the gold window.[90] He later wrote that the decision to close the gold window was probably the most commendable part of the New Economic Policy (NEP) that he announced to the nation.[91]

That announcement closing the gold window on August 15, 1971 also included a 90-day wage and price freeze, a 10 percent import surcharge, and a 10 percent investment tax credit. The "Nixon shock," as it came to be known, successfully catalyzed the diplomatic effort to adjust exchange rates. At the Smithsonian Conference held in Washington in December 1971, the U.S. devalued the dollar to $38 per oz., or an 8 percent devaluation among industrialized economies. Nixon soon after lifted the import surcharge.[92]

The U.S. in 1971 faced an overvaluation of the dollar and a worsening current account, which finally turned negative that year. The Nixon Administration used the suspension of gold convertibility and the import surcharge as a roundabout way to effect devaluation by arranging for Germany and Japan to revalue their currencies at the Smithsonian Conference. The emerging reality of fiat facilitated this process. The transition to fiat beginning with the two-tiered system in 1968 helped make possible Nixon's decision to suspend convertibility for official payments in 1971. An unsaid rationale in August 1971 was that if private parties no longer needed to recognize gold as legal tender, then official institutions did not need to do so either. The suspension of convertibility created a fiat standard, and the Nixon Administration used the fiat standard in an attempt to bring about changes in U.S. trade and competitiveness. Unlike the import surcharge, suspension of convertibility remained permanently in effect.

NOTES

1. William H. Branson, "Trends in United States International Trade and Investment since World War II," in *The American Economy in Transition*, ed. Martin Feldstein (Chicago: University of Chicago Press, 1980), 185–86.
2. Michael D. Bordo, "The Bretton Woods International Monetary System: A Historical Overview," in *A Retrospective on the Bretton Woods System: Lessons for International Monetary Reform*, ed. Michael D. Bordo and Barry Eichengreen (Chicago: University of Chicago Press, 1993), 61–65.
3. Board of Governors, *Thirty-Fourth Annual Report of the Board of Governors of the Federal Reserve System: Covering Operations for the Year 1947* (Washington, D.C.: Federal Reserve System, 1948), 27.
4. BoG, *Thirty-Fourth Annual Report*, 5.
5. Board of Governors, *Thirty-Fifth Annual Report of the Board of Governors of the Federal Reserve System: Covering Operations for the Year 1948* (Washington, D.C.: Federal Reserve System, 1949), 85–86.
6. BoG, *Twenty-Fifth Annual Report*, 90.
7. Ibid., 15.
8. Board of Governors, *Thirty-Sixth Annual Report of the Board of Governors of the Federal Reserve System: Covering Operations for the Year 1949* (Washington, D.C.: Federal Reserve System, 1950), 11.
9. BoG, *Thirty-Sixth Annual Report*, 8.
10. Ibid., 10.
11. Eichengreen and Garber, "Before the Accord," 184–85.
12. FOMC Minutes, March 4, 1953, Federal Reserve Open Market Committee, Federal Reserve Transcripts and other historical materials, Board of Governors, 41.
13. March 4, 1953 Minutes, 37.
14. NBER, "U.S. Business Cycle."
15. FOMC Minutes, August 2, 1955, Federal Reserve Open Market Committee, Federal Reserve Transcripts and other historical materials, Board of Governors, 14.
16. August 2, 1955 Minutes, 13.
17. FOMC Minutes, August 19, 1958, Federal Reserve Open Market Committee, Federal Reserve Transcripts and other historical materials, Board of Governors, 58–59.
18. Board of Governors, *Forty-Second Annual Report of the Board of Governors of the Federal Reserve System: Covering Operations for the Year 1955* (Washington, D.C.: Federal Reserve System, 1956), 86.
19. BoG, *Forty-Second Annual Report*, 87–88.
20. Board of Governors, *Forty-Fifth Annual Report of the Board of Governors of the Federal Reserve System: Covering Operations for the Year 1958* (Washington, D.C.: Federal Reserve System, 1959), 60.
21. BoG, *Forty-Fifth Annual Report*, 82.
22. Council of Economic Advisers, *Economic Report of the President* (Washington, D.C.: Government Printing Office, 1954), 52.
23. Council of Economic Advisers, *Economic Report of the President* (Washington, D.C.: Government Printing Office, 1958), 8.
24. Council of Economic Advisers, *Economic Report of the President* (Washington, D.C.: Government Printing Office, 1959), 40–42.
25. John M. Firestone, "The 1954–1958 Cycle," in *Federal Receipts and Expenditures During Business Cycles, 1879–1958*, ed. John M. Firestone (Princeton: Princeton University Press, 1960), 56.

26. "Employment Act of 1946," Federal Reserve Archival System for Economic Research, St. Louis Federal Reserve, https://fraser.stlouisfed.org/scribd/?title_id=1099&filepath=/files/docs/historical/congressional/ employment-act-1946.pdf, accessed September 2017.
27. J. Bradford De Long, "Keynesianism, Pennsylvania Avenue Style: Some Economic Consequences of the Employment Act of 1946," *Journal of Economic Perspectives* 10, no. 3 (1996): 42.
28. De Long, "Keynesianism," 47.
29. Athanasios Orphanides and John C. Williams, "Monetary Policy Mistakes and the Evolution of Inflation Expectations," in *The Great Inflation: The Rebirth of Modern Central Banking*, ed. Michael D. Bordo and Athanasios Orphanides (Chicago: University of Chicago Press, 2013), 259.
30. Council of Economic Advisers, *Economic Report of the President of the United States: Together with the Annual Report of the Council of Economic Advisers* (Washington, D.C.: Government Printing Office, 1962), 85.
31. CEA, 1962 *ERP*, 85–86.
32. John F. Kennedy, "Address at Yale University, 11 June, 1962," John F. Kennedy Presidential Library, https://www.jfklibrary.org/Asset-Viewer/Archives/JFKPOF-039-001.aspx, accessed August 2017.
33. De Long, "Keynesianism," 47.
34. CEA, 1962 *ERP*, 82–83.
35. Council of Economic Advisers, *Economic Report of the President of the United States: Together with the Annual Report of the Council of Economic Advisers* (Washington, D.C.: Government Printing Office, 1963), 18.
36. Arthur F. Burns, "The Quest for Full Employment and Economic Stability: 1960–1966," in *The Business Cycle in a Changing World*, ed. Arthur F. Burns (New York: National Bureau of Economic Research, 1969), 263.
37. Burns, "Full Employment and Economic Stability," 264–65.
38. "President Kennedy's News Conferences: News Conference 30, April 11, 1962," John F. Kennedy Presidential Library, https://www.jfklibrary.org/Research/Research-Aids/Ready-Reference/Press-Conferences/News-Conference-30.aspx, accessed August 2017.
39. Burns, "Full Employment and Economic Stability," 265–67.
40. J. Bradford De Long, "Fiscal Policy in the Shadow of the Great Depression," in *The Defining Moment: The Great Depression and the American Economy in the Twentieth Century*, ed. Michael D. Bordo, Claudia Goldin, and Eugene N. White (Chicago: University of Chicago Press, 1998), 82.
41. FOMC Minutes, October 25, 1960, Federal Reserve Open Market Committee, Federal Reserve Transcripts and other historical materials, Board of Governors, 57–58.
42. CEA, 1962 *ERP*, 86.
43. FOMC Minutes, February 7, 1961, Federal Reserve Open Market Committee, Federal Reserve Transcripts and other historical materials, Board of Governors, 45.
44. February 7, 1961 Minutes, 57.
45. Board of Governors, *Forty-Ninth Annual Report of the Board of Governors of the Federal Reserve System: Covering Operations for the Year 1962* (Washington, D.C.: Federal Reserve System, 1963), 150.
46. Board of Governors, *Fifty-First Annual Report of the Board of Governors of the Federal Reserve System: Covering Operations for the Year 1964* (Washington, D.C.: Federal Reserve System, 1965), 226.
47. Thomas E. Holland, "'Operation Twist' and the Movement of Interest Rates and Related Economic Time Series," *International Economic Review* 10, no. 3 (1969): 264.
48. NBER, "U.S. Business Cycle."
49. Council of Economic Advisers, *Economic Report of the President* (Washington, D.C.: Government Printing Office, 1960), 111.
50. CEA, 1962 *ERP*, 159.

51. Council of Economic Advisers, *Economic Report of the President: Together with the Annual Report of the Council of Economic Advisers* (Washington, D.C.: Government Printing Office, 1968), 312.
52. Francis J. Gavin, *Gold, Dollars & Power: The Politics of International Monetary Relations, 1958–1971* (Chapel Hill: University of North Carolina Press, 2004), 38.
53. Gavin, *Gold, Dollars & Power*, 40–41.
54. Ibid., 49.
55. Bordo, "Bretton Woods," 56.
56. Jeffrey A. Frankel, "International Capital Flows and Domestic Economic Policies," in *The United States in the World Economy*, ed. Martin Feldstein (Chicago: University of Chicago Press, 1988), 566.
57. Council of Economic Advisers, *Economic Report of the President: Together with the Annual Report of the Council of Economic Advisers* (Washington, D.C.: Government Printing Office, 1965), 76.
58. Council of Economic Advisers, *Economic Report of the President: Together with the Annual Report of the Council of Economic Advisers* (Washington, D.C.: Government Printing Office, 1964), 128.
59. CEA, 1968 *ERP*, 173–75.
60. Board of Governors, *Fiftieth Report of the Board of Governors of the Federal Reserve System: Covering Operations for the Year 1963* (Washington, D.C.: Federal Reserve System, 1964), 38–39.
61. Bordo, "Bretton Woods," 59.
62. Council of Economic Advisers, *Economic Report of the President: Together with the Annual Report of the Council of Economic Advisers* (Washington, D.C.: Government Printing Office, 1969), 50.
63. Branson, "International Trade and Investment," 191.
64. Ibid., 196.
65. Ibid., 226.
66. Ibid., 216.
67. CEA, 1968 *ERP*, 312.
68. Peter M. Garber, "The Collapse of the Bretton Woods Fixed Exchange Rate System," in *A Retrospective on the Bretton Woods System: Lessons for International Monetary Reform*, ed. Michael D. Bordo and Barry Eichengreen (Chicago: University of Chicago Press, 1993), 466–67.
69. Garber, "Collapse of Bretton Woods," 464.
70. Bordo, "Bretton Woods," 69–70.
71. Ibid., 70.
72. Garber, "Collapse of Bretton Woods," 464.
73. Council of Economic Advisers, *Economic Report of the President: Together with the Annual Report of the Council of Economic Advisers* (Washington, D.C.: Government Printing Office, 1970), 131–32.
74. Council of Economic Advisers, *Economic Report of the President: Together with the Annual Report of the Council of Economic Advisers* (Washington, D.C.: Government Printing Office, 1972), 150–51.
75. Douglas A. Irwin, "The Nixon Shock after Forty Years: The Import Surcharge Revisited," *World Trade Review* 12, no. 1 (2013): 31.
76. Irwin, "The Nixon Shock," 33.
77. Ibid., 32.
78. Ibid., 33.
79. CEA, 1972 *ERP*, 109.
80. Richard Nixon, *RN: The Memoirs of Richard Nixon* (New York: Grosset & Dunlap, 1978), 518.
81. Irwin, "The Nixon Shock," 34–35.
82. Nixon, *Memoirs*, 518.
83. Irwin, "The Nixon Shock," 35.
84. Ibid., 35–36.

85. Nixon, *Memoirs*, 518.
86. Paul W. McCracken, "Economic Policy in the Nixon Years," *Presidential Studies Quarterly* 26, no. 1 (1996): 173.
87. Nixon, *Memoirs*, 519.
88. McCracken, "Economic Policy," 173–74.
89. Nixon, *Memoirs*, 519.
90. McCracken, "Economic Policy," 174.
91. Nixon, *Memoirs*, 520.
92. Irwin, "The Nixon Shock," 43.

TEN

The Great Inflation

Only in the narrow time frame of 1971 to 1973, when currencies moved to a float, did the Nixon Administration use fiat as an instrument for attempting to improve the trade deficit. The dawn of fiat in the 1970s more broadly coincided with accumulating inflation, which evolved into the most visible and agonizing economic problem as the decade wore on. The Great Inflation overshadowed the period in which governments adopted fiat standards. That inflation and the adoption of fiat occurred simultaneously left policymakers especially anxious about the inflationary dangers inherent to a currency with no link to gold. Further sharpening the worries over the inflationary aspects of fiat might have been the fact that the Great Inflation itself took hold in a policy and academic environment that was inconsistent with gold orthodoxy.

Congress did not completely ignore the importance of price stability. The 1946 Employment Act sought maximum purchasing power as an end goal in addition to employment and production. But CEA economists influenced by the New Economics were more willing to allow fiscal policy to produce moderate inflation if this led to full employment and elimination of the output gap. Demand side economists based their views on the Phillips curve, which empirically correlated employment and inflation since the 1800s. Using Phillips curve analysis, Paul Samuelson and Robert Solow concluded in 1960 that a lowering of unemployment from 5.5 percent to 3 percent required an inflation rate of 4.5 percent.[1] If economists believed that targeting an optimal rate of inflation would lead to unemployment outcomes, then at least some of them also believed the reverse, that targeting unemployment would lead to inflation outcomes. Economist Herbert Stein of the Nixon CEA in retrospect thought that the targeting of a 4 percent natural rate of unemployment was hugely misguided because it led to the view that inflation could be checked merely by allowing unemployment in excess of the natural rate.[2]

Yet while the demand side economists shaped the intellectual climate, real world events overtook monetary policy in the mid-1960s, from balance of payments turmoil, to the growing threat of a convertibility crisis, to the Vietnam War. In the wake of these events, nothing prevented the Martin Fed from returning to its stop-go policies of the 1950s after four years of Twist. The FOMC's consistency in forestalling inflation in the 1950s had in fact been exemplary, despite some instances of price rises during expansions. But just as importantly, the Martin Fed of the 1950s had achieved credibility as a force for disinflation. According to the Livingston Survey among economists, inflation expectations hovered at 1 percent from the mid-1950s into the early 1960s.[3] That kind of credibility with employers and other wage and contract setters safeguarded against an unstoppable wage and price spiral.

A return to some form of leaning against the wind looked appropriate by the end of 1965. Consumer prices had increased by 2 percent, up from a range of 1 percent to 1.5 percent in previous years. Fixed investment expanded by 15 percent and corporate profits by about 20 percent.[4] Yet perhaps the most important factor was increasing defense spending as the U.S. escalated its involvement in the Vietnam War, which contributed to a $2.5 billion budget deficit late in the year.[5] In an address from 1968, Arthur Burns refuted the assumption that the Vietnam War was alone to blame for rising inflation in 1965. Burns noted that wholesale prices increased by 3 percent from mid-1964 to mid-1965, before major hostilities on the part of U.S. ground forces. He also emphasized that increased domestic spending exceeded war-related spending and therefore shouldered more of the responsibility for inflation.[6]

At a meeting in late November 1965, the FOMC discussed whether to pursue tightening. Members of the committee invoked the Vietnam War as an argument for or against tightening depending on their viewpoint. Harry Shuford of the St. Louis Bank favored tight policy because of rising Vietnam War spending and its impact on aggregate demand.[7] On the other hand, Sherman Maisel, a member of the Board of Governors, commented that the Fed should hold off on tighter policy for the time being because of an absence of rising inflation. The war also provided an independent reason for continued ease. Now that the government was requesting companies to forgo price hikes, the Federal Reserve would be deviating from the "national effort" by raising the discount rate, which could upset business expectations.[8]

Although Maisel was on the losing side of the debate, his remarks reflected how at times the Fed needed to subordinate monetary policy to national security interests. The FOMC was no longer operating in a normal, peacetime economy. According to this view, while perhaps the Fed was not required to keep bond yields pegged as it had been during

World War II, monetary ease still needed to facilitate funding for the war and to demonstrate that the Federal Reserve was fulfilling its obligation to the "national effort." But continued ease would have only accelerated inflationary pressures and created new dilemmas for the FOMC, so the question really centered on whether the government should have assumed a comprehensive war footing, involving pegged yields and wage and price controls, or attempted to fight the war under mainly normal economic conditions.

The FOMC unsurprisingly opted for the latter course by pursuing monetary tightening to prevent domestic inflation and a convertibility crisis. The Johnson Administration had sent U.S. forces to wage an apparently limited war that many expected to last for only a few years at most, so that the imposition of extreme command-and-control measures seemed unnecessary. In December 1965, the Board of Governors hiked the discount rate from 4 percent to 4 ½ percent.[9] In June 1966, the Board raised reserve requirements for time deposits from 4 percent to 5 percent.[10] The Board again raised requirements for time deposits in August from 5 percent to 6 percent.[11] In April 1967, the Board relapsed by lowering the discount rate from 4 ½ percent to 4 percent "to provide for orderly economic growth."[12] But after the devaluation of sterling, the Board raised the discount rate back up to 4 ½ percent in November. In December, the Board raised reserve requirements for demand deposits half a percentage point to 17 percent.[13] The Board made additional efforts at tightening in 1968, the primary objective now being the fight against inflation. The Board raised the discount rate to 5 percent in March and then to 5 ½ percent in April.[14] Because of an increase in taxes, the Board again wavered by lowering the discount rate to 5 ¼ percent in August but then brought it back up to 5 ½ percent in December.[15]

Monetary policy from 1965 to the end of 1968 failed to check inflation. Though Martin continued to serve as chair during these years, the Fed did not adequately stop intensifying inflationary pressures. The Fed raised short-term nominal interest rates, but these interest rate increases did not outpace the inflation rate. As a result, the Fed did not effectively raise real interest rates adjusted for inflation. Consumer prices increased by 4.2 percent during 1968 and wholesale industrial prices by 2.5 percent.[16] The Fed initially succeeded in contracting the money supply, defined as M1 (currency in circulation plus demand deposits), from about 6 percent growth in the first quarter of 1966 to negative growth in the third quarter. But M1 spiked again to nearly 10 percent growth in the third quarter of 1967 and reached 9 percent growth in the third quarter of 1968.[17] If the FOMC had decisively kept to its policies from the 1950s, then it would have regained its disinflationary credibility and driven down price expectations. According to the Livingston Survey, however, expectations increased with actual inflation in the late 1960s.[18] But any serious, overriding attempt to check inflation by the Fed could have potentially caused the Treasury's borrowing costs to skyrocket at the height of the Vietnam War. While the Federal Reserve had regained its autonomy since the 1951 Accord, it was in no position to completely disregard the interests of the Treasury, all the more so in the midst of an increasingly divisive war to stop the spread of communism.

The incoming Nixon Administration promised a policy of gradual withdrawal from the war predicated on Vietnamization. Withdrawal in turn implied lower defense expenditures. Reducing deficit spending served as one way to alleviate inflationary pressures. But more importantly, withdrawal from Vietnam in theory relieved the Federal Reserve of its burden as an agent of debt management. Whatever the fluctuations in deficit spending, the Federal Reserve remained the institution best equipped to counteract inflation by credibly contracting the money supply through a well-communicated open market policy that drove down price and wage expectations. Reserve authorities would not truly engage in these policies until October 1979, well after the economy had transitioned to entirely peacetime conditions.

Probably the best time for the Fed to have aggressively tackled inflation was early in 1969, immediately after Nixon assumed office. Deflationary policies would have resulted in a deeper recession, but this was the cost of having allowed inflation to gain strength for four straight years. Nixon tapped Arthur Burns to lead the Fed in late 1969. Because Burns had already worked for a year as Counselor in the White House, Nixon envisioned him continuing to serve the Administration's interests in his capacity as Fed chair. The conflict between the Fed and the Administration reached a critical point in 1971, with the economy recovering from recession but unemployment still high. Burns expressed skepticism towards the need for further easing in February because market confidence was more warranted at this stage of the business cycle. Connolly disagreed and bluntly told Burns in a March meeting that he needed to reduce interest rates.[19] By July, Nixon let Burns know through intermediaries that he might appoint an inflationist politician to a vacant seat on the Board of Governors. Nixon then instructed his political advisers to leak a plan that would in a sense pack the Board of Governors with Nixon appointees more susceptible to the Administration's influence.[20]

Nixon by all accounts pressured Burns to continue easing the economy through 1971. He was mindful of how recession and unemployment affect electoral outcomes and could look to his own defeat in the 1960 presidential election as evidence for this. That the unemployment rate obstinately remained over 6 percent even during recovery in the early 1970s only aggravated his worries. No president wanted a recession or high unemployment going into a reelection campaign. Burns, on the other hand, chaired for all intents and purposes a central bank ostensibly independent of White House control whose primary mandate was arguably the containing of inflation. But in all fairness to Burns, the most opportune time to act against inflation was literally right at the beginning of the Nixon Administration, in much the same way as the Fed would eventually act against inflation in earnest at the outset of the Reagan Administration in 1981.

Nixon attempted to replace the need for tighter monetary policy with a 90-day wage and price freeze imposed in August 1971 pursuant to authority granted under the Economic Stabilization Act of 1970. The freeze was highly unusual in that the Nixon Administration imposed controls as the U.S. was trying to withdraw from a foreign war and not during the height of the conflict itself. A Cost of Living Council (CLC) administered the freeze and mandated that wages, prices, and rents during the freeze period from August until November were capped at levels during a base period of one month before the announcement of the freeze on August 15.[21] Because the Economic Stabilization Act had not granted authority to cap interest rates or dividends, the Commerce Department successfully requested over 1,000 corporations to refrain from paying higher dividends on their stock.[22] The freeze succeeded in temporarily clamping down on prices, with consumer prices rising by only 1.7 percent in November, unlike 4 percent or higher earlier in the year, and wholesale industrial prices declining by 1.3 percent.[23]

That a president as seemingly free market-oriented as Richard Nixon imposed these kinds of controls and new layers of bureaucracy demonstrated how far he was willing to go in order to avoid tighter monetary policy. Phases II–IV of the controls lasted until April 1974. The first oil shock, caused by OPEC's embargo on oil to the U.S., rendered them wholly impractical. Even before the embargo, consumer prices rose by 8.3 percent and wholesale prices by 22.2 percent from January to June 1973.[24]

Though the controls briefly stopped a renewed surge in prices, they did not eliminate inflationary pressures. Private sector firms knew that the Administration would inevitably remove the controls at some future point, and when they did inflation expectations would kick back into gear. From an abstract standpoint, peacetime wage and price controls might even exacerbate inflationary pressures by forcing firms to raise prices and wages higher than they normally would in anticipation of a reimposition of controls. In any event, inflation persisted through the recession of 1974, creating conditions of "stagflation." A year later, Congress passed a resolution for the Board of Governors to regularly disclose targets for its monetary aggregates.[25] But this provision did little to galvanize the Fed into curbing monetary growth.

After Volcker became Fed chair, the Fed raised the discount rate by a full percentage point up to 12 percent in October 1979 and revised its daily open market operating procedures. The FOMC had been targeting the federal funds rate, the interest rate charged by member banks on overnight loans to each other made up of excess reserves. Targets for bank reserves now needed to conform to the targets for the monetary aggregates.[26] The new operating procedures essentially allowed the FOMC to cause a spike in the federal funds rate without overtly having to set such a target. The Fed abandoned its newfound policy in the spring of 1980 after M1 and M2 (M1 plus time and savings deposits, among a handful of other types of accounts) grew below their targets and the economy entered a recession. An assumption held that the FOMC should have followed its new operating procedures as rigidly as possible, so that if M1 and M2 were below target, then policy needed to be looser. The presidential election that year also constrained the Fed's ability to aggressively pursue disinflation. The Fed did not want to alienate itself with politicians on both sides of the aisle by causing gyrations in the money supply.[27]

Only with the election of Ronald Reagan did the FOMC commit itself to an all-out struggle to contract the money-stock and push down prices and wages, even at the cost of sending the economy into the worst contraction since the Great Depression up to that time. The monetary base, the narrowest gauge of the money supply computed as currency in circulation and total bank reserves, increased by 8.8 percent in 1980 but by only 4.9 percent in 1981. Non-borrowed reserves increased by 7.8 percent in 1980 and by 6.8 percent in 1981. M1 increased by 7.3 percent in 1980 and by 5 percent in 1981. If adjusted for the public's shift from M2 accounts into new negotiable order of withdrawal (NOW) accounts that year, which are counted as part of M1, then M1 grew by only 2.3 percent.[28]

The roots of the Great Inflation can be traced to spending for the Vietnam War and the Great Society. The Great Inflation should therefore be characterized as a partly wartime phenomenon, but heavy wartime spending in previous conflicts had not contributed to a peacetime inflation of the same magnitude or duration. The reason for this was that unlike in previous cases a policy environment existed in the 1960s and 1970s that bred reluctance in taking decisive action against inflation for fear of encountering the associated economic costs. Such reluctance contrasted with policies at the end of previous conflicts, which had accepted inevitable adjustments after wartime. After the end of World War I and the bout of hyperinflation, for instance, Reserve Banks raised their discount rates and disinflated the economy. Immediately following World War II, high export prices contributed to inflation, but Congress convened in a special session and authorized the Fed to raise reserve requirements beyond their legal limits. While the Treasury was still trying to keep the Fed conscripted into its debt management agenda, the Fed ended up selling government bonds during the recession of 1949. After the Korean War, tight fiscal and monetary policy worked to keep inflation low over the long-term, even while prices periodically rose.

Demand side theory cannot be thought to have caused the Great Inflation, but it still assumed a permanent tradeoff in inflation and employment, legitimated budget deficits from a theoretical point of view, and influenced officials to forgo disinflation after the end of wartime.

NOTES

1. J. Bradford De Long, "America's Peacetime Inflation: The 1970s," in *Reducing Inflation: Motivation and Strategy*, ed. Christina D. Romer and David H. Romer (Chicago: University of Chicago Press, 1997), 252–53.
2. Orphanides and Williams, "Monetary Policy Mistakes," 264.
3. Andrew Levin and John B. Taylor, "Falling Behind the Curve: A Positive Analysis of Stop-Start Monetary Policies and the Great Inflation," in *The Great Inflation: The Rebirth of Modern Central Banking*, ed. Michael D. Bordo and Athanasios Orphanides (Chicago: University of Chicago Press, 2013), 219.
4. Board of Governors, *Fifty-Second Annual Report of the Board of Governors of the Federal Reserve System: Covering Operations for the Year 1965* (Washington, D.C.: Federal Reserve System, 1966), 8–9.
5. Council of Economic Advisers, *Economic Report of the President: Together with the Annual Report of the Council of Economic Advisers* (Washington, D.C.: Government Printing Office, 1966), 52.
6. Arthur F. Burns, "The Perils of Inflation," in *The Business Cycle in a Changing World*, ed. Arthur F. Burns (New York: National Bureau of Economic Research, 1969), 287–88.
7. FOMC Minutes, November 23, 1965, Federal Reserve Open Market Committee, Federal Reserve Transcripts and other historical materials, Board of Governors, 77.
8. November 23, 1965 Minutes, 68.
9. BoG, *Fifty-Second Annual Report*, 12.
10. Board of Governors, *Fifty-Third Annual Report of the Board of Governors of the Federal Reserve System: Covering Operations for the Year 1966* (Washington, D.C.: Federal Reserve System, 1967), 9.
11. BoG, *Fifty-Third Annual Report*, 10.
12. Board of Governors, *Fifty-Fourth Annual Report of the Board of Governors of the Federal Reserve System: Covering Operations for the Year 1967* (Washington, D.C.: Federal Reserve System, 1968), 22.
13. BoG, *Fifty-Fourth Annual Report*, 23.
14. Board of Governors, *55th Annual Report: 1968* (Washington, D.C.: Federal Reserve System, 1969), 10.
15. BoG, *55th Annual Report*, 11.
16. Ibid., 45.
17. CEA, 1970 *ERP*, 28.
18. Levin and Taylor, "Monetary Policies," 220.
19. Burton A. Abrams and James L. Butkiewicz, "The Political Business Cycle: New Evidence from the Nixon Tapes," *Journal of Money, Credit, and Banking* 44, no. 2–3(2012): 387.
20. Abrams and Butkiewicz, "Political Business Cycle," 393.
21. CEA, 1972 *ERP*, 77.
22. Ibid., 80.
23. Ibid., 81–82.
24. Council of Economic Advisers, *Economic Report of the President: Together with the Annual Report of the Council of Economic Advisers* (Washington, D.C.: Government Printing Office, 1975), 227.
25. Board of Governors, *62nd Annual Report: 1975* (Washington, D.C.: Federal Reserve System, 1976), 51.
26. Board of Governors, *66th Annual Report: 1979* (Washington, D.C: Federal Reserve System, 1980), 19.

27. Michael L. Mussa, "Monetary Policy," in *American Economic Policy in the 1980s*, ed. Martin Feldstein (Chicago: University of Chicago Press, 1994), 102–03.

28. Board of Governors, *68th Annual Report: 1981* (Washington, D.C.: Federal Reserve System, 1982), 15.

ELEVEN

The Fiat Era

The suspension of specie payments in August 1971 did not immediately lead to the adoption of floating exchange rates. The signatory parties to the Smithsonian Agreement attempted a final round of pegged exchange rates that lasted until 1973, when central banks finally gave up trying to withstand the downward pressure on the dollar and floated their currencies. Dollar overhang and the payments imbalance had ensured overvaluation of the dollar by 1970. Due to two official devaluations and a fall in its market value under floating rates, the dollar depreciated by 26 percent as adjusted for inflation during most of the 1970s.[1] Yet the oil embargo and other externalities caused extreme fluctuations in the dollar's real exchange rate.[2] The real depreciation of the dollar coincided with the U.S.'s increasing specialization in higher value capital merchandise, with net exports in this category reaching $15 billion during the mid-1970s.[3] Agricultural exports also turned in a surplus of over $10 billion during this time.[4] On the other hand, imports of consumer goods netted $18 billion in deficits in the later part of the decade.[5]

The 1981–82 recession caused a dramatic realignment in dollar exchange rates, with the dollar climbing to a nearly 30 percent appreciated value.[6] Administration economists concluded that the dollar was hugely misaligned and a major driver of the trade deficit.[7] Working to reverse dollar appreciation in the mid-1980s required the multilateral coordination of monetary policy, while direct interventions played a comparatively minor role. Dollar appreciation reached a critical point in February 1985, followed by a new dollar rally in September.[8] G-5 finance ministers convened at the Plaza Hotel in New York later that month to collaborate on efforts to adjust the dollar's value. The parties issued a communique announcing a managed depreciation of the dollar against the other major currencies. Behind the scenes, they were committed to selling $18 billion to accelerate dollar depreciation.[9]

The dollar plunged by 4 percent on the same day the G-5 issued its communique before continuing a more moderate descent.[10] The Plaza Accord serves as a textbook case for the manipulation of market reaction in order to drive down the value of a currency. The G-5 ministers made a decisive announcement that shook markets. The Treasury and other monetary authorities then began to intervene in the markets. The Treasury purchased over $3 billion in foreign exchange in late 1985 to reinforce the dollar's fall.[11] The dollar continued to fall through 1986, helped along by the ongoing U.S. current account deficit. In March 1986, the U.S., France, Germany, and Japan implemented a round of discount rate cuts, followed a month later by additional rate cuts in the U.S. and Japan.[12]

There was some thought that the dollar's fall forced other nations into pursuing expansionary policies to stall its decline, since the U.S. would take no active steps to strengthen the dollar.[13] At the Louvre summit held in February 1987, the members of an expanded G-7 bloc announced that they would maintain exchange rates in their current range.[14] The communique indicated that exchange rates were now in line with economic conditions. Japan and Germany agreed to looser fiscal policies, while the U.S. promised to reduce its budget deficit.[15] The Fed also worked to push up U.S. interest rates.[16]

The Louvre summit represented a compromise in which Japan and Germany expanded their economies in exchange for the U.S. tightening its monetary growth. Monetary and fiscal policy served as the primary means for stabilizing the exchange rates of the world's three largest industrialized economies. But officials did not ignore the utility of foreign exchange interventions. At the Louvre summit, the G-7 committed itself to purchasing billions of dollars in the key currencies if necessary, and it targeted the dollar's yen and mark exchange rates within designated bands.[17] From the time of the Louvre Accord to the crash of the New York Stock Exchange in October 1987, exchange rates stayed steady.[18] While interventions were effective, the monetary and fiscal agreements buttressed the international framework for managing exchange rates.

The adoption of floating exchange rates in the 1970s was perhaps the most conspicuous result of the turn from gold to fiat. The period ending the gold standard entered its denouement with the soaring dollar of the 1980s. If the Great Inflation coincided with the termination of specie payments, then it proximately led to the deep recession in the early 1980s and the appreciating dollar. In the roughly fifteen years from the suspension of specie in 1971, the money supply swung from inflation to deflation, and from dollar weakness to dollar strength, until conditions stabilized in 1987. The stock market crashed in October of that year, eerily similar to 1929, but this crash did not signal the start of another global depression. The flexibility of fiat currency and floating exchange rates allowed the

Federal Reserve and other central banks to initiate a timely policy of ease. In an era of increasing globalization, fiat regimes and floating exchange rates worked better than fixed gold ratios.

The U.S. might have temporarily extended the life of the gold standard through tight monetary policy, but that ignores the more important point that the world's gold supply could no longer keep up with global output. Even as early as the 1920s, international financial commissions foresaw an inadequate gold supply and that nations would be forced into economizing their gold reserves by establishing bullion standards. In a similar vein, the breakdown of the gold standard should not be equated with domestic inflation. Closing the gold window relieved the Nixon Administration and the Federal Reserve of the burden of pursuing tight fiscal and monetary policies, but that is not the same as assuming that inflation single-handedly brought down the gold standard. On the contrary, other forces were at work, including the decline in gold production, capital flows, deterioration in the merchandise trade balance, and overvaluation of the dollar. Triffin posed his dilemma before the Great Inflation, and the dilemma came into being with or without inflation, the U.S. caught between either losing its gold or reining in its dollars and threatening the world with economic contraction. Of course there was another way out, which was for the U.S. to end convertibility and hold onto its remaining gold.

As the Phillips curve broke down in the mid-1970s with the onset of stagflation, President Ford responded not with an appeal to restore convertibility to gold but to promote a new agenda of low inflationary real growth. In his Whip Inflation Now address in 1974, Ford called for a target on federal spending, a temporary surcharge on higher incomes, and increased domestic energy and food production, among other proposals. But at no point did he mention re-adoption of the gold standard.[19] While Congress passed legislation in December 1974 again authorizing the private dealing in gold bullion, this did not signal a return to convertibility.[20]

An incident occurring in 1976 helps to illustrate the attitude of policymakers towards gold in the post-convertibility world. Gerald Ford had organized an Economic Policy Board among his economic advisers that he regularly convened. At one meeting of the Board, disagreement arose as to whether the U.S. should sell off its gold stock. Treasury Secretary William Simon recommended gold sales because of rising nominal interest rates. The Department could trade in its gold for dollars and put the dollars into interest bearing accounts. Burns, still serving as Fed chair, disagreed and argued that gold functioned as a superior form of means of exchange and should remain a hedge held in reserve. After the meeting adjourned, Ford called in the Chairman of his CEA, Alan Greenspan, who had been present at the meeting, and asked him to weigh in on the discussion. Greenspan advised against gold sales, not on the same theoretical grounds as Burns but on the rationale that they might threaten to roil markets. Ford took Greenspan's advice and did nothing, and the U.S. gold stock remained generally constant in the decades ahead.[21]

The question brought before the Economic Policy Board had not been whether to restore convertibility but whether the gold reserve offered any additional revenue to the Treasury. The Treasury's gold reserve in the fiat era can be thought of as an artifact of the old commodity standards, but gold's function as a symbol of monetary stability ensured its retention in government vaults. In 1980, Congress mandated a Gold Commission to investigate the possibility of a restored gold standard in one form or another.[22] When the Commission returned its report in 1982, it favored preserving floating exchange rates and advised against reestablishing Fed gold reserves.[23] Central bank sales of gold in global markets reduced the price of gold as a commodity in the final years of the twentieth century. In September 1999, the central banks of fourteen nations entered into the Washington Agreement that capped annual gold sales in the open markets at 400 tons per year over a five-year period. The U.S. refrained from entering into the agreement or selling off its gold.

While capital outflows and the current account deficit provided the causal link from convertibility to fiat, inflation became the legacy of fiat, whether it deserved it or not. The process of transition to fiat was not fully completed until inflation ended in the early 1980s. Through this process, the notion of low inflationary growth took on new significance now that the gold standard could no longer serve as an automatic corrective. The abandonment of gold also led to floating exchange rates, which could be used as an instrument of policy at the discretion of governments. If the emerging fiat standard were to be therefore reduced to two discrete outcomes, then they would be the need for low inflationary growth and deregulated exchange rates.

Technical aspects of a fiat standard might have been put to more activist use in the trough of a depression, and something very close to this occurred in 1933. The Thomas Amendment authorized the Treasury to issue up to $3 billion in fiduciary currency if the Federal Reserve failed to purchase securities of an equal amount. But in engineering changes to the money supply, Franklin Roosevelt relied instead on nationalizing the gold stock, purchasing newly mined gold, and devaluing the dollar, all of which were consistent with public opinion at the time. Even in the depths of 1933, the U.S. was not prepared to permanently abandon its commitment to gold, and nor did the fiduciary currency provision of the Thomas Amendment signify such an abandonment. The Aldrich-Vreeland Act also made use of fiduciary currency by allowing clearinghouses to temporarily issue emergency currency before it was taxed out of existence. But the Aldrich-Vreeland legislation was of transitory duration, and clearinghouses only implemented its provisions once at the start of World War I.

That technical aspects of fiat money were not further probed for possible changes to economic policy in the 1970s is unsurprising. The U.S. was faced with inflation and two oil shocks, so that any such abstract exercise would have been completely out of step with the major economic issues of the time. But the impracticality of such an exercise at that time should not deter a reconsideration of the technical advantages of fiat in the twenty-first century, when slowing real growth and market saturation necessitate an inquiry into what additional options remain available.

NOTES

1. Branson, "Trade and Investment," 206.
2. Jacob A. Frenkel, "United States Inflation and the Dollar," in *Inflation: Causes and Effects*, ed. Robert E. Hall (Chicago: University of Chicago Press, 1982), 198–99.
3. Branson, "Trade and Investment," 216.
4. Ibid., 212.
5. Ibid., 216.
6. Jeffrey A. Frankel, "Exchange Rate Policy," in *American Economic Policy in the 1980s*, ed. Martin Feldstein (Chicago: University of Chicago Press, 1994), 296.
7. Frankel, "Exchange Rate Policy," 298.
8. Ibid., 303.
9. Maurice Obstfeld, "The Effectiveness of Foreign-Exchange Intervention: Recent Experience, 1985–1988," in *International Policy Coordination and Exchange Rate Fluctuations*, ed. William H. Branson, Jacob A. Frenkel, and Morris Goldstein (Chicago: University of Chicago Press, 1990), 200–01.
10. Frankel, "Exchange Rate Policy," 304.
11. Obstfeld, "Foreign-Exchange Intervention," 224.
12. Ibid., 201.
13. Frankel, "Exchange Rate Policy," 305.
14. Ibid., 306.
15. Obstfeld, "Foreign-Exchange Intervention," 202.
16. Frankel, "Exchange Rate Policy," 307.
17. Obstfeld, "Foreign-Exchange Intervention," 202.
18. Ibid., 207.
19. Gerald Ford, "Address to a Joint Session of the Congress on the Economy: October 8, 1974," University of California-Santa Barbara, http://www.presidency.ucsb.edu/ws/?pid=4434, accessed August 2017.
20. Dam, "Monetary Law," 528–29.
21. Alan Greenspan, interview by Richard Norton Smith, December 17, 2008, transcript, Gerald R. Ford Oral History Project.
22. Anna J. Schwartz, "Reflections on the Gold Commission Report," in *Money in Historical Perspective*, ed. Anna J. Schwartz (Chicago: University of Chicago Press, 1987), 317–18.
23. Schwartz, "Gold Commission Report," 324.

Part II

Industrial and Foreign Exchange Policy Options

TWELVE

The Need for Efficiency

The U.S.'s money supply has been increasingly managed by government. Management of the money supply means that government has worked to fully or in part regulate money flows in an effort to stabilize banking and the real economy. Had the Second U.S. Bank survived Jackson's attack, then the nation's monetary history might have turned out differently. But in fact the expiration of the U.S. Bank's federal charter turned banking regulation over to the states. Only with the crisis of the Civil War did government officials finally return their attention to federal banking. But Chase did not try to restore the U.S. Bank as a wartime measure. Such a controversial issue would have only touched off partisan debate that the Lincoln Administration could not afford to deal with in 1862, even though the Republicans dominated Congress and were able to pass other landmark legislation through their majority.

Chase instead proposed an expedient, forcing the national banks to rack up U.S. bonds in exchange for banknotes. The National Banking System, whatever its faults, still represented a new attempt by the federal government to manage the money supply. The circulation of currency was no longer controlled by state banking laws. National banknotes were pegged to U.S. bonds. New reserve requirements also meant that cash reserves piled up in New York at central reserve banks, which were supposed to double for an actual central bank. But these central reserve banks were for profit institutions, and they used the infusion of cash to invest in stock loans. The National Banking System was a failure because it only partly managed the money supply. It ordered national banks to put so much money into reserve, but it did not create new institutions committed to market stability.

The early Federal Reserve represented a step further in the management of the money supply. Member banks were required to park their cash reserves at local Reserve Banks, which cut off reserves from the stock market. Unfortunately, member banks also abused the discount window. The new asset-backed currency appeared more flexible and amenable to commerce than the bond-backed currency, but the early Federal Reserve's decentralized structure meant that it could not adequately respond to market crises. The system worked reasonably well in response to the deep recession of the early 1920s. But the system could not overcome its second challenge at the end of the decade, and it was eventually subjected to overhauls. After regaining its autonomy, the Federal Reserve aggressively purchased longer-dated bonds during Twist in the 1960s and quantitative easing after the 2008 financial crisis. But these open market operations were not sustainable as permanent programs. The Federal Reserve cannot be expected to push down interest rates indefinitely into the future.

The fact that the U.S. did not develop a central bank over the course of the 1800s was hugely consequential, but it was also unsurprising. A central bank's natural constituency is the financial services industry, which hopes to receive bailouts or easier liquidity. The broader public does not tangibly benefit enough from a central bank to provide enthusiastic support for it, and perhaps it does not even fully understand a central bank's functions. The U.S. Bank was routinely pilloried as a tool of the Eastern financial elite and foreign interests. Given the extensive stock holdings that foreigners held in the Bank, there was some shred of truth to this claim. The Bank was an easy target, and someone like Andrew Jackson could always stir up populist resentment against it. The fact that the Bank was the brainchild of a supposedly nefarious and even monarchist High Federalism, at least from the Democratic standpoint, did not help its case. What was really missing in the U.S. in the 1800s was an unambiguous monetary authority with the attributes of a bank that had the clear mandate to maintain market stability in the name of the national interest. Such an institution should have been established in the 1850s when the country was stocked with gold. Surplus revenue could have been used to invest in an open market fund, which would have given the new institution the resources necessary to focus entirely on managing the money market and responding to panics and depressions.

The Independent Treasury was an appealing idea because the Treasury Department was an inherently governmental institution. Unlike the U.S. Bank, it did not get caught up in cotton speculation and had no foreign-owned stock shares. Leslie Shaw's vision of an interventionist Treasury was not entirely off the mark. But a government treasury cannot specialize in market stability because of its manifold responsibilities and its inherently political leadership. The case against an interventionist Treasury can be summed up by its record during Shaw's tenure. As a politically appointed officer, Shaw kept easing the banks in the hopes of prolonging an expansion, which created overheated conditions by 1907.

The idea of the Treasury as a quasi central bank, which it was after Shaw declared that public deposits were de facto part of the Department, could not survive the panic of that year.

Even though it is not fully integrated into government like the Treasury, central banking must be seen as a governmental effort to maintain market stability. This attempt at maintaining market stability is in the national and even international interest, affecting the whole economy and everyone in it. Managing the money supply is therefore a public goal. But this goal is also a limited one. A central bank's mandate should be to combat recession, stabilize the banking system, and prevent against spiraling inflation. In any given situation, these objectives occasionally complement one another but they also regularly conflict with one another, especially recession versus inflation. A central bank's goal of full employment seriously complicates its mandate. No central bank should prioritize full employment over inflation unless inflation is targeted for countercyclical ends. A central bank is therefore not an agent of permanent economic expansion. It can maintain price stability, it can expand liquidity during crises, and it can work against stagnation and general deflation, but it should not be seen as a driver of long-term GDP growth.

If GDP growth is the objective, and if central banking is ultimately inadequate for this purpose, then perhaps something resembling central banking is the answer. Central banking is after all flexible, apolitical, and more responsive to changing conditions than most other forms of economic policy. A central bank is also constantly connected to the market through open market operations, the discount window, and interest on excess reserves. In fact, central banking probably seems like the only way to manage the money supply. That has been the case in the U.S. The money supply became increasingly managed to the extent there was development of a quasi or real central banking authority. The question now becomes what institutions are capable of managing the money supply in a way that generates GDP growth over the long-term.

Monetary-industrial policy, or for short industrial policy, serves as the next step after monetary policy in pumping money into the real economy. A new accounting system should be devised that transmits money into the economy outside of the financial sector and particularly into major scale economies like manufacturing. Such an industrial policy resembles central banking because it maintains constant contact with the private sector in a flexible, apolitical, and responsive way through specific institutions. Such an industrial policy inhabits a monetary side approach, as opposed to supply side or demand side alternatives. The supply side approach focuses on cutting taxes to expand capital accumulation. The demand side approach increases government spending to boost income. The monetary side, on the other hand, is based on specialized money flows used to comprehensively drive economic gains, whether affecting saving, investment, consumption, or employment. Through all of American history, the monetary side has been confined to quasi or actual central banking. The Second U.S. Bank issued banknotes and made out loans that helped fuel land-related speculation before reversing course and contracting the money supply. The Treasury attempted to operate more countercyclically by purchasing bonds in the 1870s but failed to prevent a bank panic or provide timely ease. Federal Reserve Banks automatically rediscounted eligible paper through the 1920s before eventually coordinating open market operations. In all of these cases, the monetary authorities transmitted money into the real economy with little intention of generating permanent economic change. Even the more recent quantitative easing was primarily intended to stop a second Great Depression, albeit while producing a bull market in stocks lasting for years.

Today any notion of "monetary side" simply means monetary policy and nothing else. But the term is more meaningful when considered as a framework for new industrial policy options that generate money flows. Unlike monetary policy, these options are intended to expand fixed investment over the long-term. Revising the tax code or altering spending also implicates money flows in one way or another. Yet industrial policy options more closely hew to central banking antecedents by relying on highly specific institutions and transactions that permit optimal coordination between government and the private sector and in the process eliminating friction.

Innovation drives the economy, and nowhere is this more apparent than in manufacturing. Industries are increasingly productive because of advanced robotics and artificial intelligence. As a developed nation, the U.S. needs to remain on the leading edge of new technologies and methods of production. Implementing broad-based industrial policies might seem like a waste of resources when the ultimate goal should always be innovation. But the value of these industrial policies is that they are purely macroeconomic, in that they are totally focused on boosting GDP growth and creating ripple effects throughout the larger economy. While such an agenda cannot substitute for efforts to accelerate innovation and R&D, it does provide a potentially more efficient macro concept, especially if pursued in a political environment of fiscal responsibility. This efficient macro concept seeks to produce as much GDP growth as possible with as little funding as possible. The key to doing this is injecting liquidity right into scale economies for the manufacture of goods, whether for domestic consumption or export. An efficient macro concept of this caliber is not meant to forever supplant the need for tax cuts, and budgets will periodically go into deficit. But with the national debt threatening to eclipse GDP, there is added urgency to devising new, efficient, and less costly ways for generating economic growth. The monetary side offers a way forward in this direction through greater organization and highly specific institutions and transactions.

New monetary-industrial and foreign exchange policies also benefit from operating under a fiat monetary standard. Technical aspects of fiat are relevant to new industrial and foreign exchange policies. These technical aspects may be few, but they are still important. Under fiat, government at its prerogative is able to create and sterilize fiduciary currency. Government avoids simultaneously generating net conversion rights to gold or silver as was the case under commodity standards. Government can create currency in advance of sterilization. It can also implement institutional devices that ensure currency creation is undertaken in the safest possible manner. Technical aspects of fiat allow subsidies (defined here as being funded from taxable revenue) and pseudo credit instruments and other payments to operate with greater efficiency.

Seven policy options will be outlined. Five of the seven focus on domestic industrial policy. A sixth sketches out a foreign exchange policy, and the seventh hones in on changes in existing monetary policy.

THIRTEEN

EDAS I

The first option provides for the support of private sector firms through uniform, unilateral money transfers in order to directly fund business expenditures. Payments are limited to only expenditures in connection with manufacturing activity. The option therefore serves as a highly simplified subsidy scheme. Yet this option cannot be funded through the normal budget and appropriations process. The problem is that taxable revenue and the proceeds of debt auctions must be used to fund discretionary spending every fiscal year. The federal government's obligation to actively use revenue and Treasury proceeds would coerce firms into making payments immediately upon distribution of the funds, or else the firms might lose access to the funding. Firms could not independently plan business expenditures because of their need to make out payments. Firms might even be deterred from receiving payments because of the intrusion on their planning autonomy. As a result, industrial policy based on unilateral transfers would be inefficient if funded through the appropriations process because of the conflict between private sector planning and the public need to actively use federal revenue and Treasury proceeds for discretionary appropriations. Even if Congress were to periodically appropriate funding for a multi-year operating period, such as every four years, this would inefficiently lock money away over the course of the operating period.

An industrial policy achieves optimal efficiency through creation of currency in one fiscal year and sterilization in the next fiscal year, meaning that currency creation occurs before sterilization in a given calendar year. The Treasury can spend money on certain expenses as tax withholdings accumulate in government coffers, but funding must still precede congressional appropriations per year. Congress directs in advance the creation of a uniform amount of currency while providing that only that portion of currency forwarded for payment be sterilized out of revenue. An automated procedure is legally mandated from the outset. Currency creation and sterilization is generally speaking a form of mandatory spending. But because it does not relate to entitlement programs or other benefits for individual recipients, and because it is organized in a sui generis manner, it probably should be thought of as a new form of federal spending, along with discretionary and mandatory spending and interest payments for the national debt. Such an automated procedure removes spending for the industrial policy from the budget and appropriations process. Such an automated procedure also better ensures the stability and durability of the program from the vantage point of firms that might otherwise be deterred from applying for payments. Currency creation allows firms to freely alter the rate of their payments and therefore adapt to changing economic conditions. Sterilization, meanwhile, is only triggered to the extent of payments and not to the full amount of created currency. This plan allows for maximum flexibility because choice is passed on to private sector firms. Offering payments based on demand is also efficient. The number of firms demanding currency dictates the monetary amount required to fund sterilization.

No pretense is being made that a funding scheme based on appropriations would be impossible. But such a plan could only work through a corporatist structure, such as a centralized consortium managed by a federal agency. Firms would be integrated into the consortium, but the only way to streamline payments would be to establish a public-private partnership. Any such partnership would hamper the scope of autonomy necessary in the private sector. And even if a consortium worked in purely operational terms, it would inevitably lead to inefficiency, waste, and possibly corruption. If the intent is to effectuate macroeconomic impacts, then the means for doing so should involve not a reliance on corporatism but instead a rechanneling of the money supply using currency creation and sterilization.

A plan of this kind probably could not have worked under gold convertibility. Had government created fiduciary currency in advance of sterilization, then it would have increased conversion rights in gold to the same amount and threatened depletion of the gold reserves of monetary authorities and private banks. While the legislature could have sterilized fiduciary currency in the next fiscal year, a lag of over a year would have already elapsed during which time a drain on gold might have occurred. These pressures would have exerted themselves every year after the government's initial creation of currency and probably led to a long-term depletion in the gold reserve. Even if in normal times firms and other market actors would have been willing to hold fiduciary currency instead of gold, the threat of a drain on gold would have always been present. In addition, any such program would have weakened confidence in the nation's commitment to the gold standard in the eyes of official and private institutions. The public might have as a result started pulling their gold out of the country. The gold outflows attributable to the Bland-Allison and Sherman Silver Purchase Acts around the time of the Panics of 1884 and 1893 demonstrated that nothing short of an absolute commitment to gold convertibility was necessary to ensure public confidence and prevent gold outflows.

Such a point might seem trivial or moot. But it reinforces the deeper implication that while governments abandoned gold convertibility, they did not necessarily abandon certain assumptions that could have been ended along with convertibility. As noted before, policymakers probably never attempted to formulate a new concept of economic policy based on technical aspects of fiat money because the Great Inflation dominated public attention during the period when governments switched to fiat. Inflation was not eliminated from the U.S. economy until the early 1980s, by which time convertibility had been suspended for ten years and fiat was taken for granted.

Under the EDAS I version of the Economic Development Account System, firms obtaining membership in the System hold uniform, non-interest bearing accounts in their own name. EDAS creates cash in the accounts up to a uniform amount per year. Member firms of EDAS are subject to the rule that they can only use cash held in EDAS accounts to fund business expenditures in connection with manufacturing activity at New Plant Facilities (NPF) geographically located in the U.S. NPF exclusively refer to new manufacturing establishments. Firms eligible for EDAS accounts must plan to build NPF. EDAS accounts are only available to fund expenditures in connection with NPF, or in other words net investment associated with manufacturing. EDAS automatically balances the accounts to the uniform amount per year regardless of the amount in payments made in the previous year, with the result that accounts only have to be balanced to the extent of payments. As defined by the Census Bureau, manufacturing is "the mechanical, physical, or chemical transformation of materials, substances, or components into new products," including in most cases the assembly of manufactured components.[1] The manufacture of petrochemicals is excluded from this definition because of its highly specialized nature and close connection to the energy sector.

If firms want to use EDAS cash for expenditures, then they instruct EDAS to make a forward payment directly into the bank account of the counterparty through a normal checking process. Member firms hold constructive title to their accounts, and the checks are made out in their name. But they otherwise do not handle checks or make out payments themselves.

The term business expenditure is defined to mean expenditures made in the ordinary course of business, such as for materials or implements. This definition restricts EDAS accounts from being used to pay stock dividends, stock repurchases, or corporate bonuses. At the same time, a business expenditure occurring in the U.S. probably cannot effectuate a supply chain result, in that business expenditures cannot be further limited to only purchasing goods also produced in the U.S. Putting aside WTO prohibitions, such a provision would be impractical in any event in light of the complexity of global supply chains and logistics. Provided business expenditures are transacted in the U.S. for domestic operations, they can be used for purchasing imported materials. However, suppliers might over a longer time horizon open up new infrastructure in the U.S. in order to facilitate operations with member firms. Suppliers could also become eligible to apply for EDAS money. A supply chain result would be indirectly effectuated on the assumption that suppliers would follow the primary producers into new geographic regions. Defining manufacturing activity to include the assembly of subcomponent parts could work to accelerate these supply chain trends. But nothing on global logistics networks can be asserted with any degree of certainty, except that geographic proximity is not required given today's transportation and communication technologies.

Restricting the use of payments only to costs associated with NPF mitigates a meaningless net income effect. Without an NPF requirement, firms might simply accumulate net income, which would in turn cause them to lower their prices and dump their output onto world markets. EDAS money needs to be correlated to real growth. Business expenditures must therefore be made in connection with both manufacturing activity and NPF.

Firms must also be permitted to use forward payments for the regular compensation for labor. Labor costs therefore come under the definition of business expenditures. If forward payments are directed into the employment sphere, then EDAS money is explicitly limited to wages and salaries for production workers directly onsite at NPF. Firms are not allowed to obtain an exemption from collective bargaining arrangements, though corporate management would probably not be able to deviate from preexisting contracts with organized labor in any event.

The Bureau of Labor Statistics (BLS) computed the average hourly wage in the manufacturing sector in China in 2009 at $1.74, while the U.S. hourly wage in 2012 was $35.67.[2] The disparity in these average wages produces a labor cost differential of $33.93. Chinese labor costs are rising, but these figures indicate the challenge of resourcing manufacturing. EDAS accounts work to offset labor cost differentials. Assuming workers are fully employed through the year, the annual expenditure of an EDAS account of $20 million funds about 283 workers per year in terms of the labor cost differential. But adding workers to the economy is not the sole metric of success or even the end goal. The ultimate objective is fostering real growth and development, which adds to GDP and national income.

To probe organizational aspects of the option, EDAS offers accounts based on demand. A firm is able to secure an account when it decides to build NPF. The firm is not required to take any concrete steps prior to applying for an account, such as purchasing land, materials, or hiring workers. Regulators do not need to approve NPF prior to a firm's application for an account. If regulators do not approve NPF on environmental or other grounds, or if for whatever reason the firm is unable to build NPF, then the firm loses the account, which EDAS then transfers to the next firm making an application. Eligible firms only need to submit a plan to build NPF when applying for an EDAS account. The scheme is rules-based. Unlike with public works projects, members of Congress cannot use their political influence to determine the location of NPF. Only firms make those decisions, and the purpose of EDAS is to accommodate them. An added provision may condition access to EDAS accounts upon NPF located in specified states or geographic regions. But even under these added restrictions, the plan continues to be rules-based and not susceptible to horse-trading on Capitol Hill.

When eligible firms submit a plan for NPF, they must employ onsite at least 100 production workers. EDAS may not cater to the world's largest corporations, but firms building new fixed investments must be of sufficient size to generate economic impacts. Twenty million dollar accounts cannot be made available to startups or partnerships engaged in only rudimentary manufacturing. EDAS is intended to fund major scale economies. However, a firm is allowed to downsize its workforce to under 100 production workers after NPF has been constructed. Firms must only initially hire at least 100 workers as part of a formal plan submitted to EDAS.

The total number of available accounts is capped to stabilize foreseeable costs in sterilization. A ceiling on the number of accounts introduces the issue of what might be called cap space. If a firm hypothetically stops using its account, then EDAS currency would be holed up and prevented from being more productively used in another firm's account. But the premise of EDAS is to ensure maximum adaptability on the part of member firms. Firms are allowed to control their rate of payments. This structural flexibility molds currency creation and sterilization into an efficient plan. In the end, what is most important is that firms maintain NPF, regardless of their rate of payments. Firms are prohibited from retaining their EDAS accounts after shutting down their NPF. But if firms sell their NPF to another company, and the other company maintains the NPF, then the EDAS account is transferable.

The scale and reach of EDAS is the critical underlying imponderable. To put matters in perspective, manufacturing added nearly 12 percent of value to GDP in 2016.[3] The 2012 Economic Census estimated 297,191 manufacturing establishments in the U.S. across all North American Industrial Classification System (NAICS) manufacturing codes. Of these, 63,980 establishments included 20–99 employees, and 24,333 establishments included 100 or more employees.[4] Total U.S. manufacturing employment sat at 17.2 million in 2000. It then fell to under 14 million by 2007 before bottoming out at 11.4 million in early 2010. Employment recovered to 12.3 million by early 2017.[5] In all NAICS manufacturing codes, the annual wages of production workers averaged $337.12 billion during 2011–15, rising from $313.7 billion in 2011 to $360.7 billion in 2015. The total cost of materials rose from $3.2 trillion in 2011 to $3.5 trillion in 2014 before falling back to $3.1 trillion in 2015, averaging $3.34 trillion over the five-year period. By comparison, capital expenditures for machinery and equipment averaged $139.9 billion during 2013–15. This figure far exceeded that covering capital expenditures for buildings and other structures, which averaged $34.2 billion over the same period.[6]

An EDAS I of $50 billion per year comes to roughly 15 percent of the five-year average for annual wages, well less than 1 percent of total cost of materials, and 36 percent of capital expenditures for machinery and equipment. If due to budget realities EDAS is far smaller at only $5 billion, these percentages shrink. In this scenario, EDAS accounts are about 1.5 percent of annual wages and 3.6 percent of capital expenditures for machinery and equipment. EDAS would have a greater effect on individual firms. Twenty million dollars in payments per year provides support at the margin, such as in offsetting international labor cost differentials.

But the goal of EDAS is to incentivize the construction of fixed capital investment in the form of NPF, which is far smaller year to year compared to expenditures. If firms open up accounts and direct forward payments, then they are by definition in the process of building new fixed capital investment, or else they would not be eligible for the accounts. The success of EDAS I depends on whether $20 million accounts sufficiently incentivize firms into building NPF. Corporations like General Motors, Samsung, and General Electric might build new plants worth billions of dollars or at least in the hundreds of millions of dollars. EDAS funds per year are admittedly a pittance compared to the value of these huge investments. But EDAS could entice smaller companies to build NPF, such as manufacturing contractors for multinational corporations that outsourced their operations to foreign countries.

EDAS is a function of the extent to which so many dollars in funding translate into larger sums of money spent on fixed investment. If $20 million EDAS accounts generate fixed investment worth on average only $60 million, then an EDAS in the aggregate of $5 billion generates $15 billion in fixed investment. This figure substantially increases the $34 billion in fixed investment (buildings and other structures) during 2012–15. EDAS accounts in most cases could probably not be used to entirely fund construction of NPF. But they may provide sufficient support at the margin in terms of labor and other business costs for building NPF in the first place. A boost in the investment in NPF could also cause further increases in annual wages, cost of materials, and capital expenditures for machinery and other equipment.

If demand for the accounts is weak, then EDAS accounts can be uniformly raised to $50 million, which funds 708 workers per member firm in terms of the labor cost differential cited above. The downside to this is that fewer firms are able to join EDAS. At least tentatively, accounts should be set at $20 million in order to ensure that EDAS wields macroeconomic scale. But if this is not working, changes can always be made to correlate fewer accounts to more concentrated NPF.

A tentative, small-scale option sets up accounts individually equaling $20 million per year for 250 new manufacturing establishments. These figures approximately translate into a hypothetical maximum sterilization cost of $5 billion per year. This cost is equivalent to the hypothetical maximum because sterilization is only tied to actual forward payments. Depending upon the success of EDAS, the System can be expanded by raising the ceiling on total accounts.

Regarding sterilization, currency needs to be sterilized from taxable revenue instead of through monetary policy. If monetary policy were responsible for sterilization, then the Federal Reserve would be forced into carrying out automated open market sales of Treasurys, which would needlessly tighten financial markets. Moreover, using monetary policy for sterilization would not represent greater cost efficiency than other methods. Congress would have to regularly allocate funding to the Fed in order to support Fed purchases and repo sales of Treasurys.

The option instead sterilizes an equivalent amount in forward payments through the broader base of federal revenue. The Treasury is required by law to sterilize an amount in taxable revenue equivalent to forward payments during the past fiscal year. The Treasury sterilizes this amount after revenue has been collected from taxes but before it enters the budget and appropriations process. A lag of up to one fiscal year may occur between the time in which member firms make forward payments and when the Treasury sterilizes the equivalent amount. Such a lag further means that the money supply expands over the course of the fiscal year to the extent of the forward payments.

This automatic sterilizer is intended to stabilize market attitudes. Even though the money supply may temporarily expand in the course of the fiscal year, the automatic sterilizer reduces it back to its original amount. That is not meant to suggest that the automatic sterilizer entirely eliminates inflation expectations and can alone hold down prices. But its very existence does ensure that the money supply remains stable by rule. An automatic sterilizer implemented by the Treasury prior to the budget and appropriations process is also more stable than a fiscal sterilizer, in which Congress would be required by law to sterilize created currency in the form of an appropriation year-to-year. The differences between the automatic and fiscal sterilizer may appear superficial, but the automatic sterilizer works to greater efficiency. The automatic sterilizer reduces the budget sheet in an amount equal to that sterilized. If forward payments do not reach the maximum aggregate, then the Treasury turns the balance over to Congress for budget and appropriations. One disadvantage is that because the rate of sterilization is uncertain, the balance available for spending remains indeterminate until the end of the fiscal year. But this uncertainty in the budget sheet already exists due to fluctuations in federal revenue from one year to the next, with economic expansions usually producing greater revenue than contractions.

While EDAS creates a System of constituent members, it does not entail extensive institutional architecture. Except for limited oversight capability to verify that forward payments do not run afoul of the intended criteria, EDAS exists as a computer system. EDAS does not in any way serve as a new discretionary agency. Such a discretionary agency would only hamper the Federal Reserve's autonomy over monetary policy. The troubled interactions between the Treasury and the Federal Reserve in the 1900s signify the danger of when two discretionary institutions stand at odds with each other. Working pursuant to protocol, EDAS creates cash money to accommodate interbank settlements relating to forward payments. To avoid the minor cost of creating and destroying equivalent amounts of currency per fiscal year, sterilized cash can be rerouted to EDAS after EDAS's first year of operation.

In macroeconomic terms, whether EDAS operates pro or countercyclically cannot be easily determined. That EDAS might function in either pro or countercyclical directions reflects the adaptability granted to member firms in charting their own course in the face of a changing economic environment. The accounts operate procyclically if firms reduce their forward payments in a slowdown or recession and expand payments in an expansion. EDAS includes a built-in countercyclical effect, however, if firms use EDAS payments to fund business expenditures and money wages that would otherwise contract in a recession. EDAS also functions in broader countercyclical terms because its very existence improves market expectations. Market actors know that the EDAS pipes will keep running through a recession, so that firms are more willing to place orders and avoid layoffs. EDAS can therefore be said to resemble a lender of last resort in an industrial context, except that EDAS accounts represent direct purchasing power instead of loanable funds.

Yet EDAS is foremost intended to operate anti-cyclically, that is, to raise the level of investment and output regardless of cyclical conditions. EDAS potentially boosts competitiveness and innovation because member firms are authorized to direct forward payments into R&D as a form of business expenditure, provided the R&D is associated with NPF. However, EDAS must be distinguished from attempts to plug an output gap in the same way as the demand side New Economics of the 1960s. A major point of distinction is that EDAS represents a means for expanding purchasing power and industrial capacity as opposed to an emphasis on aggregate demand. In addition, the goal of EDAS currency is not to reach a new plain of economic utopia but to offset adjustments caused by globalization. EDAS embodies an effort to compete in the global arena, while the New Economics stood for a totalistic attempt to maintain full employment at all times.

Regarding the terms of trade, EDAS more realistically induces an import substitution effect rather than significantly achieving a higher rate of export growth. Gains in import substitution require the overcoming of labor cost differentials in possibly more labor-intensive sectors. An import substitution effect helps to improve the terms of trade through a lowering of imports on goods. On the other hand, an expansion in money wages and business expenditures could contribute to a rise in imports for both consumer merchandise and producer durables.

Because forward payments are only made in connection with NPF, EDAS impacts the larger economy by increasing output, business investment, and employment. Net output and net business investment arising from NPF can be computed as monetary aggregates. Net employment is the number of workers employed onsite at NPF. Regarding other impacts, companies and individuals consume and save at varying rates. NPF will therefore lead to some increase in savings and consumption, but otherwise these impacts cannot be easily predicted. Wage-earners tend to consume more than they save, but corporate savings could expand, which might lead to investment in mutual funds in the larger economy. What can be ascertained with clarity is that a successfully implemented EDAS will generate change in terms of output, investment, and employment.

How EDAS affects definitions of the money supply is a more peripheral methodological issue. EDAS accounts should not be defined as demand deposits under M1. While EDAS accounts may have the trappings of bank deposits, member firms do not have access to created currency in the same way depositors have with their cash in checking accounts. EDAS instead pumps currency into the bank deposits of counterparties, which temporarily increases the money-stock. The most straightforward way to measure these dynamics is to set up a hypothetical reserve consisting of the aggregate of created currency furnished in EDAS accounts. The money supply expands to the extent of a fall in the hypothetical reserve, or in other words to the extent of forward payments. The reduction in the hypothetical reserve can be further understood as measuring the velocity, or turnover, in created currency, velocity being here understood as the ratio of forward payments to total created currency. The hypothetical reserve is not actually computed as part of the money-stock.

In larger terms, the fiscal advantage of creating currency in one time period and sterilizing it in a subsequent period is that the government only spends money for sterilization after it has generated growth effects and expanded taxable revenue through currency creation. No presumption is being made that currency creation pays for itself, meaning that the growth effects lead to an increase in taxable revenue great enough to fully pay for the cost of sterilization. But forward payments are intended to efficiently generate real growth and increase taxable revenue. The increased flow of revenue enters into government vaults at the same time that the Treasury automatically sterilizes currency. How long a company would take to build NPF and hire workers is not clear. Such a process would likely go on for longer than a fiscal year, but the economic impacts begin to be felt as soon as member firms direct forward payments.

EDAS might even under certain conditions serve as an alternative to deficit spending for counteracting recessions. Generally speaking, if a cash-strapped government faces protracted recession and deflation, then it can create currency, transmit the currency into the real economy through EDAS, and pay for sterilization as the tax receipts flow into its coffers instead of ramping up deficit spending to fund a countercyclical budget. A government might even refrain from conditioning payments on NPF if the recession is severe enough. EDAS I should be viewed as a specific option, but EDAS-like mechanisms organized for temporary, countercyclical purposes can be devised that exploit the fiscal advantage. Even if a government does not want to cut other spending in order to offset the increased costs of sterilization, a temporary EDAS at least presents an alternative to implementing a full-scale countercyclical budget.

For instance, firms are permanently registered with EDAS I-B, a temporary account system for forward payments (to differentiate it from EDAS I-A, which has been explained above). EDAS I-B only directs forward payments during a recession, and payments are not correlated to NPF. Because payments cease at the direction of legislative and executive authorities, EDAS I-B functions as a quasi industrial lender of last resort, except that payments are subsidies instead of loans. Yet while payments might only be temporary, enrollment in EDAS I-B is still permanent, provided member firms maintain plant facilities with at least 100 production workers in the U.S. Accounts are also smaller at only $5 million each, which might be of relatively greater real value under conditions of deflation.

Overall, EDAS I-A works best as a counter-recessionary tool if accounts are uniformly increased for a temporary period of time, and the Treasury automatically sterilizes the additional currency the next fiscal year under its normal operating procedures. A fiscal advantage may still be exploited through an increase in tax receipts due to the expanded currency. No advantage exists in delaying sterilization beyond one fiscal year. If in a recession the government were to temporarily suspend sterilization over the course of multiple years, it would only free up money for its discretionary budget. Then it would incur an increased cost of sterilization at some future point. Increasing created currency in a deep recession while suspending sterilization for the additional amount is more logical, but this would also only delay the inevitable cost.

The paradigm of creating currency in a recession and sterilizing it in a boom offers no optimal balance. As created currency accumulates with each passing year, the corresponding cost increases at the same rate, until the point is reached where officials might be reluctant to revert to full sterilization for fear of throwing the economy back into recession. The fiscal advantage of currency creation is limited to delaying sterilization after one year, by which time increased real growth may have boosted revenue. If the government wants to take special countercyclical action, then it can implement EDAS I-B.

EDAS is foremost intended to operate efficiently. In the same way that the Reserve Banks created a currency more elastic to the needs of trade in the twentieth century, EDAS creates a currency more elastic to the needs of economic growth in the twenty-first century.

NOTES

1. U.S. Census Bureau, "About the Data," USCB, https://factfinder.census.gov/faces/affhelp/jsf/pages/metadata.xhtml?lang=en&type=category&id=category.en./ECN.NAICS2012.31-33#main_content, accessed August 2017.
2. Bureau of Labor Statistics, "International Comparisons of Hourly Compensation Costs in Manufacturing, 2012," updated August 15, 2013, BLS, http://www.bls.gov/fls/ichcc.htm.
3. Bureau of Economic Analysis, "Value Added by Industry as a Percentage of GDP," released April 21, 2017, BEA, https://www.bea.gov/iTable/iTable.cfm?ReqID=51&step=1#reqid=51&step=51&isuri=1&5114=a&5102=5.
4. U.S. Census Bureau, "Manufacturing: Summary Series: General Summary: Detailed Statistics by Subsectors and Industries: 2012," released December 18, 2015, USCB, https://factfinder.census.gov/faces/tableservices/jsf/pages/productview.xhtml?src=bkmk.
5. Bureau of Labor Statistics, "Employment, Hours, and Earnings from the Current Employment Statistics Survey (National)," BLS, https://data.bls.gov/pdq/SurveyOutputServlet, accessed August 2017.
6. U.S. Census Bureau, "Annual Survey of Manufacturers: General Statistics: Statistics for Industry Groups and Industries," released February 27, 2015, USCB, https://factfinder.census.gov/faces/tableservices/jsf/pages/productview.xhtml?pid=ASM_2015_31GS101&prodType=table.

FOURTEEN

EDAS II

An outflow/inflow device serves as another organizational means by which technical aspects of fiat money can be utilized. Outflow/inflow devices generate an optimal but temporary increase in the money supply in order to foster economic impacts. The Aldrich-Vreeland Act permitting bank clearinghouses to issue currency in times of crisis resembled an outflow/inflow device. The outflow aspect of the provision allowed clearinghouses to issue currency equal to 75 percent of the value of their holdings of commercial paper. The inflow aspect mandated that this emergency currency be taxable to expedite its swift sterilization after the crisis had passed. Inflow also existed because currency could only be issued against eligible forms of paper. But Aldrich-Vreeland applied to bank panics, authorized currency exclusively issued by clearinghouse banks, and was in no way connected to a permanent industrial policy.

Under EDAS II, the EDAS structure is largely retained. Accounts are set to a uniform amount of $20 million and funded through currency creation. Firms are only eligible for opening up accounts if they plan to build NPF. Firms do not handle the money directly and must instead rely on the forward payment mechanism. As opposed to EDAS I transfers, this option sets up an outflow/inflow device that replaces sterilization from income tax revenue. Generally speaking, outflow/inflow devices must be organized so that money flows back into reserve over a specified timeframe. A specified timeframe ensures that currency is only temporarily added to the money supply within stable limits. EDAS II is intended to incentivize investment in machinery and other equipment such as robots through longer-term non-interest loans. EDAS II could very well accelerate the trend in automation and enhanced productivity that has occurred in manufacturing. After a firm directs a forward payment, it must pay a special federal tax to EDAS of an equivalent amount within five years. Like income taxes, firms must pay the tax by a specified deadline.

Firms ideally invest in capital equipment before their incomes rise as a result of the investments. Firms therefore pay the tax after an increase in their incomes. Firms are able to pay the tax incrementally, meaning they do not have to pay in one lump sum. Their accounts automatically rebalance upon payment of all outstanding taxes. This provision safeguards against monetary excess while still ensuring institutional flexibility. Firms cannot use forward payments to pay for their taxes because, like EDAS I, EDAS II only directs forward payments to fund legitimate business expenditures, which does not include taxes. Unlike EDAS I, forward payments extend exclusively to business expenditures and not labor costs.

The inflationary perils of EDAS II cannot be ignored. If all firms immediately exhaust their accounts by directing forward payments, then EDAS II adds billions of dollars to the money-stock over a five year period, depending on the aggregate cap. Over the long-term, EDAS II should be capped at no more than $10 billion. Because accounts rebalance upon payment of all outstanding taxes within a five year timeframe, the accounts effectively add to the money supply over the long-term, albeit within the stable constraints of an outflow/inflow device.

Since only firms building NPF are eligible for EDAS II accounts, this option correlates monetary expansion to real growth. When monetary expansion and real growth occur simultaneously, price inflation is in theory stifled. Such a theory assumes that additional increments of real growth absorb the monetary expansion. But the real world is far more complicated, and trying to gauge how much real economic activity will stop so much inflation is futile. In any case, real growth can set off inflation for any number of reasons, regardless of the assumptions of an isolated theory. EDAS II will clearly generate some amount of net investment. Exactly how much is less clear. For these reasons, EDAS II must be initiated on a small scale, at no more than $5 billion. If M1 is hypothetically $3 trillion at any given time and M2 is $12 trillion, then EDAS II accounts come to .16 percent of M1 and .04 percent of M2.

Firms must be sufficiently incentivized by the five year payments/repayments to open up EDAS II accounts and build NPF. The incentives are weaker than with EDAS I, since EDAS II does not offer unilateral transfers. But EDAS II can boost investment into the long-term. As with other outflow/inflow devices, EDAS II must avoid crowding out private lending. Because EDAS II payments are of a relatively longer duration, five years, they more likely threaten the crowding out of corporate bonds instead of bank loans. But tying EDAS II to net fixed investment should hopefully prevent a crowding out effect. Like EDAS I, EDAS II is intended to induce undecided firms to build new fixed investments in the U.S. EDAS II seeks to generate economic impacts that would otherwise not occur and that would otherwise not affect private lending.

FIFTEEN

EDAS III

EDAS I and II focus on boosting capital equipment. EDAS III, however, works to strengthen short-term liquidity through an outflow/inflow device. As with the two previous options, though, firms are only eligible for EDAS III accounts if they plan to build NPF.

Under EDAS III, an aggregate in currency is created up to a cap and remains unsterilized. Because no automated sterilization occurs, this aggregate must be of a much smaller scale and hypothetically hovers from $1 billion to possibly up to $3 billion. Member firms do not receive transfers to their accounts every year but only once, when the accounts are first opened up. They voluntarily rebalance their accounts in order to re-access the created currency. To access currency, firms must rebalance an amount equal to a forward payment after four weeks.

Accounts must therefore be rebalanced over a short-term time horizon. This rule holds true regardless of the amount of the forward payment. If a firm directs a single forward payment of $20 million, then it must rebalance its account to this amount in four weeks just as if it directed a payment of $20,000. But a limit can be placed on individual payments at $100,000. A firm is also unable to in effect extend a loan by directing a forward payment to fund an unbalanced item of equal amount. Forward payments can only be used to pay for legitimate business expenditures and labor compensation and not for meeting loan repayments. As with EDAS I and II, the payment is directed to a counterparty and never enters the firm's coffers.

In this option, EDAS III appears to function as a bank making out small, non-interest loans. But while EDAS III serves as a creditor in economic terms, it does not in legal terms. The legal relationship between EDAS and member firms is not that of creditor-debtor. A firm can still be excluded from EDAS because of its failure to rebalance. Reapplication at some future time is conditioned on the firm's ability to advance a sum equivalent to the unbalanced amount and its maintaining of NPF. But otherwise member firms owe no legal obligation to EDAS for repayment of a debt. Member firms instead only rebalance accounts in order to maintain their inclusion within EDAS. Unlike most loanable funds, firms are not required to pay interest after using their accounts. Member firms are also not obligated to post collateral in order to direct forward payments. There is no reason why they would have to since EDAS would never take legal action against them for failure to rebalance. Finally, by law the failure to rebalance accounts does not affect a firm's credit rating. Created currency in this context blends characteristics of subsidies and loanable funds. Because firms are required to rebalance their accounts if they want to remain in EDAS, created currency resembles non-interest, uncollateralized loans. But because firms have no legal obligation to EDAS and ultimately are not required to rebalance their accounts, with no associated effect on their credit rating, created currency shares qualities with subsidies.

This plan works if member firms are disciplined in viewing their EDAS accounts as a resource with which to secure short-term financing for future business requirements. Federal Reserve history proves that discipline cannot be assumed and moral suasion is ineffective. One problem is that the accounts not only embody characteristics of loans and subsidies but also net savings. The opening of an EDAS account represents net savings to the member firm. Member firms might just as well switch this net savings into an interest bearing private account instead of a non-interest bearing EDAS account. Firms could not do this directly, but they could substitute forward payments for their own funds and then divert the latter funds into a private account. As a result, firms optimize their savings by indirectly transferring from an EDAS account to a higher yielding account instead of retaining their EDAS account as a reserve for future requirements. The net savings problem occurs when firms plan to fund expenditures from their retained earnings in an amount equal to the forward payments. Yet the problem could still be widespread.

Firms might refuse to rebalance their accounts in a variety of additional situations. Firms could, for instance, treat an EDAS account as a handout and use it to fund isolated projects without in any way attempting to rebalance their accounts. Even firms that wanted to abide by the rules might find it increasingly difficult to rebalance their accounts during a deep recession. Also, firms that for whatever reason decide to close their accounts with EDAS have no apparent incentive to rebalance their accounts beforehand. Firms that, for instance, face liquidation or takeover by another company would see no reason to rebalance if their inclusion within EDAS is going to terminate in any event. The edifice of pseudo credit built up by EDAS could entirely dissolve if firms decided for various reasons not to rebalance. The emission of created currency would produce what might be called lost money because it would not flow back into EDAS accounts.

Certain parallels could be drawn between EDAS and the early Federal Reserve System. Member firms might consider themselves institutionally committed to EDAS, just as member banks were committed to the Federal Reserve System. But these parallels do not hold up. National banks were ordered to join the System while state banks were eligible to join. Inclusion in EDAS, on the other hand, is purely voluntary. Also, member banks rediscounted or borrowed from the Reserve Banks instead of voluntarily repaying funds. Even if a state bank hypothetically wanted to withdraw from the Federal Reserve System, it still had to repay advances like it did any other loan. It would have also already deposited collateral before accessing currency. None of these obligations apply to member firms of EDAS. EDAS does not engender strong institutional ties between the central repository and member firms. EDAS mainly functions as a computer system handled by an existing federal department. Moreover, a corporatist partnership between the government and the private sector is anathema to the need for institutional flexibility.

Paying out monthly interest on EDAS accounts to member firms could incentivize firms into rebalancing their accounts. Interest payments would in effect serve as subsidies, but they would not create regular costs to the government as with unilateral transfers under EDAS I. Congress would appropriate money for investment in a bond fund mainly consisting of Treasurys. Income earned from the bond fund would then be transferred to EDAS accounts. In this way, costs for the program would ultimately plateau, assuming that the aggregate in created currency would be capped at anywhere from $1 to $3 billion. But paying out interest is flawed for at least two reasons. First, it would not entirely eliminate the threat of a net savings effect. Because the fund would only be invested in low yielding Treasurys with limited danger of default, member firms might consider it worthwhile to switch their savings into higher yielding accounts. To meet this danger, the fund could instead be invested in lower grade, higher yielding corporate debt. But sustained losses to the fund would seriously hamper EDAS's ability to pay out interest on the accounts and probably throw the whole program into political jeopardy. More importantly, the idea of paying out interest conflicts with the goal of keeping costs to a bare minimum. De facto subsidies could be introduced in various ways, but it would dilute the focus on pure currency creation.

At the opposite extreme, EDAS III could be modeled on Aldrich-Vreeland or EDAS II by granting it authority to impose a tax on created currency. Under such a provision, firms would pay a tax equal in amount to forward payments upon their failure to partly rebalance their accounts. A tax provision would essentially turn created currency into non-interest loans. While legally the relationship between member firms and EDAS would not be that of creditor-debtor, firms would still be required to pay back the sums advanced as forward payments. Unlike income taxes, member firms would repay the amounts owed irrespective of their earnings. Firms could not re-access their accounts until they fully paid back the amounts owed to EDAS. Yet the use of a tax should not be emphasized. Armed with tax collecting powers, EDAS III would not in this scenario offer any advantages to firms beyond offering zero interest loans, which is what EDAS II is already intended to do for capital equipment.

The discipline problem cannot be easily resolved. Firms must be incentivized to rebalance their accounts. A natural incentive to rebalance exists, but it runs counter to other motivations such as taking a handout. The Reserve Banks in the 1920s failed to discipline member banks into exclusively using their discount window borrowings for so-called legitimate purposes. Moral suasion was ineffective in forcing banks to curtail their investments in stocks, just as a purely voluntary regime under EDAS III might only lead to the dissolution of accounts into lost money.

Instead of relying on interest payments or taxes, a better method uses what might be described as objective qualitative constraints. A firm's failure to rebalance is publicly available information that is disseminated at no cost to the public. EDAS III accounts are deemed sufficiently similar to credit instruments that they merit the attention of possible future creditors, even if failure to repay is not integrated into an actual credit report. If member firms fail to timely rebalance their accounts after four weeks, then they should be granted an additional month to repay. During this additional window of time, firms are not allowed to direct forward payments from their accounts. After this probationary period has lapsed, firms have officially failed to rebalance their accounts. Their accounts are shut down, and they are removed from EDAS. Because they are not debtors, firms in this situation have not defaulted and none of their assets are subject to seizure. But information regarding their failure to rebalance is published and made publicly available.

Whether such a provision can entirely resolve the discipline problem is uncertain. But a reliance on objective qualitative constraints, not subjective ones such as moral suasion, best captures created currency's blend of subsidies and loanable funds. If, on the other hand, EDAS pays out interest to firms, then the whole plan can best be characterized as a subsidy. Or if EDAS imposes a tax on unbalanced accounts, then forward payments are de facto in arrears, and EDAS is functioning as a banker. An objective qualitative constraint establishes a middle ground for ensuring compliance because it attaches stigma to a failure to rebalance an EDAS account.

The danger of lost money must still be addressed. If hypothetically all accounts went unbalanced and all firms were excluded from EDAS, then this would translate into lost sums of anywhere from $1 to $3 billion. In the end, a provision for sterilization is necessary to reclaim the funds and neutralize additions to the money supply. The Treasury by rule sterilizes from revenue an amount equivalent to total lost money from the preceding fiscal year. Money is only lost once a firm is removed from EDAS and its account closed. A firm rejoins EDAS by repaying the unbalanced amount and keeping its NPF in operation, but it now stands at the back of the line.

The economic impacts implicated in this option also need to be understood. As with EDAS I, the accounts create a hypothetical reserve used for measuring the increase in the money-stock to the extent of forward payments. The money-stock effectively increases to the number of accounts set up, even if a four-week repayment schedule works to accelerate the velocity of rebalancing. Inflationary pressures may be closely related to the rate of forward payments among individual firms.

The best safeguard against inflation is to simply assign a fixed aggregate for EDAS III in the range of $1 to $3 billion. There is no reason to, for instance, cap the total number of accounts as a percentage of a monetary aggregate, such as the monetary base. If accounts were capped as a percentage of the monetary base, then they would adjust procyclically. As the monetary base expands in a time of inflation, the accounts increase. As the monetary base contracts during deflation, the accounts shrink. Capping EDAS III to a fixed aggregate, on the other hand, more likely leads to countercyclical outcomes. As the monetary base expands and inflation ticks upwards, EDAS III accounts will not rise beyond $20 million. During deflation, the accounts will not contract but instead continue to serve as a ready valve of money while other sources of lending are tapped out. The accounts might even increase in real value as the money supply contracts. A fixed cap might appear crude, but it is probably the safest option for setting up EDAS III.

EDAS III is intended to incentivize firms into building NPF by allowing firms to secure easier financing for their business requirements. The short repayment schedule also prevents firms from becoming overleveraged. The hypothetically most far reaching goal of this option is to effect interest rate differentials that fully or partially offset labor cost differentials. This goal implies that the reduction in borrowing costs compensates for paying higher wages in the U.S. instead of a developing country. Unfortunately, labor cost differentials in all likelihood greatly exceed interest rate differentials. The regular expenditure of wages represents an ongoing labor cost, while firms might draw down their credit lines only when retained earnings can no longer cover business expenses. But EDAS III still offers added efficiencies that can strengthen competitiveness, such as allowing firms to avoid entering into indebtedness and collateralizing assets and property. In addition, interest rate differentials become more important when international labor costs are uniform in a given sector.

Probably the greatest danger is that this option does nothing but crowd out private credit lines and hurt banking profits. But as with other versions of EDAS, EDAS III is necessarily tied to net fixed investment. Firms are on the margin of decision-making when considering whether to build NPF. EDAS III payments do not supplant credit lines for existing investments.

Pure currency creation exploits a technical aspect of fiat money, which is that government creates currency without generating net conversion rights to a commodity. But an alternative to pure currency creation, particularly for outflow/inflow devices, is funding derived through gold sales. Under a fiat standard, gold only functions as a tradeable commodity in the open markets. Government is able to sell certain amounts of gold to private dealers in order to generate economic impacts. One of the secondary advantages of a fiat standard is that the nation's gold reserve can be productively used to achieve macroeconomic ends. During the gold standard, the Treasury could never have sold gold in the open markets to fund an industrial policy. Gold sales could have only been feasibly contemplated during a period of intense gold production and inflation, when such a program would have been probably unnecessary in any event. But government should never sell off gold merely to pay for regular expenditures. The underlying dynamic of an outflow/inflow device such as EDAS III is that the money is intended to return to a de facto reserve. If the program is ever discontinued, the federal government is then authorized to repurchase a largely comparable amount of gold and thereby preserve its gold holdings.

An alternative option authorizes the Treasury to sell a relatively small portion of the gold reserve, such as $1 to $5 billion in gold oz. The dollar proceeds of the gold sales are uniformly distributed to EDAS III accounts. All other provisions of EDAS III remain the same, except that currency is funded through gold instead of through pure creation. The individual EDAS III accounts are not denominated in terms of gold oz. but simply in terms of the proceeds of the gold sales. As a result, the aggregate in currency is in no way pegged to the market price for gold, since such a provision would lead to highly impractical outcomes. In this scenario, firms would earn a de facto discount in their repayment if the market price of gold fell, but their accounts would also contract. On the other hand, if the price of gold rose, firms would incur a de facto premium, but their accounts would expand. Member firms would prefer taking out cash loans at a specified rate of interest instead of gambling on the future price of gold. Setting up a gold funded EDAS III is a simple procedure because the accounts are in no way pegged to gold.

The Treasury should also be assigned a Gold Repurchase Commitment (GRC) in the event that the program is scaled or shut down. A GRC signals to markets that the federal government remains committed to maintaining the nation's gold reserve at a roughly constant amount.

After the dollar proceeds of gold sales are transferred to EDAS III, GRC guarantees that a comparable amount in gold will be repurchased at a future time if EDAS III is shut down. If the market price for gold has risen since the initial sales, then the Treasury will incur a loss if it is mandated to repurchase the same amount in gold oz. that it initially sold. However, given fluctuations in the price for gold, the Treasury should be further authorized to delay its repurchases until the market price falls below the price at the time of the sales. At the very least, the Treasury is ideally granted a window of time to delay repurchases to allow the gold price to fall. The Treasury may in that case be able to break even or earn a small profit.

Attempting to gauge the future price of gold is extremely difficult. The price of gold fluctuates around $1,000 per ounce, but its price may fall by 2 percent one year or rise 10 percent the next, depending on economic conditions and other world events. There is no certainty when the Treasury would recoup its gold, but at least GRC directs dollars back into Treasury vaults pending their conversion to gold. If markets are on notice of when the Treasury is again going to buy gold, then traders could impede a fall in the gold price by increasing their spot purchases. Such a problem can be avoided if the Treasury anonymously enters the gold markets through a broker. In that case, market actors are not on notice of the date the Treasury previously entered the market and when it plans to reenter the market pursuant to GRC.

EDAS III should only be equipped with gold funding and GRC if pure currency creation is deemed excessively dangerous. But if gold funding is not pursued, technical aspects of fiat money can be exploited through an outflow/inflow device that only marginally expands the money-stock while also generating a roughly proportionate rate of real growth. EDAS III is not as aggressive as EDAS I or even II in generating money flows, but it is still intended to drive net investment.

SIXTEEN

CNF

The EDAS III accounts are a blend of subsidies and loans. But an outflow/inflow device that promotes short-term liquidity can be of a larger scale if organized as a pure credit facility. This facility does not use accounts or forward payments. Eligible firms instead sell one-year corporate notes or six-month corporate bills in connection with NPF to a Corporate Note Facility (CNF). CNF is run by an existing government department such as the Treasury. Eligible firms form a New Plant Facility Credit Network (NPFCN). Firms must first register with NPFCN in order to access CNF. Firms are eligible to join the NPFCN if they plan to build NPF. The notes yield low interest of at least 2 percent. The bills must pay out interest of at least 1 percent. CNF is obligated to purchase the notes and bills of firms registered with NPFCN if their proceeds are invested in business expenditures in connection with NPF and are rated BB+ or higher. CNF funds its purchases through currency creation. To ensure inflow, it sells the notes and bills to the secondary market. CNF sterilizes the proceeds of the sales. The inflow element can also be fulfilled by allowing the notes and bills to mature, which by definition must occur after no later than a year. The federal department managing CNF polices firms to ensure that they properly use the proceeds of their notes and bills in connection with NPF. If they fail to do so, they are removed from the NPFCN and denied access to CNF.

Unlike EDAS II–III, CNF serves as a bona fide creditor to eligible firms. It must secure a primary lien on the fixed investments of the firms when purchasing the notes and bills. If a firm defaults, then CNF seizes its assets upon default judgment, sells the assets, and sterilizes the proceeds. If the notes and bills decline in value and CNF can only sell them at a discount, CNF decides to forgo market sales and collect principal and interest at maturity. Earned interest is deposited in a special fund used for funding any added sterilization costs.

CNF risks the creation of another monetary authority contesting the mandate of the Federal Reserve. Hopefully this can be avoided for a few reasons. First, CNF is a rules-based regime. CNF automatically purchases notes and bills of a certain grade, issued by firms in connection with NPF, for which CNF has secured a primary lien over fixed assets. To the extent that CNF is run by an existing department, there may be some latitude for discretion. For instance, in a deep recession CNF purchases zero interest notes and bills using created currency and holds them until maturity instead of trying to sell them to the market, which would probably be impractical anyway. CNF also uses its discretion when deciding the extent to which it sells notes and bills to the market, since it would need to determine under fluid circumstances its ability to sell the notes at par or at a premium instead of at a discount. Second, CNF shares the same macroeconomic objectives as the Fed in trying to boost economic growth. CNF note and bill purchases might lead to mild inflation, which would require Fed countermeasures. But these deviations pale in comparison to the raw conflicts between the Treasury and the Fed in the 1930s, when Treasury officials coerced their Fed counterparts into supporting the market for government debt.

CNF/NPFCN is structured differently than any of the versions of EDAS. CNF is not an accounting system. Firms enrolled in NPFCN do not hold accounts with CNF. Firms are instead afforded the opportunity under certain conditions of selling notes and bills to CNF. Because inflow is possible either through open market sales or maturation, CNF can be conceivably expanded on an indefinite basis. But CNF should still be subject to a capped fund of $10 billion in outstanding notes and bills at a given time. Member firms are individually capped at $5 million in outstanding notes or bills at a given time. Such a cap safeguards against CNF issuing notes and bills too quickly in too short a time. This cap works in macro terms by requiring CNF to reject notes and bills at its purchase window after total outstanding notes and bills reach $10 billion. CNF also rejects the notes and bills of individual firms after they have reached their $5 million limit. Firms do not incur any kind of penalty if their notes and bills are rejected at the purchase window. In that scenario, firms meet their credit requirements through other means. To keep monetary expansion and net fixed investment roughly correlated, enrollment in NPFCN is limited to 500 firms.

CNF is an alternative to EDAS III. Because CNF functions as a bona fide creditor, it can be more safely expanded to cover a larger number of firms and a larger swath of net investment. But even CNF should not be taken too far. Caps still need to be imposed on outstanding notes, bills, and enrollment.

SEVENTEEN

EDAS IV

Like EDAS II, EDAS IV boosts capital equipment and is based on an outflow/inflow device. Under EDAS IV, eligible firms are granted accounts of $20 million exclusively for business expenditures and not labor costs in connection with NPF. As with EDAS I, firms admitted into EDAS IV direct unilateral forward payments to fund these expenditures. But unlike EDAS I, EDAS IV accounts are fixed at a designated amount. These accounts do not automatically rebalance each year. Once firms have used up their accounts, they can no longer direct forward payments, even if they continue to maintain NPF.

The outflow component is funded either through pure currency creation or gold. If EDAS IV creates currency to fund forward payments, then the money-stock expands to the extent of these payments over time. Accounts are capped in the aggregate at $30 billion. Monetary growth is directly correlated to net investment and real growth, since EDAS IV accounts are tied to NPF. But relying on pure currency creation, especially with aggregate costs coming to $10 billion or higher, is probably too dangerous.

EDAS IV can instead be funded through gold sales. With the market value of the U.S.'s gold stock in the hundreds of billions of dollars, the Treasury sells gold and uses the proceeds to fund forward payments. The Treasury could conceivably hand over the proceeds of gold sales to EDAS IV in order to meet the demand for forward payments. But this process may be inefficient and lead to lags between when firms want to direct the forward payments and when the money is available. The Treasury should instead automatically sell gold after forward payments using created currency have been directed and sterilize an equal amount in proceeds. These operations keep the money supply stabilized.

EDAS IV sets up inflow in two different ways. The inflow component is superficially fulfilled through gold sales. But inflow is achieved at an ulterior level by treating forward payments as conditional subsidies. Firms must repay the equivalent in forward payments if they shut down their NPF. Firms make these repayments over a five year amortization schedule. NPF is determined to have been shut down if all output stops and the fixed assets and property are sold off. Because EDAS IV payments are only conditional subsidies, assigning primary liens on the property and assets of the member firms would be impractical. If firms maintain their NPF into the foreseeable future, then collateralization does not become an immediate issue. EDAS IV is granted junior interests on the property and assets of member firms.

Admittedly, organizing EDAS IV on a repayments basis threatens to fuel procyclical outcomes. Member firms are obligated to repay forward payments as they liquidate their assets and possibly downsize their workforces. They are already entering a process of contraction. Turning EDAS IV into a conditional subsidy facility will only further drive this process. To offset these disadvantages, firms are at least not required to pay interest. Forward payments therefore serve as non-interest loans in the event that firms shut down their NPF. If EDAS IV relies on pure currency creation, then conditional subsidies are absolutely required to maintain monetary stability, regardless of any consideration for the gold stock. In this case, conditional subsidies ensure that monetary expansion is by definition tied to net investment. Once the net investment is shut down, repayments siphon the money out of circulation.

But even with gold sales inflow must be ensured at an ulterior level in order to preserve the nation's gold stock. The gold stock cannot be whittled down by funding isolated programs. Treasury gold sales are therefore contingent on GRC. As firms repay their conditional subsidies, the Treasury uses the cash to repurchase gold. As with EDAS III, EDAS IV only uses gold in a way that minimizes the effect of a permanent depletion in the nation's gold stock. Gold is an asset, and the federal government currently owns the world's largest sovereign reserve of gold. This gold must only be used to fund programs that are organized in a way that keep the gold stock stabilized over the long-term.

Unlike EDAS III and CNF, the goal of EDAS IV is to fund capital equipment. EDAS IV accounts are not intended to offset labor cost differentials. Firms are indeed restricted from using these accounts to pay wages and salaries. EDAS IV is focused entirely on ramping up expenditures for machinery and other equipment. Like EDAS II, EDAS IV may very well expedite the increased use of robots and other forms of automation in manufacturing. EDAS IV is able in this respect to promote productivity and innovation.

While accounts are non-renewable, the overall program is renewable. After firms shut down their NPF and begin the repayments process,

EDAS IV offers new accounts to other eligible firms now that cap space has opened back up. GRC signifies that the Treasury stands ready to repurchase gold when the program has ended, but the program, or at least part of it, does not necessarily end when firms repay their conditional subsidies. In fact, EDAS IV can create currency to fund new accounts while firms are still in the process of repaying. It can also use repayments to directly fund new accounts. The goal of EDAS IV is to support NPF, not specific firms.

If EDAS III and IV are gold funded, then EDAS II could also be gold funded. But making EDAS II gold funded as well could mean a large chunk of the gold stock being sold off, even if tied to GRC. A gold funded EDAS II–IV might translate into a $43 billion loss in gold. Alternatively, a gold funded EDAS II and IV could be pared down at for instance only $15 billion each. This would stabilize losses in gold. But again, any gold funding for EDAS II would, like EDAS III and IV, be conditioned on GRC. If firms shut down their NPF, then their tax payments are used to recover the equivalent in gold in the event that the overall program is phased out.

EDAS IV creates new industrial money flows funded by gold. The Federal Reserve System restructured the money supply by requiring Reserve Banks to back their note circulation with 40 percent gold reserves. EDAS IV does not reorganize the money supply in such massive terms. But its redirection of money flows in industrial sectors is in a sense gold-backed. The difference is that gold serves only as a commodity under a fiat system and can be sold for cash. A gold-backed EDAS IV, along with EDAS II-III and CNF, form an industrial policy coming at relatively little cost.

EIGHTEEN

ESF

Exchange rate policy can also exploit technical aspects of fiat money by making use of an outflow/inflow device. The U.S. has never truly maintained an official exchange rate policy, besides occasionally defending dollar exchange rates, because it never seemed worth the cost. Even the ESF's original operating fund was worth only $200 million, and the Tripartite Agreement replaced the Treasury's brief involvement in forex markets during the 1930s. The Federal Reserve's swap lines in the 1960s were part of a meager attempt to preempt a run on the Treasury's gold window. Monetary policy and diplomatic announcements more than forex interventions helped to realign the dollar in the 1980s.

The very idea of competitive devaluation to improve the trade balance appears futile, at least for a developed national economy with a currency that is freely tradable in the world's markets. A nation trying to artificially devalue its currency must reduce the currency's real exchange rate adjusted for inflation. Domestic inflation or foreign deflation can throw currency depreciation out of whack. Competitive devaluation might even incentivize foreign firms to lower their prices to compete with the exports of the devaluing nation. But the most practical criticism of competitive devaluation is that developed nations should not waste their resources trying to reduce the value of their currency by entering the world markets day in and day out. Devaluation is more viable for economies such as China with inherently weaker, regulated currencies that are not fully convertible.

As a developed economy, the U.S. should instead develop countermeasures against destabilizing dollar appreciation. Exchange rate movements are tied to shifts in ulterior dynamics like the current account. Yet in a world of fluid and global money flows, exchange rates are attributable to additional factors besides the terms of trade. Also, putting aside

WTO prohibitions, targeted depreciation leads to greater cost efficiency than tax credits to exporters or other support provisions available to individual firms, even if Congress were to appropriate funding for the ESF. But in any case, countermeasures against dollar appreciation should be based on outflow/inflow devices with no cost of sterilization. As with domestic operations, foreign exchange interventions funded through pure currency creation must be treated with the utmost caution.

Under this option, the Treasury creates currency up to a given cap mandated by Congress. Currency creation is capped anywhere in the range of $50 to $75 billion. When the dollar appreciates to a certain point against bilateral rates, the Treasury sells most or all of its created dollar holdings in the spot currency markets. Its counterparties are large banks involved in institutional currency trading. The Treasury then incrementally repurchases these dollars from the market over the immediate short-term. This procedure is most effective when action is taken against a single bilateral rate. Dollar sales apportioned among a handful of bilateral rates would be less effective. The Federal Reserve does not coordinate with the Treasury in sterilizing the dollar sales through open market sales of securities. Sterilization in this context implies neutralizing forex interventions and not currency creation per se. Open market sales would only aggravate an already tight monetary policy, since higher interest rates would have contributed to dollar appreciation in the first place. Hence if the Treasury is attempting to create some divergence between currency values and interest rates, then open market sales need to be avoided since they would only further tighten monetary policy and hamper efforts at depreciation.

The major convertible currencies freely tradable around the world today are the U.S. dollar, the euro, the pound, and the yen. Other convertible currencies include the Canadian and Australian dollar and the Swiss franc. Most of the world's other currencies are restricted from offshore trading and can only be converted for current account transactions. Many important Asian exporters restrict access to their currency, and offshore trading can only be conducted through derivatives contracts called non-deliverable forwards (NDFs). The Indian rupee, the Indonesian rupiah, the Malaysian ringgit, and the Vietnamese dong are all examples of partially inconvertible currencies. The Chinese yuan is becoming increasingly internationalized as China designates offshore trading hubs where the yuan floats.

To put the proposed operations in perspective, even if the Treasury sells $50 billion on a single day, such sales only amount to 1 percent of total trading volume in currency if trading volume hypothetically reaches $5 trillion on a given day. Currency markets are the largest and most liquid in the world. Exactly how effective these operations would be is highly uncertain. But these operations are made more effective if the Treasury is authorized to renew its operations hourly over a five-day operating period. In this scenario, the Treasury sells its created dollars, for instance $50 billion, all at once on a given hour to the market. The Treasury repurchases dollars at ten-minute intervals during the hour. The Treasury then repeats this process at the beginning of the next hour with new dollar sales. Although the Treasury is authorized to only sell $50 billion in currency, it can effectively multiply that amount at least fivefold during the course of a business day. If total trading volume peaks at $5 trillion on a given day, and the Treasury renews its operations five times during the course of the day, then the Treasury cumulatively sells $250 billion that day. Treasury dollar sales are 5 percent of trading volume for the day. If the Treasury repeats these actions during the next four days, then it cumulatively sells $1 trillion. For all five days, it sells cumulatively $1.25 trillion. These sales could very well intensify total trading volume, but if trading volume hovers at around $5 trillion each day, then cumulative dollar sales consume 5 percent of end-of-week trading volume. If the Treasury sells $50 billion seven times a day for five days, then its operations reach 7 percent of end-of-week trading.

One aspect of these spot trades is that the Treasury can conceivably renew them into the future, barring other restrictions, but it should be extremely cautious in doing so. These operations work best when understood as an isolated effort to force necessary adjustments. If due to interest rate differentials and other data investors are piling into dollars, the Treasury can in a sense attempt to break the back of dollar appreciation by alerting and even shocking the market. On a designated week, the Treasury floods the market with dollars and then gradually resells its foreign exchange. The lurking possibility that the Treasury might renew its dollar sales should destabilize market expectations regarding the future value of the dollar and influence investors into reducing their dollar holdings. A relatively brief operating period gives some leeway for the Treasury to renew sales once and perhaps twice. The sooner the Treasury compels an offloading of the dollar in financial markets, the sooner it can discontinue the operations. A short operating period ensures the rapid restoration of monetary normalcy.

The repurchase of dollars neutralizes the initial sales of created currency. In this respect, these operations function as an outflow/inflow device. If the Treasury regularly renews its sales at the beginning of a new operating period, then the money supply expands to the extent of the sales over the long-term. But to reiterate, the perpetual renewal of these operations must be avoided. The money-stock increases to the extent of the dollar sales because the dollars are forwarded to the financial accounts of the Treasury's counterparties. However, created currency held by the Treasury in its own reserve does not represent a net monetary increase because official reserves are not computed as part of the money-stock. The Treasury sends currency from its reserve to a broker's account only for a pending transaction. Currency sales represent a drastic step taken under challenging scenarios. If the goal is to combat dollar appreciation, then monetary policy is already probably restrictive, with deflation outweighing inflation as a public concern.

Relying on pure spot trading poses problems. First, the Treasury incurs exchange rate risk. If the dollar strengthens instead of weakens, then the Treasury sustains a loss in its dollar holdings when it repurchases dollars with foreign exchange. So if the Treasury fails in its attempt to combat dollar appreciation, then it also loses money when it repurchases dollars. Dollar repurchases may have to be partially funded through other means in order to repurchase the extra dollars at a higher exchange rate. The Treasury and the Federal Reserve hold tens of billions of euros and yen, a large portion of which are invested in foreign securities. The returns from these investments should be used to fund extra dollar repurchases in the event of continued dollar appreciation. A part of the Fed's profits from its bond portfolio can also be allocated to such a fund. On the other hand, if the dollar does in fact weaken because of the initial sales, then the Fed earns a slight profit when it repurchases dollars. These profits can be distributed into the fund to be used later if additional cash is needed for dollar repurchases.

A second problem with pure spot trading is that spot trades are generally settled within two business days. The Treasury must deal with the administrative hassles of physically delivering dollars to its counterparties, accepting foreign exchange, and then delivering foreign exchange. Dollars are physically created once, assuming repurchases are made.

Given these complications, a second option uses structured spot trading agreements (SSTAs). SSTAs are a blend of spot trades and swaps that do not entail forward delivery. Like the spot trades, the Treasury enters into SSTAs with banks involved in institutional forex trading. SSTAs are therefore not regulated futures contracts bought and sold on formal exchanges like the Chicago Mercantile Exchange. SSTAs are organized identically to the operations based on pure spot trades. The Treasury sells its dollars all at once at the beginning of the hour, and then it incrementally repurchases them. But with SSTAs, the Treasury repurchases dollars at the original spot rate to avoid exchange rate risk. To make the SSTAs, or "special swaps," financially remunerative to the banks, the Treasury pays out a small margin, only around .05 percent interest, per contract. Physical cash is not created, and no settlement occurs. The transactions are electronic and balance out by the end of the hour, when the Treasury again holds the same amount in dollars. Interest payments can be funded through the earnings of the Federal Reserve.

Using created currency for the ESF, whether through pure spot trades or SSTAs, is subject to certain qualifications. First, multilateral cooperation among central banks works to most effectively adjust exchange rates. The Plaza Accord triggered depreciation of the dollar because currency traders knew that the G-5 was united in its commitment to driving down the value of the dollar. The agreement of Japan and Germany to expand their fiscal policies at the Louvre conference further demonstrated the multilateral commitment to keeping the dollar from falling further and to helping the major currencies stay at their current rates. Unilateral dollar sales, on the other hand, might only trigger reciprocal measures and even start a trade war. If the Treasury were to target a single exchange rate through $25 billion in dollar sales, then the other nation's monetary authority could create currency and purchase $25 billion, thereby neutralizing the effect of the sales. The end result could be turmoil in the currency markets, which might motivate investors into unloading dollars. But in operational terms central banks would easily reciprocate the Treasury's actions by creating and selling their own currency.

A multilateral framework is necessary not only to more effectively induce dollar depreciation but also because a chaotic selloff of the dollar during a currency war would only hurt business confidence. If the private sector knows that nations are coordinating their policies towards the dollar, on the other hand, then business expectations remain stable, and forex operations based on currency creation reinforce downward pressure on the dollar.

By the same token, bilateral cooperation is essential when managing dollar rates against inconvertible currencies. In these scenarios, the Treasury works with a counterpart central bank to use dollar sales to push up the value of the other nation's currency in its onshore market. These operations do not entail conventional bilateral swaps between the Treasury and the foreign central bank, since the goal is not to infuse the central bank with dollar liquidity. The Treasury instead receives authorization from the foreign central bank to sell dollars to private banks in the onshore market for the purpose of strengthening the local currency against the dollar. Whether such operations can boost a weak Asian or Latin American currency is questionable. These operations serve as no panacea when other factors affect a currency's value.

But the Treasury might be able to implement "parallel swaps" to facilitate its operations involving inconvertible currencies. The Treasury, through its broker, sells dollars for local currency in the onshore market to a broker of the foreign central bank. The brokers transfer the currency they purchased to their respective monetary authorities per commission, with dollars going to the foreign central bank and local currency going to the Treasury. The Treasury then swaps back the local currency for dollars from the foreign central bank outside, or "parallel" to, the market. The Treasury and the foreign central bank repeat these actions via their intermediaries to test market reaction and see if the dollar can be pushed down.

Markets are highly sensitive not only to releases of new data but to the statements of officials and diplomatic announcements. Currency creation in the context of the forex markets does not depart from these norms and instead only serves as an additional instrument available to monetary authorities. But the Treasury would not necessarily be precluded from using a broker to anonymously enter the market if the need arose. This option still gives the Treasury authority to delegate a broker bank to intervene in the markets on its behalf, whether or not the interventions are carried out as part of an overt regime. And if the Treasury does anonymously sell a cumulative $250 billion in created dollars on a single day in only a few key currency markets, then investors would probably be able to infer what is transpiring, even if officials made no announcement.

The Treasury can conceivably use dollar creation to purchase currency of a national economy with significantly lower labor costs. Currency would therefore be created and swapped for foreign exchange in order to target labor cost differentials. But these operations are not realistic. First of all, most of the currencies of such export economies are not freely tradable in world markets. In any event, the sustainability of such a policy must be put into question, not only on economic grounds but on political ones as well. Such a regime would have to be upheld on a near permanent basis. The money supply would expand to the extent of dollar creation over the long-term. And as noted above, the use of currency creation for such purposes might only succeed in igniting a trade war and a race to the bottom in currency pricing.

Currency creation in the context of forex operations should instead comport with multilateral initiatives that preserve the stability of financial markets and international trade. Currency creation cannot be intended as a weapon to be used against others but as a tool to assist nations in shaping a global realignment of currency prices. But even when serving only as an instrument in stopping currency appreciation, these operations can still succeed in fomenting economic impacts. Firms would be more incentivized to use a given national economy as an export or re-export base if they were confident of that government's commitment to stalling and overturning currency appreciation under designated conditions.

The use of a nation's currency as a reserve asset has been routinely equated with a position of prestige, but in a globalized economy this honor cannot be taken too far. The U.S. assumed a prestigious position within the Bretton Woods framework, since only the dollar remained linked to gold. But with renewed competition from overseas, this parity became too costly to defend. The dollar had to be devalued simply to boost the trade balance and bring down unemployment. The economic challenges facing the U.S. in 1971 might not in retrospect appear as compelling compared to the Great Depression or even the deep recession of the early 1980s. But they were important enough to moderate views towards the dollar's role as a reserve asset.

As an instrument of multilateral initiatives, these operations might still appear dangerous if only because of the threat of unleashing inflation. Even when forex operations were financed through the Treasury's operating fund, the Federal Reserve routinely sterilized the sale of dollars by selling Treasury securities in the open market. This option, on the other hand, not only forgoes sterilization but also relies on currency creation as an alternative to an appropriated fund. The uptick in inflation might fully negate any cost savings to the federal government. While these concerns cannot go ignored, forex operations would likely be implemented during a period of deflation and high interest rates in any event. At the very least, if somehow the dollar is soaring under conditions of persistent inflation, then currency creation for forex operations should probably not be contemplated.

The unique dynamics of the forex markets enable the Treasury to repurchase dollars through foreign exchange holdings that were in turn created by way of the initial dollar sales. This option relies especially on the time element, in that a far larger portion of dollars can be created and sold before their repurchase. This durational factor temporarily pushes down the value of the dollar, even when the Treasury restores the monetary status quo at the end of the operating period. None of this is meant to imply that these operations are alone able to drive gains in the trade balance. But exploiting technical aspects of fiat money allows the Treasury to prevent dollar appreciation from hurting the trade balance and GDP. Forex ops based on currency creation serve as an additional tool available to the federal government.

NINETEEN

Monetary Policy Outflow/Inflow

Outflow/inflow devices also apply to monetary policy. In 2006, Congress passed the Financial Services Regulatory Relief Act (FSRRA), which authorized the Federal Reserve to pay out interest on required reserves (IORR) and interest on excess reserves (IOER). The legislation went into effect in 2008 as the financial crisis hit markets. IOER essentially allowed the Fed to fund quantitative easing as member banks parked trillions of dollars in excess reserves at Reserve Banks. Even though the Fed paid out only .25 percent on IOER during the Great Recession and the recovery, excess reserves rose sharply from a baseline under $2 billion each year before FSRRA went into effect to $2.7 trillion by 2014.[1]

IOER hugely facilitates quantitative easing and potentially crowds out private sector lending. An outflow/inflow device offers a smaller-scale and more efficient alternative. Under this alternative, legislation authorizes the Treasury to create up to $50 billion to transfer to the Federal Reserve under designated conditions. If the Fed has exhausted its resources and cannot continue to purchase securities in a period of deflation and recession, then it issues a formal but undisclosed notice to the Treasury. In response, the Treasury transfers the currency to the Fed to fund open market purchases. Inflow is fulfilled simply by allowing the securities to mature. The Fed should not be required to sell securities equivalent in value to the created currency by a deadline because this would impede economic recovery.

Giving the Treasury authorization to help fund Fed operations is similar to the fiduciary currency provision of the Thomas Amendment. Under the Thomas Amendment, Congress sanctioned the Treasury in issuing $3 billion in fiduciary currency through bond purchases if the Fed failed to pump an equivalent amount into circulation. But in this case, the Treasury only transfers currency to the Fed upon the Fed's normal notice.

Nor is the Treasury authorized to purchase bonds using the created currency if the Fed forgoes making a request with the Treasury.

Central banks around the world pay out IOER. Repealing FSRRA in part or full is not totally necessary in normalizing monetary policy. Fed officials obviously recognize the implications of allowing member banks to rack up excess reserves in the System. But if Fed officials lower the IOER rate during mild inflation and rising nominal interest rates, this might set off a flood of deposit withdrawals and threaten the Fed's ability to accommodate member banks, depending on how much currency the Fed had on-hand. This situation could also occur if the Fed simply maintained its IOER rate in the face of rising nominal interest rates. The Fed could be forced to sell securities to come up with the money. IOER complicates the policy framework of the Federal Reserve. An outflow/inflow device simplifies it and ensures currency creation only in the depths of a recession.

NOTE

1. Federal Reserve Bank of St. Louis, "Excess Reserves of Depository Institutions," updated July 2017, Federal Reserve Economic Data (FRED), https://fred.stlouisfed.org/series/EXCSRESNS.

TWENTY

Market Stability

EDAS I (or I-A), II, and IV are intended to boost capital equipment. EDAS III and CNF provide shorter-term liquidity. All of these options are intended to incentivize NPF. Firms planning to build NPF are only able to apply for one of these options. EDAS I accounts are the most sought after, since they serve as unilateral transfers, followed by EDAS IV accounts, which are conditional subsidies. Firms most likely apply for EDAS II and III accounts and enroll in NPFCN only after EDAS I and IV accounts are used up. Once firms apply for a version of EDAS or NPFCN, they are precluded from shifting to a different version of EDAS after cap space has opened back up.

Industrial policy could be organized differently by offering packages to firms, such as EDAS I-III/CNF, EDAS II-III/CNF, and EDAS III-IV/CNF. In this case, a firm selecting a designated package accesses longer-term liquidity, whether in the form of EDAS I, II, or IV, as well as shorter-term credit-like instruments EDAS III and CNF. But basing industrial policy upon these packages causes duplication in money flows when correlated to NPF. EDAS III accounts and CNF credits would be added on top of EDAS I, II, and IV accounts for corresponding increments of NPF, meaning that monetary expansion could outpace real net investment. Firms should therefore only be eligible for a single option. This restriction keeps monetary expansion in line with real growth. EDAS I and IV accounts will be the first to be used up. If firms are still sufficiently incentivized to build NPF by accessing EDAS II, III, and CNF, then additional monetary expansion will fund real growth. If these latter accounts and credits are not sufficient in incentivizing NPF, then payments are limited to EDAS I and IV.

The potential dangers of these options cannot be ignored. The first option, EDAS I, makes use of subsidies. Government creates currency in advance of sterilization to streamline the payments process. While the advantages of fiat money in this context may appear modest, the risk of breeding monetary turmoil is also low. In the same vein, EDAS IV can only be realistically funded through gold instead of pure currency creation. On the other hand, the use of created currency without sterilization from taxable revenue for EDAS II–III, the ESF, and CNF pushes the fiscal advantages of fiat money a step further but also leads to added risks. The rationale for implementing EDAS II–III, ESF, or CNF (and EDAS IV for that matter) is to implement economic policy on a shoestring budget, so to speak, meaning that economic impacts can be generated at no or little fiscal cost. But the quandary of whether reducing fiscal costs is worth the risk in monetary turmoil will never go away.

Creating currency without sterilization from taxable revenue poses serious risks of fueling unintended consequences. Rules act as safeguards, but rules do not erase the risk of these initiatives. The assumption that following a given rule necessarily eliminates the threat of an unwanted outcome can indeed be a grave error. The risk of currency creation applies especially to the ESF, where the monetary authority, the Treasury in this case, has greater discretionary control for when and how much created currency to use for market operations. While EDAS II–III, the ESF, and CNF are set up as outflow/inflow devices, EDAS II–III exist as contraptions in the same way as EDAS I and IV, organized entirely through preconceived procedures. As for the ESF, the Treasury's actions are still constrained by rules for the type and duration of transactions into which it can enter using created currency, but otherwise the Treasury determines when and how much currency to use. CNF is generally rules-based but is allowed some room for discretion for whether to resell bills and notes to the market or let them mature.

All of these options should be implemented at a miniature level and then only steadily built up if they work. In the implementing legislation, Congress should grant executive branch departments the authority to build up these programs within stable limits and subject to both an initial and an ultimate cap. For instance, Congress provides for a $500 million initial cap each for EDAS I and IV and a $250 million cap each for EDAS II–III and CNF. The original implementing legislation should be specific enough so that the executive branch departments do not need to write their own regulations. EDAS and CNF are not intended as discretionary agencies. The legislation only leaves it to the discretion of the executive branch department to decide the number of accounts or enrollment spaces to offer to eligible firms subject to the initial and ultimate caps.

Executive branch departments can also at their discretion request Congress to impose new intermediate caps if the initial caps are reached. Congress can only impose new intermediate caps through further legislation. Congress is also authorized to raise the intermediate caps on its own initiative. Any time Congress seeks to impose new intermediate caps, whether at the request of executive branch officials or on its own initiative, it must hear the testimony and receive the reports of executive branch and Federal Reserve officials on the matter. Congress must ensure that EDAS and CNF expand only within stable limits by successively imposing intermediate caps until the ultimate cap is reached. Original implementing legislation should also require the executive branch departments to report to Congress at least once a year on the threat that these programs may cause inflation and the crowding out of private lending.

Congress must write the ultimate caps into the original legislation. EDAS I is ultimately capped at $50 billion, EDAS II at $10 billion, EDAS III at $3 billion, EDAS IV at $30 billion, and CNF at $10 billion, with a total cap of just a little over $100 billion. This cap would not be reached until after several years. Just as important, at least some and perhaps all of the programs might never reach their ultimate caps. There is the possibility that Congress may eventually write new ultimate caps into legislation or increase accounts to adjust for inflation. Because this scenario cannot be totally avoided, the original legislation should still require that Congress hear the testimony and receive the reports of executive branch and Federal Reserve officials before voting on such legislation.

Congress stabilizes expansion in the Treasury's ESF through similar procedures. In the original legislation, Congress imposes a $5 billion initial cap for created currency that the Treasury uses to test specified swaps and other forex interventions and a $50 billion ultimate cap. The Treasury requests Congress for higher intermediate caps after testing these operations. As with EDAS and CNF, Congress must by law hold hearings with executive branch and Federal Reserve officials on whether these intermediate caps can be safely raised, as well as receive reports on the matter.

Giving Congress the responsibility to authorize increases in the intermediate caps, whether for EDAS or ESF, provides for direct legislative accountability. Raising the intermediate caps does not have to be linear, meaning that the accounts do not have to be raised at the same rate year to year. Congress can double, triple, or even quadruple the number of accounts the next year if the program is running smoothly and is not causing major disturbances. However, if congressional authorization for the intermediate caps proves unworkable, Congress can delegate this responsibility to a committee of Executive Branch and Federal Reserve officials to vote on the caps in its place. This delegation of authority comes with the caveat that Congress can always pass supervening legislation to cap or even phase out the program. But this option is just one step above giving full discretion to executive authorities for raising the intermediate caps. The dilemma is reconciling democratic government with efficient policy options. At one extreme, congressional authorization may be too cumbersome or even unnecessary, while at the opposite extreme, total departmental discretion gives the Executive Branch too free a hand. A committee formed for the specific purpose of supervising intermediate cap hikes could work as a middle ground.

At the same time, an EDAS I-B, or temporary EDAS used for counter-recessionary purposes, preemptively registers up to 10,000 firms with plant equipment staffed by at least 100 production workers. EDAS I-B accounts are much smaller, at only $5 million each, and they are also non-renewable. However, if recession is protracted, Congress can pass emergency legislation renewing the accounts. A 10,000 firm EDAS I-B with accounts of $5 million each comes to a total maximum cost of $50 billion, which may be substantially less than stimulus bills for public works projects. EDAS I-B also operates more efficiently because the system has already enrolled eligible firms. Congress only votes to temporarily activate the accounts as the economy slips into recession. Member firms are then able to direct forward payments during the window of time when accounts are activated. After Congress again votes to suspend the accounts, member firms can no longer direct forward payments, regardless of how much money is left in their accounts. Member firms would probably be incentivized to use up their accounts as quickly as possible before suspension. These payments would hopefully provide a timely jolt to the economy. Firms that are registered with any other version of EDAS or CNF are prohibited from joining EDAS I-B.

In spite of these institutional safeguards, the crowding out of corporate bonds and bank loans is still an admitted danger implicit in EDAS II, III, and CNF. But a few factors hopefully ameliorate this danger. First, the accounts and credits operate to incentivize NPF that would otherwise not be built in the U.S. Second, any crowding out is confined to designated increments of NPF. Once EDAS II, III, and CNF stop expanding, any crowding out effect, if it ever existed at all (which is unlikely), ceases to exist. At the same time, EDAS I and IV could very well strengthen the demand for bank loans as eligible firms expand their private credit lines as a source of short-term liquidity for their new investments.

If executive branch departments and Congress cooperate to steadily build up EDAS, CNF, and ESF, then these programs will impact the larger economy. The automatic sterilizer under EDAS I-A stabilizes growth in the money-stock, but it does not necessarily contain inflationary pressures. The transmission of currency into industrial sectors can set off a wage and price rise for any number of reasons, whether because of market expectations, the bidding up of prices for productive resources, or a rise in labor costs. An overheating economy unleashes inflation and rising nominal interest rates. The extent to which the transmission of created currency is responsible for accelerating these conditions depends on the scale of EDAS I. If EDAS I is built for scale and entails an aggregate of created currency worth $50 billion per year, then the economic impacts it generates in terms of fixed investment may be robust, with inevitable consequences for inflation.

EDAS I is not alone in its ability to unleash inflationary pressures. The most inflationary of all versions of EDAS is EDAS II, which potentially translates into a $10 billion addition to the money supply. But even EDAS II is correlated to NPF. If firms shut down their NPF, then they are no longer able to access their EDAS II accounts. EDAS IV may also be inflationary, even if EDAS IV accounts are non-renewable.

The Federal Reserve must stand positioned to safeguard against inflation through its normal policy tools. A moderately inflationary industrial policy and a tight monetary policy provide the best assurance for sustainable, low inflationary economic growth. Industrial policy stimulates real growth over the long-term, while monetary policy assumes its proper function of preserving price stability. A more dynamic and even inflationary industrial policy potentially relieves the central bank of the burden of attempting to meet targets for unemployment and GDP. In addition, while industrial policy is inherently rules-based, monetary policy remains discretionary. A mildly inflationary industrial policy and a central bank committed to price stability provide the most effective framework for maintaining market stability.

A moderately inflationary industrial policy can also be counterbalanced by tight fiscal policy. An industrial policy of scale negates deficit spending as a justification for stimulating the economy. Depending on its scale, EDAS I-A serves as a clear alternative to deficit spending through the fiscal advantage of directing payments in advance of the collection of tax revenue. EDAS II is similarly equipped to boost income before EDAS taxes are paid. While EDAS IV accounts are finite, Congress can still opportunely implement EDAS IV when it is balancing the budget, especially for the first time after a long period of deficits. EDAS III and CNF, along with EDAS II, do not compete with other programs for funding. A mildly inflationary industrial policy is entirely compatible with balanced budgets. Government can in fact more safely test the possibilities of inflationary unilateral payments and outflow/inflow devices when it is committed to fiscal responsibility.

Of course a major problem with EDAS I-A is that it adds to long-term costs, which might be considered inconsistent with the goal of deficit reduction. EDAS I-A is the ultimate option because it unconditionally supports industry with unilateral transfers. But due to budget realities it could be scaled back to a I-C version. Under EDAS I-C, firms are granted $20 million accounts per year for four years. Payments then cease at the end of four years, regardless of the amount in currency directed for forward payment on the part of member firms. Firms are then automatically registered with EDAS I-B in the event of a downturn. An EDAS I-B/I-C combination cannot permanently offset labor cost differentials, but it could be a sufficient inducement for reshoring plant facilities. EDAS I-C tentatively comes in the aggregate to $40 billion per year for 2,000 firms. I-B is larger at up to $50 billion in total registration and incorporates the I-C firms. An EDAS I-B/I-C combination could also be useful when implemented in conjunction with an effort to balance the budget.

New industrial and foreign exchange policies are foremost intended to be sustainable over the long-term. Among other reasons, these policies are sustainable because they do not seek to upend the international trade framework. EDAS I–IV, CNF, and a resuscitated ESF comply with the WTO. The WTO expressly prohibits subsidies that are linked to exports or the purchase of domestic goods instead of imports. Competitively devaluing a currency through "currency retention schemes" qualifies as an export subsidy. Specific subsidies that are tied to individual firms or geographic regions may also be actionable in trade court. But non-specific subsidies are not actionable, even if the subsidies cause serious prejudice to another nation.[1]

The system of payments set up under EDAS I–IV and CNF count as subsidies under the WTO's definition, which includes unilateral transfers and loans. But EDAS and CNF payments do not fall under the WTO's definitions for prohibited or specific subsidies. EDAS and CNF are in no way tied to exports, and they do not mandate that eligible firms purchase domestic goods instead of imports for their business expenditures. An earlier supply chain provision was hypothecated for EDAS I in which eligible firms would be required to exclusively purchase materials from domestic firms. This hypothetical proposal was deemed unreasonable on economic grounds, and it would also violate the WTO. EDAS and CNF cannot also be thought of as specific subsidies because they are broad-based. They are not linked to individual firms or specified sectors. Enrollment in these programs is only conditioned on the building of NPF.

The ESF's use of currency creation for specialized swaps also does not fall under the WTO's definition of an export subsidy. The ESF avoids permanently retaining currency over the long-term in the same way as competitive devaluation. The ESF only responds to dollar appreciation and smooth over dollar exchange rates. Because the ESF creates currency with which to purchase foreign exchange, it must eventually resell the foreign exchange, either through spot sales or more specialized swaps, in order to offset the earlier dollar infusion. The ESF does not permanently retain foreign exchange. In any event, the Treasury must work constructively with other nations in maintaining stable exchange rates. The Treasury would never act unilaterally to any major extent and alienate itself with counterpart institutions in other countries.

New monetary-industrial and foreign exchange policies avoid protectionism, coordinate with the central bank in maintaining market stability, and are compatible with balanced budgets. These policies aim to generate solid economic expansion through an efficient but stable mechanism. They are part of the historical pattern of an increasingly managed money supply. The U.S. Banks, the National Banking System, the Treasury, and the Federal Reserve System greatly affected money and banking during four different centuries. These structures unavoidably caused major changes in the banking sector. Most of the options making use of fiat money reach beyond monetary policy and central banking in generating economic change. But unlike their predecessors, EDAS I–IV, CNF, and the ESF do not attempt to build what might be called monuments, or governmental structures entirely altering practices within the private sector. No behemoth is being imposed upon American business. These options should instead be thought of as possible tools that, if prudence allows, can be expanded with time. Each of the options shares a flexible design that permits free adaptability on the part of private firms. Most importantly, the power of decision-making rests with the market, and those who decide hold the key to their future.

NOTE

1. World Trade Organization, "Uruguay Round Agreement: Agreement on Subsidies and Countervailing Measures," WTO, https://www.wto.org/english/docs_e/legal_e/24-scm_01_e.htm, accessed August 2017.

Glossary

Corporate Note Facility (CNF)*	Purchases short-term notes and bills of firms enrolled in NPFCN.
Council of Economic Advisers (CEA)	Created under Employment Act of 1946 to institutionalize White House staff economists.
Economic Development Account System (EDAS) I-A*	Unilateral payments on behalf of eligible firms. Renewable accounts.
EDAS I-B*	Temporary unilateral payments for countercyclical purposes. Not correlated to NPF.
EDAS I-C*	Unilateral payments tied to accounts that are nonrenewable after four years. Firms subsequently registered in I-B.
EDAS II*	Eligible firms repay forward payments through federal taxes. Renewable accounts.
EDAS III*	Eligible firms voluntarily rebalance accounts. Renewable accounts.
EDAS IV*	Unilateral payments on behalf of eligible firms. Nonrenewable accounts. Firms repay if they shut down NPF.
Exchange Stabilization Fund (ESF)*	Managed by Treasury Department to fund foreign exchange operations and loans to developing nations. Can be equipped with outflow/inflow device.
Federal Open Market Committee (FOMC)	Responsible for Federal Reserve open market operations. Made up of all seven members of the Board of Governors and five Reserve Bank presidents.
Foreign Direct Investment (FDI)	Investment reflecting a company's ownership or control over business assets in a foreign country. Distinguishable from portfolio investment in securities.

Gold Repurchase Commitment (GRC)*	Treasury Department's guarantee to repurchase gold in the commodity markets if a gold-funded outflow/inflow device is shut down or scaled back.
Gross Domestic Product (GDP)	Gross product of goods and services within national borders. Combined total of household consumption, business expenditures, government expenditures, and net exports.
Gross National Product (GNP)	Gross product of goods and services of a nation's residents and companies. Combined total of household consumption, business expenditures, government expenditures, and net exports, including goods and services produced by nation's residents and companies abroad and excluding goods and services produced by foreign residents and companies within national borders.
Interest on Excess Reserves (IOER)	Interest payable to member banks on their excess reserves held at Federal Reserve Banks.
Interest on Required Reserves (IORR)	Interest payable to member banks on their required reserves held at Federal Reserve Banks.
M1	Narrow definition of the money supply. Components are currency in circulation (excluding the Federal Reserve, the Treasury Department, and depository institutions), demand deposits, other checkable deposits (OCDs), and traveler's checks issued by non-banks.
M2	Broader definition of the money supply. Components are M1, savings deposits, time deposits under $100,000, and shares in retail money market mutual funds.
Monetary Base	Narrowest definition of the money supply. Components are currency in circulation (excluding the Federal Reserve and the Treasury Department but including bank vault cash) and bank reserves held at Federal Reserve Banks.

Negotiable Order of Withdrawal (NOW)	Interest bearing account counted as a type of OCD under M1. Withdrawals can be made on demand. Checks can be written out against NOW accounts.
New Plant Facilities (NPF)*	Net fixed investment. In Census Bureau terminology, buildings and other structures. Criterion for eligibility in most versions of EDAS.
New Plant Facility Credit Network (NPFCN)*	Eligible firm enrollment in order to access CNF.
North American Industry Classification System (NAICS)	Industry codes used for compiling and releasing U.S. economic statistics.
parallel swaps*	Funded through currency creation. Treasury Department and a foreign central bank swap currencies through bank intermediaries. Dollars ultimately rerouted to Treasury.
Open Market Investment Committee (OMIC)	First open market committee of Reserve Bank governors. Set up in 1923 with initially five seats.
Open Market Policy Conference (OMPC)	Direct precursor to FOMC. Replaced OMIC in 1930 and made up of all twelve Reserve Bank governors.
outflow/inflow device*	Institutional means for creating relatively small sums of currency under stable conditions.
Reconstruction Finance Corporation (RFC)	Charged with purchasing newly mined or foreign gold in 1933 in order to raise gold prices. Also responsible for bailouts to distressed financial institutions during the Great Depression.
Structured Spot Trading Agreements (SSTAs)*	Funded through currency creation. Treasury Department pays out interest on short-term swaps with financial institutions in institutional forex market.

*In reference to policy options in part II of the text.

Bibliography

Abrams, Burton A. and James L. Butkiewicz. "The Political Business Cycle: New Evidence from the Nixon Tapes." *Journal of Money, Credit, and Banking* 44, no. 2–3 (2012): 385–399.

Agger, E.E. "The Development of an Open Market for Commercial Paper." *The Annals of the American Academy for Political and Social Science* 99 (1922): 209–217.

Ailes, Milton E. "National Banking System and Federal Bond Issues." *The Annals of the American Academy of Political and Social Science* 36, no. 3 (1910): 114–128.

Aldrich, Nelson W. *Suggested Plan for Monetary Legislation: Submitted to the National Monetary Commission, Revised Edition*. Washington, D.C.: National Monetary Commission, 1911.

Allen, William H. "The Election of 1900." *The Annals of the American Academy of Political and Social Science* 17 (1901): 53–73.

American Delegates to the International Monetary Conference. *Report of the Commissioners on Behalf of the United States, and Journal of the Sessions of November 22, 1892, to December 17, 1892*. Washington, D.C.: Government Printing Office, 1893.

Andrew, A. Piatt. "The Treasury and the Banks Under Secretary Shaw." *The Quarterly Journal of Economics* 21, no. 4 (1907): 519–568.

———. "The United States Treasury and the Money Market. The Partial Responsibilities of Gage and Shaw for the Crisis of 1907." *American Economic Association Quarterly* 9, no. 1 (1908): 218–231.

Andrews, E. Benjamin. "The Monetary Conference of 1892." *Political Science Quarterly* 8, no. 2 (1893): 197–219.

Austin, O.P. "The Public Debt of the United States." *The North American Review* 175, no. 552 (1902): 701–720.

Bloomfield, Arthur I. "Operations of the American Exchange Stabilization Fund." *The Review of Economics and Statistics* 26, no. 2 (1944): 69–87.

Board of Governors. *Twenty-Second Annual Report of the Board of Governors of the Federal Reserve System: Covering Operations for the Year 1935*. Washington, D.C.: Government Printing Office, 1936.

———. *Twenty-Third Annual Report of the Board of Governors of the Federal Reserve System: Covering Operations for the Year 1936*. Washington, D.C.: Federal Reserve System, 1937.

———. *Twenty-Fourth Annual Report of the Board of Governors of the Federal Reserve System: Covering Operations for the Year 1937*. Washington, D.C.: Federal Reserve System, 1938.

———. *Twenty-Fifth Annual Report of the Board of Governors of the Federal Reserve System: Covering Operations for the Year 1938*. Washington, D.C.: Federal Reserve System, 1939.

———. *Thirty-Second Annual Report of the Board of Governors of the Federal Reserve System: Covering Operations for the Year 1945*. Washington, D.C.: Federal Reserve System, 1946.

———. *Thirty-Fourth Annual Report of the Board of Governors of the Federal Reserve System: Covering Operations for the Year 1947*. Washington, D.C.: Federal Reserve System, 1948.

———. *Thirty-Fifth Annual Report of the Board of Governors of the Federal Reserve System: Covering Operations for the Year 1948*. Washington, D.C.: Federal Reserve System, 1949.

———. *Thirty-Sixth Annual Report of the Board of Governors of the Federal Reserve System: Covering Operations for the Year 1949*. Washington, D.C.: Federal Reserve System, 1950.

———. *Forty-Second Annual Report of the Board of Governors of the Federal Reserve System: Covering Operations for the Year 1955*. Washington, D.C.: Federal Reserve System, 1956.

———. *Forty-Fifth Annual Report of the Board of Governors of the Federal Reserve System: Covering Operations for the Year 1958*. Washington, D.C.: Federal Reserve System, 1959.

———. *Forty-Ninth Annual Report of the Board of Governors of the Federal Reserve System: Covering Operations for the Year 1962*. Washington, D.C.: Federal Reserve System, 1963.

———. *Fiftieth Report of the Board of Governors of the Federal Reserve System: Covering Operations for the Year 1963*. Washington, D.C.: Federal Reserve System, 1964.

———. *Fifty-First Annual Report of the Board of Governors of the Federal Reserve System: Covering Operations for the Year 1964*. Washington, D.C.: Federal Reserve System, 1965.

———. *Fifty-Second Annual Report of the Board of Governors of the Federal Reserve System: Covering Operations for the Year 1965*. Washington, D.C.: Federal Reserve System, 1966.

———. *Fifty-Third Annual Report of the Board of Governors of the Federal Reserve System: Covering Operations for the Year 1966*. Washington, D.C.: Federal Reserve System, 1967.

———. *Fifty-Fourth Annual Report of the Board of Governors of the Federal Reserve System: Covering Operations for the Year 1967*. Washington, D.C.: Federal Reserve System, 1968.

———. *55th Annual Report: 1968*. Washington, D.C.: Federal Reserve System, 1969.

———. *62nd Annual Report: 1975*. Washington, D.C.: Federal Reserve System, 1976.

———. *66th Annual Report: 1979*. Washington, D.C: Federal Reserve System, 1980.

———. *68th Annual Report: 1981*. Washington, D.C.: Federal Reserve System, 1982.

Bordo, Michael D. "The Bretton Woods International Monetary System: A Historical Overview." In *A Retrospective on the Bretton Woods System: Lessons for International Monetary Reform*, ed. Michael D. Bordo and Barry Eichengreen, 3–108. Chicago: University of Chicago Press, 1993.

Branson, William H. "Trends in United States International Trade and Investment since World War II." In *The American Economy in Transition*, ed. Martin Feldstein, 183–257. Chicago: University of Chicago Press, 1980.

Bronson, S.A. *John Sherman: What He Has Said and Done, Being a History of the Life and Public Services of the Hon. John Sherman, Secretary of the Treasury of the United States*. Columbus, OH: H.W. Derby & Co., 1880.

Bryan, William J. *The First Battle: A Story of the Campaign of 1896*. Chicago: W.B. Conkey Co., 1896.

Burns, Arthur F. "The Quest for Full Employment and Economic Stability: 1960–1966." In *The Business Cycle in a Changing World*, ed. Arthur F. Burns, 254–85. New York: National Bureau of Economic Research, 1969.

———. "The Perils of Inflation." In *The Business Cycle in a Changing World*, ed. Arthur F. Burns, 286–302. New York: National Bureau of Economic Research, 1969.

Cagan, Philip. "High-Powered Money." In *Determinants and Effects of Changes in the Stock of Money*, 1875–1960, ed. Philip Cagan, 45–117. New York: NBER, 1965.

Calomiris, Charles and David Wheelock. "Was the Great Depression a Watershed for American Monetary Policy?" In *The Defining Moment: The Great Depression and the American Economy in the Twentieth Century*, ed. Michael D. Bordo, Claudia Goldin, and Eugene N. White, 23–66. Chicago: University of Chicago Press, 1998.

Catterall, Ralph C.H. "The Issues of the Second Bank of the United States." *Journal of Political Economy* 5, no. 4 (1897): 421–457.

Catteral, Ralph C.H. *The Second Bank of the United States*. Chicago: University of Chicago Press, 1903.

Cleveland, Grover. *The Public Papers of Grover Cleveland: Twenty-Second President of the United States, March 4, 1885 to March 4, 1889*. Washington, D.C.: Government Printing Office, 1889.

———. *Grover Cleveland: Addresses, State Papers, and Letters*, ed. Albert Ellery Bergh. New York: The Sun Dial Classics Co., 1909.

Conant, Charles A. "Fluctuations in the Secured Circulation of the National Banks and Their Relations to the Prices and Investment Values of Bonds." *Publications of the American Statistical Association* 3, no. 24 (1893): 471–476.

Cordell, William H. and Kathryn Coe Cordell. "Unions among the Unemployed." *The North American Review* 240, no. 3 (1935): 498–510.

Council of Economic Advisers. *Economic Report of the President*. Washington, D.C.: Government Printing Office, 1954.

———. *Economic Report of the President*. Washington, D.C.: Government Printing Office, 1958.

———. *Economic Report of the President*. Washington, D.C.: Government Printing Office, 1959.

———. *Economic Report of the President*. Washington, D.C.: Government Printing Office, 1960.

———. *Economic Report of the President of the United States: Together with the Annual Report of the Council of Economic Advisers*. Washington, D.C.: Government Printing Office, 1962.

———. *Economic Report of the President of the United States: Together with the Annual Report of the Council of Economic Advisers*. Washington, D.C.: Government Printing Office, 1963.

———. *Economic Report of the President: Together with the Annual Report of the Council of Economic Advisers*. Washington, D.C.: Government Printing Office, 1964.

———. *Economic Report of the President: Together with the Annual Report of the Council of Economic Advisers*. Washington, D.C.: Government Printing Office, 1965.

———. *Economic Report of the President: Together with the Annual Report of the Council of Economic Advisers*. Washington, D.C.: Government Printing Office, 1966.

———. *Economic Report of the President: Together with the Annual Report of the Council of Economic Advisers*. Washington, D.C.: Government Printing Office, 1968.

———. *Economic Report of the President: Together with the Annual Report of the Council of Economic Advisers*. Washington, D.C.: Government Printing Office, 1969.

———. *Economic Report of the President: Together with the Annual Report of the Council of Economic Advisers*. Washington, D.C.: Government Printing Office, 1970.

———. *Economic Report of the President: Together with the Annual Report of the Council of Economic Advisers*. Washington, D.C.: Government Printing Office, 1972.

———. *Economic Report of the President: Together with the Annual Report of the Council of Economic Advisers*. Washington, D.C.: Government Printing Office, 1975.

Coxey, Jacob S. *The Coxey Plan: Medium of Exchange Without Cost, Public Bonds Without Interest, Common Carriers Without Private Profit*. Massilon, OH: Jacob. S. Coxey, 1914.

Dam, Kenneth W. "From the Gold Clause Cases to the Gold Commission: A Half Century of American Monetary Law." *University of Chicago Law Review* 504, no. 50 (1983): 504–532.

David, Paul A. "The Growth of Real Product in the United States Before 1840: New Evidence, Controlled Conjectures." *Journal of Economic History* 27, no. 2 (1967): 151–197.

De Long, J. Bradford. "Keynesianism, Pennsylvania Avenue Style: Some Economic Consequences of the Employment Act of 1946." *Journal of Economic Perspectives* 10, no. 3 (1996): 41–53.

———. "America's Peacetime Inflation: The 1970s." In *Reducing Inflation: Motivation and Strategy*, ed. Christina D. Romer and David H. Romer, 247–80. Chicago: University of Chicago Press, 1997.

———. "Fiscal Policy in the Shadow of the Great Depression." In *The Defining Moment: The Great Depression and the American Economy in the Twentieth Century*, ed. Michael D. Bordo, Claudia Goldin, and Eugene N. White, 67–86. Chicago: University of Chicago Press, 1998.

Dewey, Davis Rich. *Financial History of the United States*. Sixth Edition. New York: Longmans, Green and Co., 1918.

Dutton, John. "The Bank of England and the Rules of the Game under the International Gold Standard: New Evidence." In *A Retrospective of the Classical Gold Standard, 1821–1931*, ed. Michael D. Bordo and Anna J. Schwartz, 173–202. Chicago: University of Chicago Press, 1984.

Eichengreen, Barry. "International Policy Coordination in Historical Perspective: A View from the Interwar Years." In *International Economic Policy Coordination*, ed. William H. Buiter and Richard C. Marston, 139–83. Cambridge: Cambridge University Press, 1985.

Eichengreen, Barry and Peter M. Garber. "Before the Accord: U.S. Monetary-Financial Policy, 1945–51." In *Financial Markets and Financial Crises*, ed. R. Glenn Hubbard, 175–206. Chicago: University of Chicago Press, 1991.

Federal Reserve Act: As Amended to December 24, 1919. New York: National Bank of Commerce in New York, 1920.

Federal Reserve Board. *Sixth Annual Report of the Federal Reserve Board: Covering Operations for the Year 1919*. Washington, D.C.: Government Printing Office, 1920.

———. *Seventh Annual Report of the Federal Reserve Board: Covering Operations for the Year 1920*. Washington, D.C.: Government Printing Office, 1921.

———. *Eighth Annual Report of the Federal Reserve Board: Covering Operations for the Year 1921*. Washington, D.C.: Government Printing Office, 1922.

———. *Ninth Annual Report of the Federal Reserve Board: Covering Operations for the Year 1922*. Washington, D.C.: Government Printing Office, 1923.

———. *Tenth Annual Report of the Federal Reserve Board: Covering Operations for the Year 1923*. Washington, D.C.: Government Printing Office, 1924.

———. *Eleventh Annual Report of the Federal Reserve Board: Covering Operations for the Year 1924*. Washington, D.C.: Government Printing Office, 1925.

———. *Fourteenth Annual Report of the Federal Reserve Board: Covering Operations for the Year 1927*. Washington, D.C.: Government Printing Office, 1928.

———. *Fifteenth Annual Report of the Federal Reserve Board: Covering Operations for the Year 1928*. Washington, D.C.: Government Printing Office, 1929.

———. *Seventeenth Annual Report of the Federal Reserve Board: Covering Operations for the Year 1930*. Washington, D.C.: Government Printing Office, 1931.

———. *Eighteenth Annual Report of the Federal Reserve Board: Covering Operations for the Year 1931*. Washington, D.C.: Government Printing Office, 1932.

———. *Nineteenth Annual Report of the Federal Reserve Board: Covering Operations for the Year 1932*. Washington, D.C.: Government Printing Office, 1933.

———. *Twentieth Annual Report of the Federal Reserve Board: Covering Operations for the Year 1933*. Washington, D.C.: Government Printing Office, 1934.

———. *Twenty-First Annual Report of the Federal Reserve Board: Covering Operations for the Year 1934*. Washington, D.C.: Government Printing Office, 1935.

Firestone, John M. "The 1954–1958 Cycle." In *Federal Receipts and Expenditures During Business Cycles, 1879–1958*, ed. John M. Firestone, 55–59. Princeton: Princeton University Press, 1960.

Frankel, Jeffrey A. "International Capital Flows and Domestic Economic Policies." In *The United States in the World Economy*, ed. Martin Feldstein, 559–658. Chicago: University of Chicago Press, 1988.

———. "Exchange Rate Policy." In *American Economic Policy in the 1980s*, ed. Martin Feldstein, 293–366. Chicago: University of Chicago Press, 1994.

Frenkel, Jacob A. "United States Inflation and the Dollar." In *Inflation: Causes and Effects*, ed. Robert E. Hall, 189–210. Chicago: University of Chicago Press, 1982.

Gallman, Robert E. "Gross National Product in the United States, 1834–1909." In *Output, Employment, and Productivity in the United States after 1800*, ed. Dorothy S. Brady, 1–90. New York: National Bureau of Economic Research, 1966.

Garber, Peter M. "The Collapse of the Bretton Woods Fixed Exchange Rate System." In *A Retrospective on the Bretton Woods System: Lessons for International Monetary Reform*, ed. Michael D. Bordo and Barry Eichengreen, 461–94. Chicago: University of Chicago Press, 1993.

Gavin, Francis J. *Gold, Dollars & Power: The Politics of International Monetary Relations, 1958–1971*. Chapel Hill: University of North Carolina Press, 2004.

Gidney, R.M. "Relations of Reserve Banks to Member Banks and Inter-Relations of Federal Reserve Banks." *The Annals of the American Academy of Political and Social Science* 99 (1922): 87–95.

Groseclose, Elgin. *America's Money Machine: The Story of the Federal Reserve*. 1966. Reprint. Auburn, AL: Ludwig von Mises Institute, 2009.

Gurdon, Alexander. *John Tyler: President of the United States, Up to the Close of the Second Session of the Thirty Seventh Congress*. New York: Harper & Brothers, 1843.

Hamilton, Alexander. "On the Establishment of a Mint." In *The Works of Alexander Hamilton: Comprising His Correspondence, and His Political and Official Writings, Exclusive of the Federalist, Civil and Military*, vol. III, ed. John C. Hamilton, 149–88. New York: John F. Trow, 1850.

———. "National Bank." In *The Works of Alexander Hamilton: Comprising His Correspondence, and His Political and Official Writings, Exclusive of the Federalist, Civil and Military*, vol. III, ed. John C. Hamilton, 106–46. New York: John F. Trow, 1850.

Harrison, Benjamin. *The Public Papers and Addresses of Benjamin Harrison: Twenty-Third President of the United States, March 4, 1889 to March 4, 1893*. Washington, D.C.: Government Printing Office, 1893.

Hart, Albert Bushnell. *American Statesman: Salmon Portland Chase*. New York: Houghton, Mifflin, and Co., 1899.

Holdsworth, John Thom. "Lessons of State Banking before the Civil War." *Proceedings of the Academy of Political Science in the City of New York* 1, no. 2 (1911): 210–224.

Holland, Thomas E. "'Operation Twist' and the Movement of Interest Rates and Related Economic Time Series." *International Economic Review* 10, no. 3 (1969): 260–265.

Hoover, Herbert. *The Memoirs of Herbert Hoover: The Great Depression, 1929–1941*. New York: The Macmillan Company, 1952.

Howard, Oliver Otis, Thomas Byrnes, and Alvah H. Doty. "The Menace of 'Coxeyism.'" *The North American Review* 158, no. 451 (1894): 687–705.

Huffman, Wallace E. and James R. Lothian. "The Gold Standard and the Transmission of Business Cycles, 1833–1932." In *A Retrospective on the Classical Gold Standard: 1821–1931*, ed. Michael D. Bordo and Anna J. Schwartz, 455–512. Chicago: University of Chicago Press, 1984.

Irwin, Douglas A. "The Nixon Shock after Forty Years: The Import Surcharge Revisited." *World Trade Review* 12, no. 1 (2013): 29–56.

Johnson, Emory R., T.W. Van Metre, G.G. Huebner, and D.S. Hanchett. *History of Domestic and Foreign Commerce of the United States*. Washington, D.C.: Carnegie Institution, 1915.

Juglar, Clement. *A Brief History of Panics and Their Periodical Occurrence in the United States*. New York: G.P. Putnam's Sons, 1916.

Kemmerer, E. W. "Causes and Progress of Inflation." *Proceedings of the Academy of Political Science in the City of New York* 9, no. 1 (1920): 1–15.

———. *Gold and the Gold Standard: The Story of Gold Money Past, Present, and Future*. New York: McGraw Hill Co., 1944.

Kerr, Winfield S. *John Sherman: His Life and Public Service*, vol. II. Akron, OH: Werner Co., 1907.

Knox, John J. *A History of Banking in the United States*. New York: Bradford Rhodes & Co., 1900.

Kuznets, Simon. "Long-Term Changes, 1869–1938." In *National Income: A Summary of Findings*, ed. Simon Kuznets, 31–72. New York: National Bureau of Economic Research, 1946.

Laughlin, J. Laurence. "The 'Baltimore Plan' of Bank-Issues." *Journal of Political Economy* 3, no. 1 (1894): 101–105.

———. "The Aldrich-Vreeland Act." *Journal of Political Economy* 16, no. 8 (1908): 489–513.

Leech, Edward O. "Silver Legislation and Its Results." *North American Review* 157, no. 440 (1893): 42–51.

Levin, Andrew and John B. Taylor. "Falling Behind the Curve: A Positive Analysis of Stop-Start Monetary Policies and the Great Inflation." In *The Great Inflation: The Rebirth of Modern Central Banking*, ed. Michael D. Bordo and Athanasios Orphanides, 217–44. Chicago: University of Chicago Press, 2013.

McCracken, Paul W. "Economic Policy in the Nixon Years." *Presidential Studies Quarterly* 26, no. 1 (1996): 165–177.

Meade, Edward S. "The Deposit-Reserve System of the National-Bank Law." *Journal of Political Economy* 6, no. 2 (1898): 209–224.

———. "The Recent Production of Silver and Its Probable Future." *Annals of the American Academy of Political and Social Science* 14 (1899): 43–59.

Miller, A.C. "Federal Reserve Policy." *The American Economic Review* 11, no. 2 (1921): 177–206.

Mitchell, Wesley C. "The Suspension of Specie Payments, December 1861." *Journal of Political Economy* 7, no. 3 (1899): 289–326.

———. "The Circulating Medium During the Civil War." *Journal of Political Economy* 10, no. 4 (1902): 537–574.

———. "The Crisis of 1920 and the Problem of Controlling Business Cycles." *The American Economic Review* 12, no. 1 (1922): 20–32.

Morrison, Rodney J. "The London Monetary and Economic Conference of 1933: A Public Goods Analysis." *The American Journal of Economics and Sociology* 52, no. 3 (1993): 307–321.

Mussa, Michael L. "Monetary Policy." In *American Economic Policy in the 1980s*, ed. Martin Feldstein, 81–145. Chicago: University of Chicago Press, 1994.

Newbach, Harvey E. *William Jennings Bryan: A Concise But Complete Story of His Life and Services*. Lincoln, NE: The University Publishing Co., 1900.

Nixon, Richard. *RN: The Memoirs of Richard Nixon*. New York: Grosset & Dunlap, 1978.

North, Douglass. "The United States Balance of Payments, 1790–1860." In *Trends in the American Economy in the Nineteenth Century*, ed. Conference on Research in Income and Wealth, 573–628. Princeton: Princeton University Press, 1960.

Noyes, Alexander D. "The Treasury Reserve and the Bond Syndicate." *Political Science Quarterly* 10, no. 4 (1895): 573–602.

Oberholtzer, Ellis Paxson. *Robert Morris: Patriot and Financier*. New York: The Macmillan Co., 1903.

Obstfeld, Maurice. "The Effectiveness of Foreign-Exchange Intervention: Recent Experience, 1985–1988." In *International Policy Coordination and Exchange Rate Fluctuations*, ed. William H. Branson, Jacob A. Frenkel, and Morris Goldstein, 197–246. Chicago: University of Chicago Press, 1990.

Orphanides, Athanasios and John C. Williams. "Monetary Policy Mistakes and the Evolution of Inflation Expectations." In *The Great Inflation: The Rebirth of Modern Central Banking*, ed. Michael D. Bordo and Athanasios Orphanides, 255–88. Chicago: University of Chicago Press, 2013.

Patton, Eugene B. "Secretary Shaw and Precedents as to Treasury Control over the Money Market." *Journal of Political Economy* 15, no. 2 (1907): 65–87.

Perkins, Edwin J. "Langdon Cheves and the Panic of 1819: A Reassessment." *The Journal of Economic History* 44, no. 2 (1984): 455–461.

Putnam, J.W. "An Economic History of the Michigan and Illinois Canal." *Journal of Political Economy* 17, no. 5 (1909): 272–95.

Rockoff, Hugh. "Some Evidence on the Real Price of Gold, Its Costs of Production, and Commodity Prices." In *A Retrospective on the Classical Gold Standard: 1821–1931*, ed. Michael D. Bordo and Anna J. Schwartz, 613–50. Chicago: University of Chicago Press, 1984.

Rostow, W.W. "The Take-Off Into Self-Sustained Growth." *The Economic Journal* 66, no. 261 (1956): 25–48.

Rothbard, Murray. *The Panic of 1819: Reactions and Policies*. 1962. Reprint. Auburn, AL: Ludwig von Mises Institute, 2007.

———. *A History of Money and Banking in the United States: The Colonial Era to World War II*. Auburn, AL: Ludwig von Mises Institute, 2002.

Rousseau, Peter L. "Monetary Policy and the Dollar." In *American Economic Policy in the 1790s*, ed. Douglas Irwin and Richard Sylla, 121–49. Chicago: University of Chicago Press, 2010.

Schwartz, Anna J. "Alternative Monetary Regimes: The Gold Standard." In *Money in Historical Perspective*, ed. Anna J. Schwartz, 364–90. Chicago: University of Chicago Press, 1987.

———. "Reflections on the Gold Commission Report." In *Money in Historical Perspective*, ed. Anna J. Schwartz, 317–32. Chicago: University of Chicago Press, 1987.

Secretary of the Treasury. *Report of the Secretary of the Treasury on the State of the Finances for the Year Ending June 30, 1862*. Washington, D.C.: Government Printing Office, 1863.

———. *Annual Report of the Secretary of the Treasury on the State of the Finances for the Year 1872*. Washington, D.C.: Government Printing Office, 1872.

———. *Annual Report of the Secretary of the Treasury on the State of the Finances for the Year 1874*. Washington, D.C.: Government Printing Office, 1874.

———. *Annual Report of the Secretary of the Treasury on the State of the Finances for the Fiscal Year Ended June 30, 1906*. Washington, D.C.: Government Printing Office, 1906.

Simon, Mathew. "The United States Balance of Payments, 1861–1900." In *Trends in the American Economy in the Nineteenth Century*, ed. Conference on Research in Income and Wealth, 629–716. Princeton: Princeton University Press, 1960.

Sprague, O.M.W. *History of Crises under the National Banking System*. Washington, D.C.: Government Printing Office, 1910.

———. "Proposals for Strengthening the National Banking System." *The Quarterly Journal of Economics* 24, no. 2 (1910): 201–242.

———. "The Discount Policy of the Federal Reserve Banks." *The American Economic Review* 11, no. 1 (1921): 16–29.

Sylla, Richard. "The Financial Foundations: Public Credit, the National Bank, and Securities Markets." In *Founding Choices: American Economic Policy in the 1790s*, ed. Douglas Irwin and Richard Sylla, 59–88. Chicago: University of Chicago Press, 2010.

Taussig, F.W. *The Tariff History of the United States*. Fifth Edition. New York: G.P. Putnam's Sons and the Knickerbocker Press, 1910.

Warburg, Paul M. "Defects and Needs of Our Banking System." In *Essays on Bank Reform in the United States*, 7–22. New York: Academy of Political Science, Columbia University, 1914.

———. "A Plan for a Modified Central Bank." In *Essays on Bank Reform in the United States*, 23–29. New York: Academy of Political Science, Columbia University, 1914.

———. "A United Reserve Bank of the United States." In *Essays on Bank Reform in the United States*, 75–115. New York: Academy of Political Science, Columbia University, 1914.

Wolman, Leo. "Changes in Union Membership, 1889–1923." In *The Growth of American Trade Unions, 1880–1923*, 29–66. New York: National Bureau of Economic Research, 1924.

COLLECTIONS

Federal Open Market Committee. Federal Reserve Transcripts and other historical materials. Board of Governors of the Federal Reserve System.
Minutes of the Meetings of the Open Market Investment Committee. Federal Reserve Archival System for Economic Research. St. Louis Federal Reserve.
Minutes of the Meetings of the Open Market Policy Conference. Federal Reserve Archival System for Economic Research. St. Louis Federal Reserve.

Index

About the Author

William Mannen is a lawyer living in Virginia. He has previously written about the national debt and other policy issues. He holds a BA from Trinity College in Connecticut and a JD from Washington University in St. Louis.

www.ingramcontent.com/pod-product-compliance
Ingram Content Group UK Ltd.
Pitfield, Milton Keynes, MK11 3LW, UK
UKHW041629031026
15587UKWH00001B/160

9 781498 560023